MONTANA

History Weekends

Fifty-two Adventures in History

BY DAVE CONKLIN

The Globe Pequot Press

Guilford, Connecticut

Maps: Trapper Badovinac
Text design: Lisa Reneson
All interior photos by the author except where noted.
Front/back background photograph by Mark Windham/Index Stock
Front inset photo by Index Stock
Back inset photograph by Dave Conklin
Cover design by Libby Kingsbury

Library of Congress Cataloging-in-Publication Data is available.

ISBN 0-7627-1161-2

Manufactured in the United States of America
First Edition/First Printing

Contents

Introduction, 1

How to Use This Book, 1

Montana's Frontier Legacy, 1

Tips for History Explorers, 3

Be Prepared, 4

A Word about Ethics, 5

Trip Locator Map, 6

Legend, 7

1 Looking for the Mother Lode, 8
Marysville Ghost Town

2 Four Billion Years of History, 13
Museum of the Rockies

3 Homeland of "The People," 18
The People's Center

4 The Ghosts of Garnet, 22
Garnet Ghost Town

5 Monuments in Conservation, 27
Gardiner Roosevelt Entrance Arch

6 A Company Town Grows Up, 32
Anaconda Historic District

7 The Gold Is Gone but the Elk Aren't, 36
Elkhorn Ghost Town

8 High Plains Buffalo Culture, 40
Ulm Pishkun State Park

9 From Cowboy to Artist, 44
Charles M. Russell Museum, House, and Studio

10 Towns Where the West Is Still Wild, 48
Landusky and Zortman

11 Still the Richest Hill on Earth, 54
Butte Historic District

12 Lewis and Clark's Indian Highway, 58
    Lolo Trail National Historic Landmark

13 Captain Clark Leaves His Mark, 64
    Pompeys Pillar National Monument

14 The Cradle of Montana Civilization, 68
    Fort Owen and St. Mary's Mission

15 Raising the Fastest Horses in the World, 73
    Marcus Daly Mansion

16 Pioneers in Forestry, 77
    Savenac Tree Nursery

17 The Valley of the Mission, 81
    St. Ignatius Mission

18 Steamboat's a Comin', 85
    Upper Missouri River Breaks National Monument

19 If Cattle Were Kings, Sheep Were Queens, 91
    Charles M. Bair Family Museum and Ranch

20 General Miles's Frontier Outpost, 95
    Miles City Historic District

21 Guarding the Whoop-Up Trail, 99
    Fort Assinniboine

22 Bear's Tooth Meets Sleeping Giant, 104
    The Gates of the Mountains

23 Where the Sister Saved Her Brother, 109
    Rosebud Battlefield State Park

24 Fur Traders and Free Trappers, 113
    Fort Union National Historic Site

25 Custer's Last Stand, 118
    Little Bighorn Battlefield National Monument

26 Homesteading the Medicine Line, 123
    Scobey Pioneer Town

27 The Wild Bunch Goes Shopping, 127
    The Great Train Robbery

28 Nation of the Plains Indian, 133
    North American Indian Days

29 The Sheriff Was a Road Agent, 137
    Bannack Ghost Town State Park

30 The Golden Gulch, 142
    Virginia City and Nevada City

31 Liver Eatin' Johnston Slept Here, 147
    Red Lodge Historic District

32 Surprise Attack on the Nez Perce, 152
    Big Hole National Battlefield

33 They Call Them the Apsaalooke, 157
    Crow Indian Fair

34 The Frenchman Becomes a Cowboy, 162
    Pierre Wibaux House

35 The Last Chief of the Crows, 167
    Chief Plenty Coups State Park

36 The Steel Rail Crosses the West, 172
    The Charlie Russell Railroad

37 Where Low Rent Means High Spirits, 176
    Havre Beneath the Streets

38 Reflections of Glaciers, 180
    Lake McDonald Lodge

39 A River Runs Through It, 184
    Lewis and Clark National Historic Trail Interpretive Center

40 I Will Fight No More Forever, 189
    Bear Paw Battlefield, Nez Perce National Historical Park

41 Growing Up Like Huckleberry Finn, 193
    Fort Benton National Historic Landmark

42 The Great Indian Council of 1855, 197
    Judith Landing Historic District

43 Christmas at the Mansion, 201
    The Charles Conrad Mansion

44 Last Chance Gulch Becomes the First City, 205
    Helena Historic District

45 The Cavemen of Bitter Creek Coulee, 210
    Pictograph Cave State Park

46 Teddy Roosevelt's Hunting Ground, 215
    Medicine Rocks State Park

47 They Said It Couldn't Be Done, 219
    Fort Peck Dam

48 Victorian Christmas at the Ranch, 224
    Grant-Kohrs Ranch National Historic Site

49 Guideposts of the Great Plains, 229
    Sleeping Buffalo Rock

50 The Bloody Bozeman, 233
    The Bozeman Trail

51 Lewis and Clark Reach the Headwaters, 237
    Missouri Headwaters State Park

52 Prairie Tycoon with a Vision, 241
    The Moss Mansion

Best Bets by Chapter

    For Families, 246

    For Scenery and Photography, 246

    For Living-History Demonstrations, 247

    For Avoiding the Crowds, 247

    For the Mobility Impaired, 248

    For a Tight Budget, 248

    For Native American Culture, 249

    For Explorer Trails, 249

    For Forts and Fights, 249

    For Ghost Towns, 250

    For Frontier Architecture, 250

Further Reading, 251

Index, 262

Acknowledgments/About the Author, 265

Introduction

Montana, the heart of the Old West, where you can turn your imagination loose to range the dry coulees, golden gulches, picturesque prairies, and magnificent mountains. Here the panorama of history is peopled with larger-than-life phantoms of the past: Captains Meriwether Lewis and William Clark, John Colter, Liver Eatin' Johnston, John Bozeman, Father Anthony Ravalli, Chief Plenty Coups, Chief Joseph, Crazy Horse, Sitting Bull, Lieutenant Colonel George Custer, General George Crook, Pike Landusky, Butch Cassidy and the Sundance Kid, Charlie Russell, Marcus Daly, and the list goes on. So stop reading about history, and start experiencing it. There is something happening somewhere to make every weekend a history weekend in Montana. If you've ever wanted to spin yarns with the fur trappers, pan gold with prospectors, ride with the 7th Cavalry, or dance at the Victorian Ball, this book will get you there when it's happening.

How to Use This Book

For each trip in this book, a short history of the destination is provided, along with suggestions for what to do and where exactly to go to get the most out of the experience. The trips are presented in such a way that you get all the details at a glance: how to get there, when to go, any required admission fees, and the minimum amount of time you need to see what there is to see, as well as a list of suggested equipment, clothing, and other items you might want to bring along to more fully enjoy your outing. Also included are unique or historic places to find food and lodging, and addresses, phone numbers, and Web sites where you can get more information about the area. In the back of the book, Further Reading provides a list of references so you can learn more about each destination.

Unless otherwise noted, all the places described in this guide are accessible by standard passenger vehicles with average clearance.

Montana's Frontier Legacy

Montana's history begins with its prehistory. The fossil record of life stretches from the Precambrian trilobites of the Rocky Mountains to the Cretaceous *Tyrannosaurus rex* of the eastern plains and more. Both man and mammoth may have entered what is now Montana more than 20,000 years ago during the last Ice Age. By 7000 B.C., these "Paleo-Indians" were pursuing bison, or buffalo, with spears. By 5000 B.C., a newer "Archaic" culture developed. At Pictograph Cave near Billings, members of this culture created new tools, began gathering and preparing plant foods, and developed the seasonal migration patterns later observed by the first explorers. The "Late Hunters" (A.D. 500–1800) also depended on the buffalo and were responsible for most of the rock art and stone piles in Montana.

The introduction of the horse from the Shoshone tribe in the early 1700s made buffalo hunting and tribal contact easier. This in turn produced the culture and the warriors known to history. These tribes were nomadic, and tribal boundaries changed frequently. Only the Salish, Kootenai, and Pend d'Oreille tribes of Western Montana have lived in that region for centuries. Every tribe now in Montana east of the continental divide came into the region after A.D. 1600.

The first white exploration to leave written records was the Lewis and Clark Expedition of 1804–06. Ordered to explore the vast Louisiana Purchase of 1803 by President Thomas Jefferson, their perilous journey remains an outstanding achievement in the history of land exploration. They were soon followed by businessmen—fur trappers and traders who wished to capitalize on the rich resources of the Upper Missouri River. In the 1830s Fort Union and other trading posts traded manufactured goods to the Indian tribes in exchange for furs for the fashion and clothing industries. Father Pierre Jean DeSmet built the first permanent white settlement of St. Mary's Mission in the Bitterroot Valley in 1841.

By 1853, a military expedition under General Isaac Stevens began exploring and mapping routes for a transcontinental railroad and connecting roads to the great waterways of the Missouri and Columbia Rivers. This and the discovery of gold in 1858 paved the way for the major gold strikes of Bannack, Alder Gulch, Last Chance Gulch, and Confederate Gulch in 1862–65. A torrent of immigrants, including men like Charles Conrad, began a chain of events that created the cultural and political landscape we see today. Between 1863 and 1865, Montana produced more than $35 million in placer gold. The need for government, industry, and transportation became vital, but resulted in squeezing out the resources, lands, and culture of the Indian tribes. As soon as the Civil War ended, Washington responded with treaties, and force if necessary, to end the tribal migrations, with a disastrous climax at the Battle of the Little Bighorn in 1876 and the Battle of the Bear's Paw in 1877.

Freeing the range from Indian control marked the beginning of the cattle and sheep empires of men like Pierre Wibaux, Conrad Kohrs, and Charles Bair, who took full advantage of the open and "free" range. Within twenty years, however, low prices, severe winters, and homesteader fences caused those who remained to turn to better feeding, breeding, and fencing their stock.

Montana became the forty-first state in 1889 and Montana politics, never calm, became quite raucous when it came time to select members of Congress and choose the location of state institutions. The "Copper Kings," Marcus Daly and William Clark, even used their considerable finances to battle for votes over where to locate the state capital. In 1914 Montana women gained the right to vote. Montana's Jeanette Rankin became the first woman elected to Congress in 1917, and she was the only member of Congress to vote against entering into both World Wars.

As the mining and timber industries went into decline after the turn of the twentieth century, Montana became more dependent on agriculture. A flood of homesteaders arrived just in time to experience the drought years of 1917–20 and 1930–36. But oil and coal discoveries in eastern Montana began to produce the raw materials for refining and power generation industries, followed by hydropower in northwestern Montana. Today these industries continue to ebb and flow and affect the cultural fabric of the land and the people.

Montana's frontier legacy is a precious and perishable commodity. Cherish it and protect it, because losing the special places where these historic events occurred would mean losing our sense of the present and future—and our ability to connect with our roots.

Tips for History Explorers

Knowing where to go and when to go are key ingredients in experiencing and learning about Montana's history. That is what this book is all about. But knowing what to do when you get there can make all the difference in the quality of your visit. Here are some tips to help you get the most out of each outing.

This book has all the information you need to get where you want to go, but there is no substitute for the experience of the site managers, park rangers, and others who work full-time in these historic locations. Don't be afraid to check Web sites and call ahead before you start out or to ask questions of on-site staff when you arrive. Although many events are scheduled for the same time each year, sometimes construction, weather, or even economic conditions may cause schedules and events to change. Also, Montana is a state of extremes, and that includes the weather. Getting up-to-date information on weather and road conditions can help you plan your trip for maximum enjoyment and minimum disappointment.

You do not need special equipment to appreciate history, but there are a few things that will help. A camera and notebook are useful for recording your experiences for the future. Binoculars are very handy for seeing the details of large landscapes or tall buildings. Even a tape recorder is a welcome partner for preserving the unique sounds of historical events and reenactments.

History books are indispensable for a full understanding of the location and events. Most of the references provided in Further Reading can be checked out from a public library before your trip. The most useful items to bring along are curiosity, patience, and a desire to learn. When you use these tools, you will begin to understand why things happened the way they did to weave the fabric of history, year by year, into what you see today. Although each trip description suggests a minimum amount of time to spend, the longer you stay the more you are likely to see, and the more you are likely to understand and appreciate those who came before us.

Be Prepared

Some of the trips in this book will take you off the beaten path, so take some basic precautions and use common sense to avoid any unplanned adventures. First of all, dress for the weather and always be prepared for the worst. Even in the summer, thunderstorms and heavy rain can occur at any time. Snowstorms can hit mountain areas, and nighttime temperatures can fall below freezing, even on the high plains.

Dress in layers to control your comfort by adding or removing clothing as conditions change. Winter wear could include wool or polypropylene underwear, wool shirt and pants, down vest, winter parka, wool hat, gloves or mittens, and arctic pack boots. Summer wear could include shorts, T-shirt, lightweight pants, long-sleeved shirt, fleece vest, rain jacket, hat, gloves, and sturdy boots. And don't forget to take some carbohydrate-rich snacks and water.

When taking trips into snow country, be prepared for winter driving conditions by bringing tire chains, a shovel, and a survival kit with flares, which may even come in handy to help someone else. Don't forget to check road conditions before leaving home. In the summer, take extra jugs of water when driving in the eastern prairies. When visiting some of the more out-of-the-way places, ask locally about current road conditions. Roads in the remote gumbo clay areas in the eastern prairies that were perfectly good yesterday may be as slippery as a wet bar of soap for days after a thunderstorm. Mountain roads could be washed out by heavy rain or blocked by rock slides. Cell phones are useful in emergencies, but keep in mind that they may not always be able to pick up a signal away from major cities.

A Word about Ethics

As you explore the historical places described in this book, you will see why they are valuable beyond measure. Our ancestors, both Native American and immigrant alike, lived, worked, played, and died here. All of the land and gravesites are sacred, many of the structures are private, and some of the buildings are residences. Respect the rights of the owners and the people who live there. When in doubt, always ask for permission to enter or photograph land or buildings, and to photograph people.

Follow the basic rule of "take only pictures and leave only footprints." To do otherwise is unethical. Artifact hunting and grave robbing are illegal, whether you are on private, state, or federal property, and the penalties are embarrassing as well as costly. Do not write or carve on any part of a building. If you smoke, do so in your vehicle. Old buildings and even landscapes, once burned, are irreplaceable. If pets are allowed, keep yours on a leash, and if you spot any litter, pick it up and take it with you.

These historical resources are weathering away too fast as it is; don't help them go faster. Removing artifacts and souvenirs from abandoned sites only accelerates the deterioration, depriving others of a historical excursion into the past, and minimizing the success of any future scientific investigations. Remember that many people have worked to protect and preserve this heritage for present and future generations. Be one of them. Join a preservation organization, volunteer to clean up a historic site, and teach your children the value of preserving our past, our roots. With your help, these historic places will still be around for generations to come.

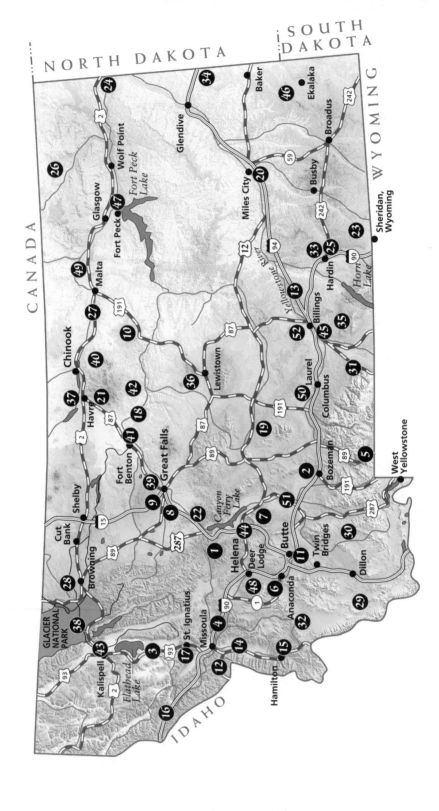

State boundary

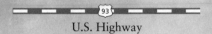

U.S. Highway

Interstate

State/County Road

Local/Secondary Road

Main Attraction

Town Locator

Point of Interest

Map Orientation

1

Looking for the Mother Lode
Marysville Ghost Town

Marysville, the mile-high mining town on the eastern edge of the Continental Divide, owes its history to an illiterate Irish immigrant. Enjoy a day out in the snow, scenery, and blue skies, and learn how Thomas Cruse struck it rich and became the richest man in Montana.

The history

The history of Marysville is the history of Thomas Cruse and his Drumlummon Mine, named after the parish of Drum Lummon in his native Ireland. Cruse came to Montana after failing to find his fortune in the gold fields of California, Nevada, and Idaho. In 1868 he was placer mining on Trinity Gulch when he met William Brown, who later gave him one of his five gold claims. Cruse soon began "looking for the mother lode" farther up the hillside; he found it in 1876. The town of Marysville arose as people rushed in to stake their claims when word of Cruse's strike got out.

An astute businessman, Cruse realized that lots of money and modern mining equipment would be needed to follow the 50-foot-wide gold vein farther into the earth. So in 1883 he sold the Drumlummon Mine to investors from London for $1.5 million, retaining a one-sixth interest. Cruse moved to Helena, established a bank, and became one of the richest men in Montana at the time. Cruse donated to a number of civic causes, including the construction of Montana's capitol and St. Helena's Cathedral.

By 1887 Marysville claimed to have 4,000 residents, two railroads, two newspapers, and twenty-seven saloons. In 1889 the owners of the Drumlummon Mine became engaged in a long battle with the adjacent St. Louis mine, similar to the underground war that later plagued the mines in Butte. The most notable battle, however, was between the Northern Pacific

A few brick buildings including the Masonic Hall still survive
on Marysville's Main Street.

and the Great Northern Railroads. Both wanted the mining district's business
and began building spur lines up Silver Creek. The Northern Pacific arrived
in 1887, bridged the creek, and prevented the Great Northern from building
under its 85-foot-high trestle. By 1900 Marysville had spewed out $60 mil-
lion worth of gold and silver ore, but by 1925 only fifty families remained.

The fun

As you drive toward Marysville, look for both old and new mine tailings left
over from mining along the creek bottom. The road follows the general route
of the Great Northern railway into the town of Marysville. Look to the left
just before town to see the foundations of the Drumlummon Mine and
stamp mill. In Marysville, stop to read the weathered sign, then go another
block and turn north on Main Street, where the Masonic Hall and other sub-
stantial buildings still remain.

If you've brought your skis or snowmobile, about halfway up the street
on the west side is a parking lot and trailhead. From here you can explore the
entire valley on skis or snowmobile when conditions permit.

Drive or walk through Marysville, read the signs in front of the more
important buildings, and explore the old log cabins on the outskirts of town.

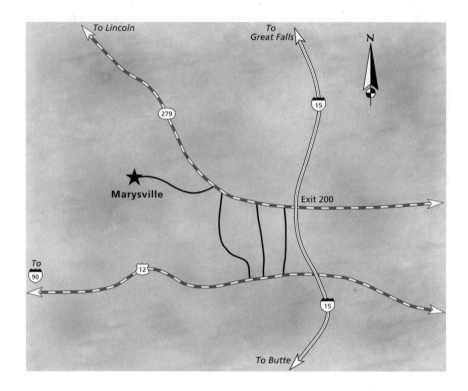

After you've seen the town, drive another 1.5 miles to the Great Divide Ski Area. For a fee you can take the chairlift up Mount Belmont (elevation 7,330 feet) for a great view of the valley, then ski, walk, or take the chair back down. The ski area also has a lodge and equipment shop.

If you get hungry on your way back to Marysville, stop on the east side of Main Street at the Marysville House restaurant. This rustic but not so historic eatery also offers wood-paneled walls where patrons have carved a record of their visit, hopefully here instead of on a historic building. As you drive back to Helena, you can reflect on the fact that Marysville was named by Thomas Cruse in honor of Mary Ralston, the wife of one of the first Cornish miners in the area, mother of eleven children, and a friend to all. For more local history, at Silver City turn right onto the Birdseye Road and go south to Helena. This is the route of the old Fort Benton Stage Road and Captain John Mullan's Wagon Road. After you cross the railroad tracks you pass Fort Harrison, where the Canadian-American First Special Service Force, "the Devil's Brigade," was trained during World War II.

Next best

If you'd like to meet some Marysville Pioneers, attend the Pioneer Picnic held every year on a weekend in mid-July.

Unique food and lodging

The **Marysville House** restaurant on Main Street serves such specialties as fresh lobster and a crab leg and seafood skillet. But be prepared to wait for up to two hours; they don't take reservations since they don't have a phone. For accommodations, the only place in town is the **Overnighter.** Located on the east side of town on Atwood Place, this rustic wood- and electric-heated bunkhouse was moved here in 1997 from a local ranch. If you want to stay in a house Mary Ralston would like to have had for her eleven children, on your way back to Helena stop at the **Mountain Meadow Inn,** north of Country Club Avenue near Fort Harrison. This brick bed-and-breakfast was once the Masonic Retirement Home. Here you can stay in a fully remodeled single room, suite, or even a tepee. They also offer a country store with herbs and spices.

Practical information

Site: Marysville, near Helena.

Recommended time: First weekend in January.

Minimum time commitment: Three hours, plus driving time.

What to bring: Warm clothes, sturdy waterproof winter boots, hat, gloves, sunblock, sunglasses, camera, and binoculars. Cross-country or downhill skis are also fun accessories.

Admission fee: None.

Hours: The town is accessible year-round. The Great Divide Ski Area is open from November into April on weekends and some weekdays depending on snow conditions. Hours are 9:00 A.M. to 4:00 P.M. on weekends, with night skiing until 9:00 P.M. The Marysville House is open year-round for dinner. Hours are Tuesday through Saturday 5:00 to 10:00 P.M.

Directions: From Helena, go 7 miles north on Interstate 15 and take the Lincoln Road exit 200. Go west 9.6 miles on Secondary Road 279. Turn left onto the gravel Marysville Road and go 6 miles to the town.

For more information

Helena Chamber of Commerce
225 Cruse Avenue, Helena, MT 59601
(406) 447–1530, (800) 743–5362
www.helenachamber.com, www.downtownhelena.com

Great Divide, 7385 Belmont Drive
P.O. Box Ski, Marysville, MT 59640
(406) 449–3746
www.greatdividemontana.com

The Overnighter
Doug and Linda Peterson, Marysville, MT 59640
(406) 449–0854

Mountain Meadow Inn
2245 Head Lane, Helena, MT 59602
(406) 443-7301, (888) 776-6466

2

Four Billion Years of History
Museum of the Rockies

Be a time traveler and journey through the history of the Northern Rockies in a big way. See the 4.5-billion-year-old "big bang" in the world-class Taylor Planetarium, then take a walk among the dinosaurs at the Museum of the Rockies.

The history

A walk through the Museum of the Rockies is a walk through more than 4 billion years, from the beginning of time to the present. Located at the geographic center of the Northern Rocky Mountain region, which includes the states of Montana, Idaho, Wyoming, and portions of Canada and the Dakotas, the museum interprets the natural and cultural history of this vast, sparsely populated area.

It all began in 1957 as a part of Montana State University and grew with the help of a distinguished Montana physician, Dr. Caroline McGill, and the head of the university history department, Dr. Merrill Burlingame. The museum originally focused on cultural history, but within a decade amended its mission to include the study and interpretation of the region's rich natural history as well. Adult learning is another special emphasis of the museum, as are partnerships with groups such as the Nature Conservancy, Yellowstone National Park, the Lewis and Clark Trail Heritage Foundation, and the Army Corps of Engineers.

Today the 94,000-square-foot Museum of the Rockies has become the largest natural history museum in the region and is nationally recognized by the Society for Vertebrate Paleontology and the American Association of Museums. It also has the only Digistar planetarium in the Northern Rockies. Outside the museum is the Tinsley House, an eleven-acre fully interpreted living-history farm.

The Tinsley Pioneer House and Living History Farm are popular
with young and old alike.

The fun

Start your travel through time 4.5 million years ago with the "big bang" at
the Taylor Planetarium, where live narrated tours of the night sky change
quarterly. Next stop at the spectacular *Landforms/Lifeforms* dioramas to learn
about the geology of the region. Don't miss the video on Pangea and the
artifacts and activities. See dinosaurs and fossils from current research projects
on display in the Berger Dinosaur Hall, where you'll also find mammoths
from the Great Ice Age 10,000 years ago. The origins of Native Americans
are described in *Enduring Peoples: Native Cultures of the Northern Rockies and
Plains.* The next stop should be the Paugh History Hall for the *Montana on
the Move* exhibits describing the lifestyles of trappers and early settlers, as well
as artifacts from the only scientifically verified Lewis and Clark campsite in
Montana.

Don't leave without seeing the three-dimensional presentation in the
Hager Auditorium or visiting the museum store, which has an excellent
selection of books on Montana geology, dinosaurs, and history. Children will
enjoy the Martin Discovery Room interactive play area.

No trip to Bozeman is complete without a visit to the Gallatin County

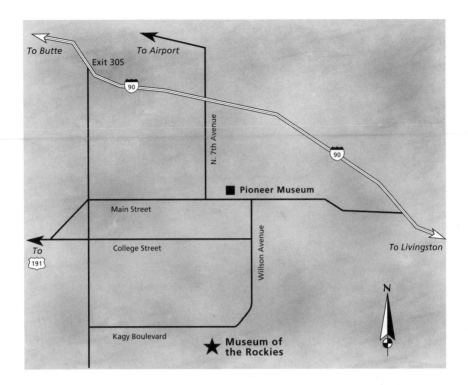

Pioneer Museum in the historic jail on Main Street. Admission is free, and exhibits include the famous Big Horn Gun, a model of Fort Ellis, a Bozeman Trail fort, an 1870s log cabin, and a great resource library and bookstore.

Next best

Another good time to visit is during the summer, when you can see the Tinsley House Living History Farm's pioneer garden in full bloom and get a lesson in churning butter. From 9:30 A.M. to 5:00 P.M., volunteers bake bread, feed the chickens, and tend the garden, complete with period seeds. Make sure you try some fresh cornbread made by the volunteer pioneer family. The museum also conducts a number of weeklong camps for the kids.

Unique food and lodging

Accommodations include several restored Victorian and Revival style homes: The **Lehrkind Mansion** bed-and-breakfast (1897), 719 North Wallace Avenue; the **Lindley House** bed-and-breakfast (1889), 202 Lindley Place; and **The Voss Inn** bed-and-breakfast (1883), 319 South Willson.

The Mysterious Big Horn Gun

Resting on a gun carriage in the Gallatin County Pioneer Museum is a piece of Montana history known as the Big Horn Gun. For many years it sat as a yard ornament outside the Gallatin County Courthouse, its barrel plugged in 1957 after pranksters used it to shoot the windows out of the high school across the street. No one knows when or where it was made, but this cannon played a fascinating role in the history of Montana and the West. Some even say it was the catalyst for the Sioux War of 1876–77.

The cannon is similar to the twelve-pound mountain howitzers the military used during the 1800s, but it has no military or manufacturer's markings. Some say it was probably cast during the late 1700s. The gun may have been used in the Mexican War in 1848 and brought north over the Chihuahua and Santa Fe Trails afterward, or used to protect the crews building the Union Pacific Railroad on its way to Promontory, Utah, in 1869. What is known is that in 1870 the gun showed up in Cheyenne, Wyoming, acquiring its name when it was brought down the Big Horn River to the Yellowstone and then to the town of Bozeman with a party of miners.

The citizens of Bozeman purchased the gun to defend the town from hostile Sioux and Cheyenne Indians, who made travel east along the Yellowstone River very dangerous. In the spring of 1874, some 150 well-armed men formed the Yellowstone Wagon Road and Prospecting Expedition for the unstated purpose of starting a war that would require the U.S. military to drive out the Indians. There were no cannonballs for the gun, so before the expedition members left Bozeman, they bought a stock of canned oysters and filled the cans with nails and scrap iron to use as ammunition. The Big Horn Gun was used with devastating results against 600 Sioux who attacked the wagon train on April 4 and again on April 12.

A year later, a similar expedition took the cannon down the Yellowstone River on a flatboat, which capsized. Walter Cooper, a Bozeman gun shop owner, succeeded in retrieving the cannon from the bottom of the river. The gun was mounted on the walls of Fort Pease and used against attacks by a band of 500 Sioux. The Sioux continued to harass the fort until a rescue party was sent to retrieve the survivors in March 1876. The gun was left behind and the Sioux burned the fort to the ground. A few years later, Cooper, the gun shop owner, found the cannon in the remains of the fort and had it shipped back to Bozeman, thus saving the mysterious gun and preserving its fascinating history.

Practical information

Site: Museum of the Rockies, Bozeman.

Recommended time: Mid-January.

Minimum time commitment: Four hours, plus driving time.

What to bring: Camera with flash attachment.

Admission fee: $7.00 adults, $4.00 ages 5 to 18, under age 5 free; $3.00 for planetarium.

Hours: Winter: 9:00 A.M. to 5:00 P.M. Monday through Saturday; 12:30 to 5:00 P.M. Sunday. Memorial Day through Labor Day 8:00 A.M. to 8:00 P.M. daily.

Directions: Take Interstate 90 to exit 305 1 mile west of Bozeman. Go south 5 miles on 19th Avenue (Montana Highway 412) to Kagy Boulevard. Turn left on Kagy and follow the signs to 600 West Kagy Boulevard.

For more information

Museum of the Rockies, Montana State University
600 West Kagy Boulevard, Bozeman, MT 59717
(406) 994–2251
www.museumoftherockies.org

Gallatin County Historical Society and Pioneer Museum
317 West Main, Bozeman, MT 59715
(406) 522–8122
www.pioneermuseum.org

Lehrkind Mansion
719 North Wallace Avenue, Bozeman, MT 59715
(406) 585–6932, (800) 992–6932
www.bozemanbedandbreakfast.com

Lindley House
202 Lindley Place, Bozeman, MT 59715-4833
(406) 587–8403, (866) 587–8403
www.lindley-house.com

Voss Inn
319 South Willson, Bozeman, MT 59715
(406) 587–0982
www.bozeman-vossinn.com

3

—

Homeland of "The People"
The People's Center

Visit the homeland and culture of the ancient inhabitants of these mountains and learn how their traditions, rituals, and skills were handed down through the centuries in a language unlike any other in the world.

The history

The Salish, Pend d'Oreille, and Kootenai tribes together form the sovereign people of the Flathead Nation. Kootenai is derived from a Blackfoot word meaning "water people," a reference to their lifestyle on the waterways of western Montana, their aboriginal name was the Ktunaxa, but they call themselves simply "The People." They have inhabited western Montana for centuries, and they speak a language unrelated to other tribes. There are seven bands of Kootenai, the Ksanka band resides on the shores of Flathead Lake in present-day Montana.

The first "modern" Indians to occupy Montana with the Kootenai were the Crow, Salish, and Pend d'Oreille. Lewis and Clark called the Salish "Flathead" Indians, and now the name is applied to lakes, rivers, and valleys. The Salish and Pend d'Oreille spoke different languages from the Ksanka and occupied territory as far east as the Bighorn Mountains. These tribes shared common hunting grounds during the 1700s and seasonally crossed the mountains to hunt buffalo and clash with their hereditary enemies, the Blackfeet. They were also known as skilled canoeists, trappers, anglers, tobacco growers, and buckskin clothing makers.

Although the Salish lived in the Bitterroot Valley to the south of the Kootenai, the Hellgate Treaty of 1855 required that all three tribes live together on the 1.2 million acres that today comprise the Flathead Indian

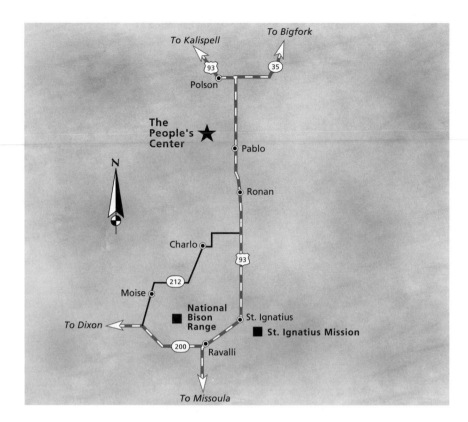

Reservation. About 60 percent of the 6,885 enrolled tribal members now live on the reservation. The official languages of the reservation are Salish and Kootenai, and the tribes are working to preserve them from extinction. Many of the Scotch and French family names of tribal members came from marriages with the Hudson Bay Company trappers and traders during the fur trade era.

The fun

The People's Center is a great place to visit during the winter when many outdoor areas are closed and the crowds are gone. You must either come on a weekday or call ahead for a tour by one of the Center's Native EdVentures native guides. Tours can be as short as three hours or as long as a day, and you can learn more about the Flathead Indian Reservation or even visit local powwows that are held many times during the year.

Start your trip at the center, which features exhibits on the history and culture of these tribes both before and after contact with the white man. You

Paintings of Salish and Kootenai chiefs adorn the entrance of the People's Center.

can also see the text and hear narration in the native language. The center has a good selection of books on Native Americans not found in many bookstores, as well as gifts and artwork by local Indian artisans.

To see more of the history and beauty of the reservation, from the People's Center drive 14 miles south on U.S. 93 to historical highway marker 13 at milepost 40. Here the view of the Mission Mountains is spectacular when there has been a fresh snow. Go 1 mile farther south to historical highway marker 14. Here on Post Creek is Fort Connah, the last Hudson Bay trading post established south of the forty-ninth parallel. A log storehouse still remains at the post, which Scotsman Angus McDonald completed in 1847. His son, Duncan McDonald, spoke twelve Indian languages and helped chronicle the history of the local tribes.

Next best

Another good time to visit is during one of the annual powwows on the Flathead Indian Reservation. The Salish and Pend d'Oreille hold their powwow at Arlee on the first weekend in July. The Kootenai tribe holds its powwow at Elmo on the third weekend in July. During the summer months, the

Ninepipes Museum of Early Montana, 6 miles south of Ronan, also chronicles the history and culture of the Flathead Reservation.

Practical information

Site: The People's Center, Pablo.

Recommended time: Mid-January.

Minimum time commitment: Three hours, plus driving time.

What to bring: Warm clothes, hat, gloves, sturdy boots, water bottle, binoculars, and camera.

Admission fee: $3.00 adults, $1.50 seniors and students, $5.00 family.

Hours: 9:00 A.M. to 5:00 P.M. Monday through Friday, plus 10:00 A.M. to 6:00 P.M. Saturday and Sunday during the summer.

Directions: Pablo is 6 miles south of Polson on U.S. 93. The People's Center is located at milepost 54, on the west side of the highway.

For more information

The People's Center
P.O. Box 278, Pablo, MT 59855
(406) 883–5344
www.peoplescenter.org

Polson Area Chamber of Commerce
P.O. Box 667, Polson, MT 59860
(406) 883–5969
www.polsonchamber.com

4

—

The Ghosts of Garnet
Garnet Ghost Town

Some say the ghosts are real and they have seen them. Others say it's only "electromagnetic radiation." You can ski, snowshoe, or snowmobile to the town in the winter, stay in a rustic cabin, and, on a quiet starlit evening, find out for yourself.

The history

One of Montana's premier ghost towns, Garnet was named after a Montana gemstone because of the brown garnet rock outcrops in the area. The real boom on First Chance Gulch came in the 1890s with advances in hard rock mining and smelting technologies for complex ores. Larger mining companies consolidated claims, and in 1895 Dr. Armistead Mitchell built a stamp mill that led to the founding of the town of Mitchell, which was later renamed Garnet. Soon Samuel Richey discovered rich gold ore in an old shaft of the Nancy Hanks Mine. Within a few years, miners gouged $1.4 million worth of gold, copper, and silver from mines in the district. By 1897 Garnet had four hotels, thirteen saloons, and a daily stagecoach. In 1898 Garnet had a population of 1,000, but by 1905 only 150 remained. Half of the town was burned in a raging fire in 1912. The last mines operated sporadically until 1954.

Garnet is also a ghost town of legends. One tells of a winter when the town was snowed in and supplies were running low. A miner took his lamp and disappeared into the tunnels, emerging 10 miles away in Bearmouth, where he made arrangements for supplies to be sent in. Another says that the steep China Grade as you approach Garnet from the south is named after a Chinese miner who left a sizable fortune in gold buried in a baking powder can nearby.

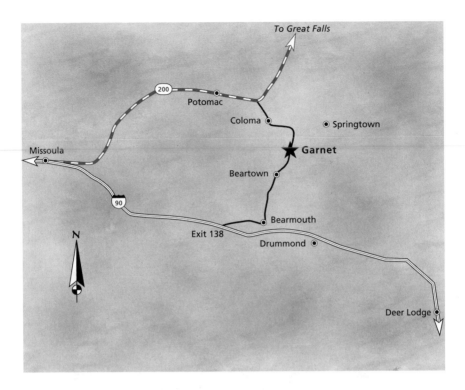

But the real mystery began on a cold night in January 1972, when the town's only resident and caretaker heard piano music and laughter coming from Kelly's Saloon. When he walked into the long-deserted building, the sounds stopped. On another cold night in December 1975 sometime after midnight, another caretaker heard the same sounds from his cabin and took his dog, Whiskers, with him to investigate. As he approached the saloon he could even hear glasses clinking, but as soon as Whiskers touched his nose to the building, all the sounds stopped. Today about thirty-five buildings remain, including Kelly's Saloon, the J. K. Wells Hotel, the general store, and twenty or so log cabins, thanks to the long life of the town and its winter isolation.

The fun

Garnet is one of the last surviving "boom and bust" historic ghost towns that have almost vanished in recent years. The best time to see and appreciate it is during the winter when you have to do it the old-fashioned way—on skis or snowshoes (or by snowmobile). In fact, there are more than 116 miles of snowmobile/ski trails in the Garnet area. The 26-mile road through Garnet has also been designated a scenic Backcountry Byway.

Snowmobilers take a break above Kelly's Saloon in Garnet.

Once you get to town, head for the visitor center in Ole's Tavern, an old Depression-era bar at the end of the street. You can pick up a self-guided tour brochure for a quarter, and also a snow trails map. (During the summer, you can also get a guided tour for an additional $2.00.) Take time to see each of the buildings and read the interpretive panels installed during the summer of 2000. There is even a picnic table, a toilet, and drinking water available from freeze-proof water hydrants. If you have time, I highly recommend making a cabin reservation and staying overnight to experience what a "real" ghost town feels like. Popular weekends are reserved even before the season starts, but most weekdays usually go unreserved and provide the best experience. Who knows, maybe you'll see the ghosts too!

Next best

If you don't mind crowds and you like children's games, gold-panning demonstrations, and homemade pies, attend Garnet Ghost Town Day, usually held every year or two on the last Saturday in July.

Unique food and lodging

Those who like rustic accommodations can stay right in Garnet. Two historic wood-heated log cabins are available (the wood and the ax are provided). The **Dahl House** sleeps eight to ten people, and the smaller **Wills Cabin** with two double beds sleeps up to four. They are available December through April by reservation only.

Practical information

Site: Garnet Ghost Town, 42 miles east of Missoula.

Recommended time: Late January.

Minimum time commitment: One day.

What to bring: Warm clothes, sturdy waterproof winter boots, hat, gloves, sunblock, sunglasses, camera, and binoculars. A snowmobile, cross-country skis, or snowshoes are also recommended.

Admission fee: None during the winter season; $2.00 for adults, free for children under 12, and free with federal Golden Age, Golden Access, or Golden Eagle Pass during the summer season.

Hours: The town is open year-round, but only accessible by skis or snow-mobile during the winter. The visitor center is open 8:00 A.M. to 6:00 P.M. daily from Memorial Day through September and on weekends during the winter.

Directions: Call the Bureau of Land Management for current road conditions. From Missoula, take Interstate 90 32 miles east to Bearmouth exit 138. Drive 5.5 miles east to Bear Gulch gravel road. Turn left and go 7.5 miles north to the winter trailhead parking area at the site of Beartown, a one-hour trip from Missoula. In the winter you must ski or snowmobile the last 3 miles to Garnet from the parking area, traveling up Bear Gulch and the China Grade in First Chance Gulch. It's a two-hour trip with a 1,200-foot gain in elevation. For those who think getting there is half the fun, there is also a parking area north of Garnet on Montana Highway 200 east of Potomac between mileposts 22 and 23. From there it is a 12-mile, five-hour trip to Garnet on skis.

For more information

Cabin Rentals, Garnet Preservation Association
3255 Ft. Missoula Road, Missoula, MT 59804-7293
(406) 329–1031
www.garnetghosttown.org

Bureau of Land Management, USDI, Missoula Field Office
3255 Ft. Missoula Road, Missoula, MT 59804-7293
(406) 329–3914

5

Monuments in Conservation
Gardiner Roosevelt Entrance Arch

Drive through the great stone arch as the stagecoaches did, into
the world's first national park, a winter wonderland of wild
and silent beauty. Follow the elk and bison on their winter
migrations or ski the grounds of old Fort Yellowstone, where
hoarfrost from the hot springs turns trees into ghosts.

The history

In April 1903 President Theodore Roosevelt came to Gardiner to dedicate
the cornerstone to the Roosevelt Arch at the original entrance to Yellowstone
National Park. The arch is made of local basalt rock and is inscribed with the
words, "For the Benefit and Enjoyment of the People," a quote from the law
creating the nation's and the world's first national park in 1872. The establishment of Yellowstone was a turning point in man's relationship with nature.
For the first time, the preservation of America's unique wildlands became as
much a priority as conquering and taming them.

When Teddy Roosevelt delivered his dedication speech to more than
4,000 people, Gardiner had been a mining town for twenty years, and was
about to become a tourist town. By 1904 the Northern Pacific Railroad was
bringing visitors to Gardiner, where stagecoaches would carry them under
the arch and into the park. Gardiner is still the only year-round drive-in
entrance to Yellowstone National Park.

When Yellowstone was established in 1872, there was no park service to
protect the park or the visitors. In fact, in 1877 the Nez Perce Indians captured several tourists in the park, and trappers and poachers operated with
impunity. From 1886 until the National Park Service was established in 1916,
the U.S. Army at Fort Yellowstone protected the park. Today, the park headquarters at Mammoth preserves what is left of Fort Yellowstone.

Views of Gardiner are spectacular from Mammoth Hot Springs.

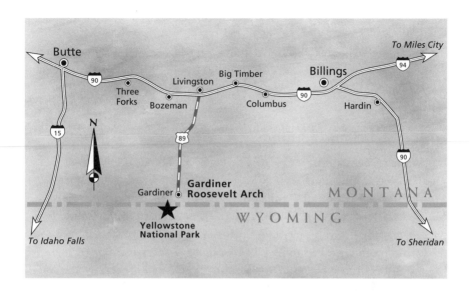

The fun

Start your trip by driving south from Gardiner to the Roosevelt Arch and the new Arch Park and pavilion. Stop to read the historical signs, then drive 5 miles up the Gardiner River Canyon toward Mammoth Hot Springs. This is the winter range for elk, bighorn sheep, antelope, coyotes, and wolves, so watch out for them. At Mammoth, make your first stop at the Albright Visitor Center to see the exhibits and learn about the history of Yellowstone and Fort Yellowstone. Don't miss the film or the bookstore, and be sure to pick up a *Winter Guide to Yellowstone* here. Don't touch the elk—they are real.

You can take a two-hour ranger-led snowshoe walk (beginners welcome) or rent some skis at the lodge and ski the lower or upper travertine terrace loops around the hot springs. The hoarfrost from the steam makes them even more incredibly beautiful than in the summer. There is also a warming hut nearby, with vending machine snacks and cold drinks. From Mammoth you can also take a snowcoach tour to Old Faithful, or throw the skis in the car and drive another 47 miles to Cooke City beyond the northeast entrance. This is the only road open to cars in the winter, and you're sure to see buffalo and other wildlife in the Lamar Valley. There are a number of short side trips you can take on snowshoes or skis, if you have the time and energy. Remember, daylight is short this time of year, so head back to Mammoth for dinner, and stick around for the hour-long program at 8:30 P.M. Thursday through Saturday. Relax in the hotel's hot tub, or return to Gardiner for the night—but watch out for elk on the road if you drive at night.

Next best

Most winter activities can be enjoyed from mid-December to the end of February. Or visit during Gardiner's Buffalo Days on the fourth Saturday in August for an old-fashioned community celebration complete with a rodeo, parade, barbecue, and street dance.

Unique food and lodging

In downtown Gardiner you can get free coffee with your breakfast at the **Two Bit Saloon.** Pamper your sweet tooth at a 1920s soda fountain at **Minnie's Old Fashioned Fountain and Candy.** Completed in 1930, the **Mammoth Hot Springs Hotel,** at the park headquarters in Mammoth, is the only park hotel with year-round drive-in access. Special winter events in the dining room include Sunday breakfast buffets and theme dinners in January and February. Finally, if you want to experience winter like the trappers did, **Mammoth Campground** is open year-round also.

Practical information

Site: Roosevelt Arch, at the entrance to Yellowstone National Park near Gardiner.

Recommended time: Late January.

Minimum time commitment: One day.

What to bring: Warm clothes, sturdy waterproof winter boots, hat, gloves, sunblock, sunglasses, camera, and binoculars. A snowmobile, cross-country skis, or snowshoes are also recommended.

Admission fee: $20 per vehicle, or $50 per vehicle for a twelve-month passport to all national parks, $10 Golden Age lifetime pass for seniors 62 and older, free for blind or disabled persons.

Hours: Open daily, year-round. Albright Visitor Center hours are 9:00 A.M. to 5:00 P.M. daily during the winter. Warming hut hours are 8:00 A.M. to 5:00 P.M. daily during the winter.

Directions: From Gardiner, follow signs south to Yellowstone Park.

For more information

Yellowstone National Park, WY 82190
(307) 344–7381
www.nps.gov/yell

Gardiner Chamber of Commerce
P.O. Box 81, Gardiner, MT 59030
(406) 848–7971
www.gardinerchamber.com

Mammoth Hot Springs Hotel
Yellowstone National Park Lodges
Yellowstone National Park, WY 82190
(307) 344–7311

6
—

A Company Town Grows Up
Anaconda Historic District

See the showcase town that Copper King Marcus Daly built
for his Anaconda Mining Company and as a site for the state
capital. Get your Valentine's Day chocolate at the chocolate festival and take in a movie at one of the most beautiful theaters
in America.

The history

In June 1883, Butte Copper King Marcus Daly founded Anaconda as a
smelter and company town for his Butte mines. His rival William Andrews
Clark already controlled the water rights around Butte, so Daly chose a
location in the Deer Lodge Valley 27 miles away. Within two months it had a
population of 1,500 and by October the new smelter could operate at a
capacity of 500 tons of ore per day. In 1886 the capacity of the plant was
doubled, and a second plant was built in 1888. Three years later, the railroad
refused to haul ore to the smelter from Butte over a rate dispute, so Daly
built his own railroad—the Butte, Anaconda, and Pacific—which he later
electrified.

Daly built a magnificent hotel in the center of Anaconda in 1888. On
the floor of the bar was a mosaic of Daly's racehorse, Tammany. It was said
that anyone found standing on it was obliged to buy drinks for the house.
The hotel was finished just before Montana became a state, and Daly planned
to make his company town the permanent capital in the 1894 election. He
had the cash to do it too, by buying votes with cigars, drinks, and five-dollar
bills. But William Andrews Clark was able to buy more votes for Helena than
Daly could for Anaconda.

By the turn of the century, Daly had built the gigantic Washoe Smelter,
which could treat 15,000 tons of ore a day, and in 1918 the world's largest

Only the bottom two floors remain of Marcus Daly's Montana Hotel.

smokestack was erected at the plant. The smelter finally closed in 1980, but the stack remains as a state park. At 585 feet tall, you could hide the Washington Monument inside of it. The "Smelter City" of Anaconda still lives on, but with a new image as an open-air history museum and gateway to the outdoors.

The fun

Try visiting Anaconda in early February during the Chocolate Festival. This is also the best time to enjoy the area's many winter activities. Start at the old railroad depot/visitor center building downtown—the one with a railroad car parked in front. Here you can visit the museum, see a sixteen-minute video of local attractions, get directions, and pick up a self-guided walking tour brochure. The visitor center also offers a ninety-minute antique bus tour of the city at 10:00 A.M. and 2:00 P.M., and you can pick up some one-of-a-kind items, such as slag ink pens or a "bag o' slag." Ask for directions to the new Anaconda Stack Interpretive Site, where you can stand inside a full-scale replica of the base of the stack.

Then walk, drive, or ride to see Anaconda's outstanding turn-of-the-twentieth-century architecture while you check out the shops for Valentine's

Day chocolates at the Chocolate Festival. Across from the depot is the recently restored Davidson Building, now a tearoom, gift shop, and beauty salon. The old city hall building to the east was restored and is now the community's art center, cultural center, and Copper Village Museum. Marcus Daly's Montana Hotel at the corner of Main and Park Streets had two floors removed and now houses offices and a sandwich shop, but it still retains its redbrick exterior and arches. Other historic architecture includes the Hearst Free Library, St. Mark's and St. Peter's churches, and the county courthouse at the top of Main Street. Even Anaconda's streetlights are historic, designed after lamps in Washington, D.C., and made in 1913 in the Anaconda Foundry. If you brought your ice skates, take a spin on the outdoor skating rink at the Kennedy Common.

Round out your tour with a walk on the paved historical trail at the Old Works Golf Course and the site of the first smelter. This 18-hole course was designed by pro-golfer Jack Nicklaus as a centerpiece of the effort to clean up this industrial site. Then see the wildlife displays and feed the trout at the 1908 Washoe hatchery, the oldest fish hatchery in Montana. After dinner, be sure to take in an 8:00 P.M. show at the most popular historic site in Anaconda, the Washoe Theater on Main Street. Built in 1931 and ranked by the Smithsonian as the fifth most beautiful theater in the nation, the Washoe is one of the few classic art deco theaters still operating in America today.

Get your full quota of art deco by finishing up with a visit to Club Moderne at the corner of Park and Ash Streets. The club was built in 1937 by "Skinny" Francisco, who also designed his home on Fourth and Walnut Streets in the same style. Always a popular gathering place for the "after shifters," the back room still has a working jukebox.

If you can spend another day, try downhill skiing at Discovery Basin or cross-country skiing or snowmobiling at Mount Haggin Wildlife Management Area, then finish with a soak in a hot pool or a trip on the waterslide at nearby Fairmont Hot Springs.

Next best

If you have never seen a white golf ball hit from a black sand trap made of mine slag, a great time to visit is the second week in August when the Old Works Golf Course hosts the Montana Cup.

Unique food and lodging

Try some Scottish scones and tea for lunch at **Rose's Tea Room** in the historic Davidson Building, 301 East Park Avenue. The **Hickory House Inn** bed-and-breakfast, 608 Hickory Street, is a restored century-old home that offers rooms complete with claw-foot bathtubs.

Practical information

Site: Anaconda Historic District, Anaconda.

Recommended time: Early February.

Minimum time commitment: One day.

What to bring: Warm clothes, sturdy waterproof winter boots, hat, gloves, sunblock, sunglasses, camera, swimsuit, ice skates, and skis.

Admission fee: None.

Hours: The Anaconda Visitor Center is open Monday through Friday 9:00 A.M. to 5:00 P.M.

Directions: Anaconda is 27 miles northwest of Butte and 105 miles southeast of Missoula, Montana. From the south, take Interstate 90 to Montana Highway 1, exit 208. Follow the signs 7.5 miles to the city. From the north, take Interstate 90 to Montana Highway 48, exit 201. Follow the signs 9.6 miles to the city.

For more information

Anaconda Chamber of Commerce
306 East Park Avenue, Anaconda, MT 59711
(406) 563–2400
www.anacondamt.org

Hickory House Inn
608 Hickory Street, Anaconda, MT 59711
(406) 563–5481
www.mtrdp.org/hickoryhouseinn

Fairmont Hot Springs Resort
1500 Fairmont Road, Fairmont, MT 59711
(800) 332–3272
www.fairmontmontana.com

7

—

The Gold Is Gone but the Elk Aren't

Elkhorn Ghost Town

Wake up to the howl of huskies, enjoy a winter's day on the edge of the Elkhorn Wilderness exploring the most picturesque ghost town in America, and finish up with a dip in a historic hot pool or a tour of a health mine.

The history

Swiss immigrant Peter Wys discovered the rich Elkhorn silver lode in 1870, naming it after the surrounding mountains. During the boom years of the 1880s, the town of Elkhorn grew up around the mines and swelled to more than 2,500 inhabitants. Many of them were Scandinavian, French, Irish, Dutch, and German immigrants. Giant stamp mills were built to crush the ore, and 1,500 mules worked the mines while 500 woodsmen cut timbers for them.

In 1889 the Northern Pacific Railroad built a spur line to the town. Elegant homes, hotels, and fraternity halls seemed to appear overnight, as well as a number of bawdy houses and fourteen saloons. The 1893 silver collapse put an end to the boom, and the 1910 silver market crash put an end to the town. But by the time the railroad pulled up its tracks in 1931, more than $32 million in silver and gold ore and 9 million pounds of lead had poured out of the local mines. Since then, the pine and spruce trees have grown back, the Rocky Mountain elk have returned, and a few cabins continue to be occupied year-round.

The fun

If you want to catch the frontier spirit and all of its sights and sounds, stop in Helena in the early afternoon to watch hundreds of dogs and mushers begin

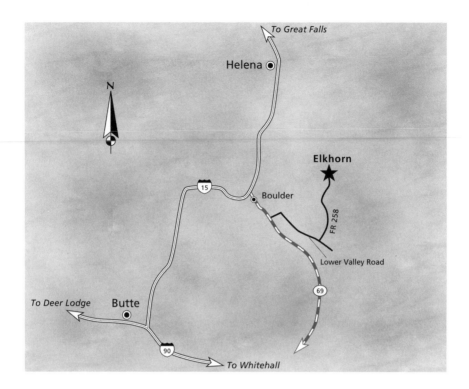

the 350-mile Race to the Sky sled dog race. Then drive south into the picturesque nineteenth-century ghost town of Elkhorn. As you approach the town, look for the old mine tailings on your left. Stop at the Forest Service picnic area on your right and read the interpretive sign. You can continue by car, foot, or ski up the main road into town. The names of many of the buildings are on signs in front of them. Elkhorn's most imposing buildings are Gillian and Fraternity Halls, designated as a state park. Built in the 1890s, Fraternity Hall, with its Greek Revival false front and ornate neoclassical balcony, is said to be the most photographed ghost town building in the nation. These halls were the center of the town's social activities, hosting dances, theater performances, boxing matches, and at least one murder.

The cemetery lies on the eastern ridge above the town. The dates and ages on the tombstones underscore the hardships of the miners. As you drive, walk, or ski through town, remember that the buildings are private property. People still live here and if it weren't for them, souvenir hunters would have taken much of the town home with them by now. Head back toward Boulder and, if you brought your swimsuit, finish up the day in one of the 104-degree hot pools at Boulder Hot Springs. First developed in the 1860s, it

An old wagon frame guards the entrance to Elkhorn Ghost Town.

was rebuilt in the California mission architectural style in 1909. If you didn't bring your swimsuit and want to see the inside of a real mine, you can get a tour of one of the abandoned mine tunnels in the area that is now operated as a "radon health mine." Radon is a radioactive gas given off by the rocks. While long periods of exposure can be dangerous, many people swear by its therapeutic value for chronic arthritis pain and other ailments.

Next best

If you like fall colors, one of the most beautiful times of the year to visit Elkhorn is during early October.

Unique food and lodging

If you ever wondered who invented Fletcher's Castoria, you can find the answer at the **Castoria Motel** bed-and-breakfast, 211 South Monroe, in Boulder. Stay in the 1889 Victorian house of the famous tonic inventor, Dr. Fletcher. The historic **Boulder Hot Springs,** 3 miles south of Boulder on Montana Highway 69, offers hotel rooms, a bed-and-breakfast, and a Sunday buffet as well as geothermal pools. For something outdoors, **The Free**

Enterprise Health Mine 2 miles west of Boulder has seasonal RV camping as well as health mine tours.

Practical information

Site: Elkhorn Ghost Town, near Boulder.

Recommended time: Second Saturday in February.

Minimum time commitment: Four hours, plus driving time.

What to bring: Warm clothes, sturdy waterproof winter boots, hat, gloves, sunblock, sunglasses, camera, and binoculars. A swimsuit, towel, and cross-country skis are also fun accessories.

Admission fee: None.

Hours: The town is accessible year-round, depending on snow conditions.

Directions: From Helena, go 29 miles south on Interstate 15 and take the Boulder exit 164. Go south 7.3 miles on Montana Highway 69 and look for the sign to Elkhorn. Turn left onto the gravel Lower Valley Road and go 3.2 miles southeast. Turn left on Elkhorn Forest Road 258 and go 8 miles north to the town.

For more information

Park Manager, Elkhorn State Park
930 Custer Avenue West, Helena, MT 59601
(406) 444–4720
www.fwp.state.mt.us/parks/

Castoria Motel
211 South Monroe Street, Boulder, MT 59632
(406) 225–3549

Boulder Hot Springs
P.O. Box 930, Boulder, MT 59632
(406) 225–4339
www.boulderhotsprings.com

The Free Enterprise Health Mine
P.O. Box 67, Boulder, MT 59632
(406) 225–3383
www.radonmine.com

8

High Plains Buffalo Culture
Ulm Pishkun State Park

The story of the Plains Indian culture is the story of the American bison, or buffalo. It is hard to say where one ended and the other began. See, touch, listen, and learn why the end of the buffalo also meant the end of a way of life.

The history

For thousands of years, before the horse changed the Native American culture, prehistoric men and women of the Great Plains hunted the American bison, or buffalo, by driving them over cliffs or "jumps." Bison kill sites, called *pishkuns* by the Indians, were essentially "factories" for creating shelter, tools, and food. The Indians did not need rifles or horses to chase the buffalo. This buffalo jump near the town of Ulm is possibly the largest in the world, the top of the cliff being more than a mile long. It was used for about 600 years until the 1500s. At the base of the cliffs, compacted bison bones have been found nearly 13 feet deep. In fact, the bone deposits were so extensive that the state of Montana, which owns the site, at one time allowed the bone deposits to be mined and sold for fertilizer.

The same procedure was used at most buffalo jumps. It involved finding a herd of buffalo and decoying them into stampeding over a nearby hidden cliff. In 1805, the Lewis and Clark Expedition saw one such buffalo jump on the Missouri River. Lewis noted, "the part of the decoy I am informed is extreamly dangerous, if they are not fleet runers the buffaloe tread them under foot and crush them to death, and sometimes drive them over the precipice also, where they perish in common with the buffaloe."

With the introduction of the horse in the 1600s, the Plains Indian no longer needed to rely on natural cliffs and elaborate planning, and no longer risked starvation if the plan didn't work.

The Ulm Buffalo Jump or "Pishkun" is more than a mile long.

The fun

You can visit this site any time of the year, but try a late February trip when the sky is cobalt blue and the snow is sparkling with the sun's reflection like a million diamonds. It's the best medicine I know of for cabin fever. If you call and make an appointment during this time of year, you can have the visitor center practically to yourself. Start there and take the time to see all the exhibits. Bring the kids because there are a lot of hands-on displays that demonstrate how Montana's native peoples relied on the bison economy. Exhibits show how the families worked together to butcher the bison; how hides were used for tepees, clothing, and blankets; how horns became hand tools and spoons; and why meat that wasn't needed immediately was dried to make jerky and sometimes mixed with berries to carry as emergency provisions for long journeys. Ask to see the visitor center's book selection and gift shop for items that focus on the history of the bison and Native American culture.

You can see the extensive cliffs from the window of the visitor center, but the best way to see how the buffalo perished is to drive the 2.7-mile gravel road to the top and walk the trail to the edge. The 360-degree view is spectacular, and there are interpretive signs along the trail. If the ground is

Indian Cattle

The Plains Indians' most important natural resource was the American bison. Writer Ernest Thompson Seton estimated that there were 60 million of these huge beasts in America at the beginning of the nineteenth century. The Indians hunted many different animals, but only the buffalo provided them with all of their basic food, clothing, and shelter. Tepees made from buffalo hides could be put together and taken down quickly and easily, allowing the Plains tribes to follow the seasonal migrations of the buffalo. The tepee could also be packed up and dragged behind a dog or horse on a travois when the Indians moved their village.

Buffalo meat was an excellent source of protein. The fresh meat was either roasted on a stick or boiled, sometimes with fresh vegetables. The Indians also made a sausage by stuffing meat and herbs into the buffalo's gut. The meat that could not be eaten fresh was cut into strips and hung on racks to dry. Dried buffalo jerky and pemmican could then be kept for months until it was eaten.

The buffalo's hide was also made into clothing decorated with beads, porcupine quills, and feathers. No part of the buffalo went to waste. Horns were used as spoons, cups, and toys. Bones were used as tools and weapons. The tail was used as a fly brush or horse whip. The stomach, intestines, and bladder were cleaned and used to carry water.

The white man found that as long as there were buffalo, the Indians could not be subdued. It was only when these great herds of "Indian cattle" had been decimated that the Plains Indians could be forced onto reservations. By 1900, when the nomadic life of the Plains Indian had been ended, less than 300 wild buffalo remained in North America.

dry, you can walk to the bottom of the cliff for another view. The top of the jump has a black-tailed prairie dog town that is quite active during the summer. You can finish your trip here, or if you want a longer outing, ask at the visitor center for a number of additional historic sites in the area that you can visit.

Next best

If you can't get to the park during February, try visiting in late September when the World Atlatl Association has their spear-throwing competition and the prairie dog town is active.

Unique food and lodging

For a dinner of cultural cuisine that is considerably more modern, return to Great Falls and take U.S. 87 exit to Black Eagle. The 1946 art deco **3D International** (Drink-Dine-Dance) Club features Italian, American, and Asian menus nightly.

Practical information

Site: Ulm Pishkun State Park, 10 miles southwest of Great Falls.

Recommended time: Late February.

Minimum time commitment: Three hours, plus driving time.

What to bring: Warm clothes, hat, gloves, sturdy boots, water bottle, binoculars, and camera.

Admission fee: $2.00 adults, $1.00 children ages 6 to 12, or $24.00 for an annual state park passport.

Hours: The park is accessible year-round, depending on snow conditions. The visitor center is open Wednesday through Saturday from 10:00 A.M. to 4:00 P.M., and Sunday from 2:00 to 4:00 P.M. from October 1 to Memorial Day weekend, daily from 10:00 A.M. to 6:00 P.M. from Memorial Day through September.

Directions: From Great Falls, go 10 miles south on Interstate 15 to Ulm exit 270. Follow signs 3.5 miles on a paved county road west from Ulm to the park visitor center. From the visitor center, it is 2.7 miles by gravel road to the top of the Buffalo Jump.

For more information

Park Manager, Ulm Pishkun State Park
P.O. Box 109, Ulm, MT 59485
(406) 866–2217
www.fwp.state.mt.us/parks, www.lewisandclarktrail.com/section3/montanacities/greatfalls/ulmpishkun/index.htm

Great Falls Chamber of Commerce
P.O. Box 2127, Great Falls, MT 59403
(406) 761–4434
www.greatfallsonline.net

9
—

From Cowboy to Artist
Charles M. Russell Museum, House, and Studio

Visit the log cabin studio of the legendary "cowboy artist" Charles M. Russell and see the most complete collection of his finest masterpieces, which portray the colorful, quickly vanishing frontier and its inhabitants: cowboys, Indians, trappers, mule skinners, mountain men, moose, buffalo, and bear.

The history

Although Charles M. Russell grew up in St. Louis, stories of the Wild West lured him to Montana. In 1880, when Charlie was sixteen, his industrialist father let him visit a friend's sheep ranch in Montana. He soon became a night wrangler on the Judith River and worked for eleven years for various cattle outfits in central Montana.

Russell was much better at sketching and modeling than wrangling. His hobby was painting, and he gave away his pictures as gifts for friends and sometime to pay for a drink or two. Only in 1893, when his paintings were displayed at the Chicago World's Fair, did he decide to make a career of art. He soon married Nancy Cooper, who handled the business end of their partnership. Before he died in 1926, Russell had created more than 4,000 paintings, sculptures, and sketches depicting the rugged, unspoiled West of Indians, trappers, mountain men, and cowboys.

The Charles M. Russell Museum contains the world's most complete collection of Russell's original art and personal objects, as well as works of his contemporaries. The 46,000-square-foot museum was built near Charlie's 1900 home, and the 1903 log cabin studio he made from telephone poles. Many historians believe that Russell's art portrays the Old West perfectly. This

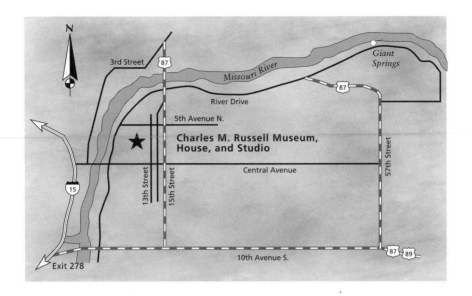

legendary artist and sculptor spent most of his adult life here in Montana. Some say only someone like Russell, who actually lived the life of a cowboy, could have captured the realism and emotion of Montana in the late nineteenth and early twentieth centuries the way he did.

The fun

This is a great trip for that winter weekend when it is too cold to be outside but not too cold to want to see and learn about great western art and a great western artist and sculptor. Russell's bronzes, watercolors, oil paintings, and illustrated letters are a treat for any history buff as well as those who appreciate great art.

A commemorative bronze statue of Russell greets you at the entrance to the museum. Walk through Russell's studio. His home is open May through September. Then see Russell's greatest pieces in the museum, which also contains works from such renowned artists as O. C. Seltzer, Joseph Henry Sharp, E. I. Couse, Winold Reiss, E. E. Heikka, Olaf Wieghorst, and Edward Curtis. The museum also has a noteworthy Browning firearms collection and a miniature wagon collection. You can finish your trip in the museum gift shop, which has a great selection of reproductions of Russell's work. If you want a longer outing, pick up a *Historic Saloons Tour* guide at the museum or chamber of commerce and check out some of Charlie Russell's favorite local watering holes.

Charlie Russell built his log cabin studio using telephone poles.

Next best

If you prefer crowds and excitement and have some extra cash to burn, time your visit for the third week in March during the annual C. M. Russell Auction of Original Western Art. You can buy an original painting or bronze at this fund-raiser that has grossed $12.6 million for the museum since 1969.

Unique food and lodging

If you want to have lunch in the downtown block of taverns where Charlie Russell spent some of his time, on weekdays try the "no-frills grill" at the **Club Cigar Saloon and Eatery,** 208 Central Avenue. One of Great Falls' oldest taverns, its gilded electric fans and massive mahogany back bar are worth a look. The 1939-era **City Bar and Casino,** 709 Central Avenue, with its huge Brunswick back bar and nickel-plated hotel parlor stove, offers a daily lunch special. For overnight accommodations in a century-old Period Revival manor, try the **Charlie Russell Manor** bed-and-breakfast, 825 Fourth Avenue North, in the original townsite.

Practical information

Site: Charles M. Russell Museum, House, and Studio, Great Falls.

Recommended time: Late February.

Minimum time commitment: Three hours, plus driving time.

What to bring: Camera; no flash attachments allowed.

Admission fee: None for the museum gift shop. Admission to the museum and studio is $6.00 adults, $4.00 groups and seniors over 60, $3.00 students, under age 5 free.

Hours: October through April: 10:00 A.M. to 5:00 P.M. Tuesday through Saturday, 1:00 to 5:00 P.M. Sunday; May through September: 9:00 A.M. to 6:00 P.M. Monday through Saturday, noon to 5:00 P.M. Sunday.

Directions: Take Interstate 15 to Great Falls exit 278. Go east on 10th Avenue South, turn left on 15th Street South, and go to 4th Avenue North. Turn left and continue 2 blocks to the museum at 400 13th Street North.

For more information

C. M. Russell Museum
400 13th Street North, Great Falls, MT 59401-1498
(406) 727–8787
www.cmrussell.org

Great Falls Chamber of Commerce
P.O. Box 2127, Great Falls, MT 59403
(406) 761–4434
www.greatfallschamber.org/cmrussel.htm

Charlie Russell Manor
825 Fourth Avenue North, Great Falls, MT 59401
(877) 207–6131, (406) 455–1400
www.charlie-russell.com

10

Towns Where the West Is Still Wild
Landusky and Zortman

If you want to experience what frontier legends are made of, there is nothing better than a late winter visit to the boom and bust mining camps of Landusky and Zortman, rich in Indian lore, gold strikes, cattle ranching, and outlaw tales.

The history

The beautiful, isolated Little Rockies were named when the Lewis and Clark Expedition mistook them for the Rocky Mountains. The mining camps of Landusky and Zortman sprang up in 1894 after Powell "Pike" Landusky and Oliver "Pete" Zortman made separate gold discoveries in Alder and Ruby Gulches. Landusky arrived in Montana in the 1860s as a teenager with a terrible temper, which he never outgrew. He was shot down by Kid Curry in Jake Harris's saloon in Landusky on December 27, 1894. Rumor has it that the townspeople buried him 6 feet deeper than usual and piled rocks on top of his grave so he couldn't get out. Zortman was not as colorful, and lived until he was 65 years old, dying in 1933.

The Ruby Gulch Mine near Zortman produced as much as $14,000 per day in gold bullion and became the second largest cyanide mill in the world. By 1920 Landusky and Zortman had a combined population of 2,000, and Zortman had nine bars, two hotels, a hospital, bakery, newspaper, and more than one brothel. When the mines closed after a 1936 forest fire destroyed most of the operations, they had produced $125 million in gold. From 1979 to 1998 the mines were reopened and employed up to 230 miners. Since then, reclamation efforts continue. The population of Landusky has dropped to seven and Zortman to about sixty.

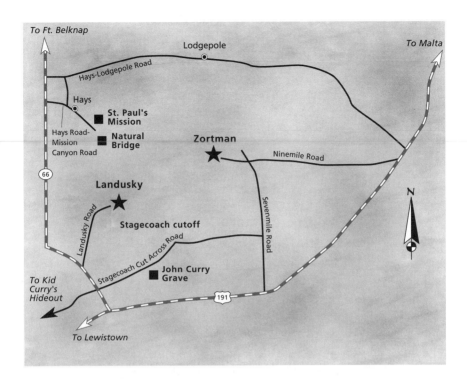

The fun

Start your trip with a lesson on outlaw history at the Phillips County Museum on U.S. 2 in Malta. Then drive to Zortman and pick up a sketch of the local roads at the Zortman Garage and Motel just below the little white church on the hill. You can try your hand at panning for gold or garnets, or looking for marine fossils in nearby Alder Gulch year-round. The folks here will show you the best locations, loan you a gold pan, and even show you how it's done indoors in the winter. Although the town today is a mishmash of metal buildings, several historic structures still exist. Be sure to see the white clapboard Catholic church, the Miner's Club oak back bar that came by way of Missouri riverboat, the old jail, the house of Charles Whitcomb, who developed the Ruby Gulch Mine, and the cemetery above the town. Remember this is private property, so ask first.

From Zortman, you can make a 50-mile loop around the Little Rockies. Take the gravel road that goes south to U.S. 191. Turn right and go south to the junction of Montana Highway 66. Turn right and go 4.3 miles north to the turnoff to Landusky; turn right and continue 3.4 miles up the gravel

This dovetail-notched log cabin was built on the south side of Zortman.

road. If you have a high-clearance vehicle, you can take the old stagecoach cutoff used by the Wild Bunch as part of the Outlaw Trail. It continues all the way to Kid Curry's hideout and the old Power Plant ferry on the Missouri River. This is private property, so stay on the road, and don't even consider this route if the weather is not dry and stable.

In Landusky, stop at the iris-choked cemetery to read the gravestones, then return to Montana Highway 66 and drive 12 miles north through scenic prairie foothills and the Fort Belknap Indian Reservation to the turnoff to Hays. Turn right and go 2.3 miles to St. Paul's Mission, built in 1886 with native stone. If you drive another half mile into Mission Canyon, you can also see the Natural Bridge. To complete the loop, go back through Hays and turn right onto the Hays-Lodgepole Road. This scenic paved road skirts the northern flank of the Little Rockies on its way to the town of Lodgepole and on to U.S. 191 just north of the Zortman turnoff where you started.

Next best

If you like your ghost towns to have a few more people and a little more excitement in them, a good time to visit is during the "Big Dig" on Memorial Day weekend. The Gold Prospectors Association of America sponsors a gold-panning contest in Alder Gulch near Zortman, with pans, sluice boxes, and trommels. After the gravel is washed, everyone combines the "concentrate" into one pile and draws out a portion. The person who finds the biggest gold nugget is the winner!

Unique food and lodging

For the full "gold miner" experience, you can camp at **Camp Creek Public Campground** 1 mile from Zortman or **Montana Gulch Public Campground** just below Landusky. The **Buckhorn Store and Cabins** in Zortman has rustic log cabins with kitchens, the **Kalamity Kafe** offers free coffee and homemade jam, and the **Miner's Cafe** has homemade pies.

Practical information

Site: Landusky and Zortman, 50 miles southwest of Malta.

Recommended time: Early March.

Minimum time commitment: One day.

What to bring: Warm clothes, water, sturdy waterproof boots, shovel, pick, gold pan, hat, sunblock, sunglasses, camera, and binoculars.

Admission fee: None.

Hours: The area is accessible year-round, depending on snow conditions.

Making Gold

Most of the early gold discoveries in Montana were placer gold, or gold taken from streambed gravel deposits. The simplest way to separate the gold was to wash the gravel in a pan until the lighter sand and gravel were washed out. An experienced panner could work forty to fifty pans per day. When traces of "color" were found, another simple but more economical method of working a placer claim was to use a sluice box, an inclined trough with riffles to catch the gold flakes, scads, and nuggets (a scad is a small flat nugget). Sluice boxes were 20 to 30 feet long and used poles from nearby trees for riffles to catch the gold. More elaborate methods used for working placer claims included hydraulic mining with large pressure hoses, and floating dredges. Both of these methods required expensive equipment but could follow the placers down to bedrock in many cases.

When the placers played out, the miners went to hard rock or lode mining deposits of gold ore in the rocks themselves. A vertical shaft or a horizontal adit was dug to follow the ore deposit into the rock. Sometimes a winze, a steeply inclined shaft, was dug to connect one mine level with another. Several methods were used to extract gold from the ore. One primitive method was the arrastra, a circular rock-lined pit with a post in the center. Extending out from the post were two arms. Attached to one arm was a horse or burro as a power source. Attached to the other arm were heavy stone blocks that ground the ore on the floor of the pit as the horse walked around. Water was slowly dripped onto the ore being ground, washing it into a sluice box where the gold was separated.

A more common method of ore extraction was the stamp mill. The stamp was a long, straight iron rod with a heavy round head. The stamps, which weighed between 500 and 900 pounds, were dropped about 8 inches onto the ore, crushing it. One stamp could deliver sixty blows per minute and could crush three tons of rock in a day. The crushed rock was then mixed with water and run through a sluice box.

Sometimes liquid mercury was sprinkled on the ore to separate the gold. The mercury would combine with the gold into a gummy amalgam alloy ball. The amalgam was then heated in a frying pan or a scooped-out potato to evaporate the mercury, leaving behind the gold.

Larger mines used a cyanide flotation method in large tanks with wooden slats and false bottoms. Heavy canvas was spread over the slats, and the crushed ore was dumped on top. Sodium cyanide was pumped into the bottom of the tank and allowed to work on the ore until all the gold was dissolved. The solution was then drawn off and dried, and the gold precipitate was melted in a furnace, poured into molds, cooled, and shipped.

Directions: From Malta, go 41 miles south on U.S. 191 (from Lewistown, go 95 miles north on U.S. 191). Turn onto the paved Ninemile Road and continue 9 miles to town.

For more information

Phillips County Museum
431 Highway 2 East, Malta, MT 59538
(406) 654–1037

Malta Area Chamber of Commerce
P.O. Box GG/MR, Malta, MT 59538
(406) 654–1776

Buckhorn Store and Cabins
P.O. Box 501, Zortman, MT 59546
(406) 673–3162

Zortman Garage and Motel
P.O. Box 302, Zortman, MT 59546
(800) 517–0372

11

Still the Richest Hill on Earth
Butte Historic District

*The War of the Copper Kings, the Gibraltar of Unionism—
the story of Butte and its ethnic diversity is one of the most
colorful episodes in the history of Montana, and the best time
to celebrate that history is on Saint Patrick's Day.*

The history

Butte began as a placer gold strike on Silver Bow Creek in 1864 and was named after the "big butte" to the north. At the peak of the placer boom in 1867, the town grew to 500, but lost half of its population over the next two years. Then quartz deposits were discovered on the "rich city on the hill," and Butte boomed as a silver camp. Soon three "copper kings" arrived on the scene: William Andrews Clark, Marcus Daly, and Fritz Augustus Heinze. Clark became rich by buying and operating silver mines. In 1881, Daly bought a played-out silver mine and turned it into a copper mine just as silver prices crashed. An economic war between the two erupted as each tried to prevent the other from getting the upper hand. Then in 1892, Heinze began buying smelters and mines, and soon began gouging ore out from underneath other mines. His legal maneuvering in the courts made him millions and kept his mines in business for more than a decade.

The miners worked around the clock and played around the clock. Nearly half the population was foreign-born, with the Irish becoming the largest ethnic group. During the 1890s, Butte's brothels on East Galena Street rivaled those of the Barbary Coast, and saloons sold a shot of whiskey with a beer chaser for a dime. In 1899, Marcus Daly merged with Rockefeller's Standard Oil Company to create the Amalgamated Copper Mining Company. It bought up smaller mining companies and changed its name to the Anaconda Copper Mining Company in 1910, the largest power in Butte and Montana. The company dominated Montana politics and business, and until the 1950s owned every newspaper in the state.

The Butte mines were so rich in copper and zinc that strip mining was introduced in 1912. Butte's landmark Berkeley Pit was started in 1955 and operated nonstop until 1983, when mining ceased for the first time in a century. No longer the largest city in Montana, Butte has gained new life by diversifying its economy.

The fun

Butte has always been known for its raucous Saint Patrick's Day celebrations. Make your first stop at the visitor center at I–90 exit 126 and pick up a *Butte Visitor's Guide* and a Saint Patrick's Day program. Wear purple on Saint Urho's Day (March 16) and celebrate the crowning of Saint Urho, the Finnish Patron Saint, in "Finntown." Then "Finnish" up with the Irish at the Friendly Sons of Saint Patrick Banquet at the Copper King Inn and a stay at a historic hotel or house in uptown Butte.

Begin Saint Patrick's Day by putting on something green and having breakfast at the M & M Bar and Cafe, a Butte landmark. Then don't miss the grand parade with its bagpipers, beer wagons, and bonnie lasses. For lunch, several cafes offer the traditional corned beef and cabbage. From the parade route you can walk to many of the city's historic sites, including the Arts Chateau in Charles Clark's century-old mansion, the courthouse with its massive copper doors, and the 1897 Saint Lawrence O'Toole Church, built with donations from miners' families. Even the 1890 Dumas Brothel is open—as a museum. Call early and you can tour William Clark's Mansion, which cost more than a quarter million dollars to build in the 1880s.

Next take a short drive to historic Centerville, Walkerville, the Anselmo Mine Yard with its headframe, and the Montana College of Technology. The Mineral Museum here has more than 1,500 specimens on display, including a 27.5-ounce gold nugget. Don't forget to see the mile-wide Berkeley Pit from its viewing stand. Anytime during the day or night, you can head back to the uptown bars and cafes to participate in the celebration and music of Saint Patrick's Day. For dinner try an ethnic Chinese, Irish, or Cornish dish.

Next best

If you can't be there on Saint Patrick's Day you can log on to www.mtstandard.com to see live pictures of the celebration. Or if you want to see how Butte's most famous citizens lived, take the Historic Homes tour on Saturday in mid-June. At that time the World Museum of Mining is also open, and the weather is likely to be better for outdoor photos.

Old mine gallows frames still punctuate the skyline of uptown Butte.

Unique food and lodging

For eats and treats at anytime of the day or night, try Butte's one-of-a-kind **M & M Bar and Cafe,** 9 North Main Street, or get an original Cornish miner's pasty and coleslaw dinner at **Nancy McLaughlin's Pasty Shop,** 2810 Pine Street (off of Continental Drive). If you treasure your dinners, you can eat them in a Bank Vault at the **Metals Banque Restaurant,** Park and Main. The upstairs Chinese **Pekin Noodle Parlor,** 117 South Main Street, is just down the street.

Accommodations in the historic uptown area include the **Finlen Hotel,** Broadway and Wyoming, where the likes of Charles Lindberg and John F. Kennedy once stayed. Bed-and-breakfasts include William Andrews Clark's 1884 Victorian **Copper King Mansion,** 219 West Granite Street, and the red- brick **Scott Inn,** 15 West Copper Street, a restored miner's boarding-house.

Practical information

Site: Butte Historic District, in uptown Butte.

Recommended time: March 16 and 17.

Minimum time commitment: Two days.

What to bring: Warm clothes (purple and green), sturdy waterproof winter boots, hat, gloves, sunblock, sunglasses, and camera.

Admission fee: None.

Hours: The Butte Chamber visitor center is open Monday through Friday from 9:00 A.M. to 5:00 P.M. The Montana College of Technology Mineral Museum's winter schedule is Monday through Friday from 9:00 A.M. to 4:00 P.M. and from 1:00 to 5:00 P.M. on weekends.

Directions: Butte is located at the crossroads of Interstates 15 and 90. Take Interstate 90 to exit 126.

For more information

Butte Chamber, Visitor, and Transportation Center
1000 George Street, Butte, MT 59701
(800) 735–6814
www.butteinfo.org

Finlen Hotel and Motor Inn
100 East Broadway, Butte, MT 59701
(800) 729–5461
www.finlen.com

Copper King Mansion
219 West Granite Street, Butte, MT 59701
(406) 782–7580

Scott Inn
15 West Copper Street, Butte, MT 59701
(800) 844–2952
www.mtbba.com

12

Lewis and Clark's Indian Highway
Lolo Trail National Historic Landmark

Few drives can compare with following the Lolo Trail along U.S. 12 for its combination of history, scenery, and recreation. You can experience the remote, rugged, wild character of the land as Lewis and Clark once did.

The history

On September 11, 1805, Lewis and Clark began the most difficult part of their journey to the Pacific Ocean: their crossing of the Bitterroot Mountains by way of the ancient Lolo Trail. The Lolo Trail is different from all other frontier American trails because fur traders, emigrants, and covered wagons didn't use it. This ancient hunting trail began to be used extensively by the Nez Perce Indians of Idaho to reach the Montana buffalo country after horses were introduced in the early 1700s. The timber was so thick and the river canyons so rugged that the trail followed the ridge tops in many places.

On September 13, 1805, Lewis and Clark were following the trail when they found Lolo Hot Springs. The springs have been measured at 111 degrees Fahrenheit with a discharge of 180 gallons per minute. Old Toby, Lewis and Clark's Shoshone guide, lost the trail here briefly as they climbed to Lolo Pass. The following day, they again lost the trail and followed a fishing trail down to the Lochsa River (lochsa is a Salish word meaning "rough water") and camped at an Indian fishing site near the present-day Powell Ranger Station. Ten days later—wet, tired, cold, and hungry—they finally reached Idaho's Weippe Prairie. The Expedition returned eastward on the trail in 1806.

In 1866 the Lolo Trail was surveyed and improved, but it never became more than a pack trail. Then in 1877 after years of pressure by the U.S. government to force the Nez Perce Indians to give up their nomadic ways and

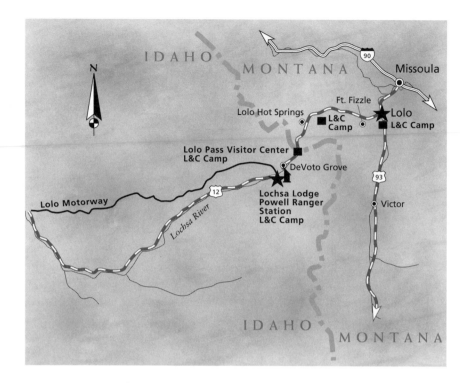

move onto a reservation, the Nez Perce war broke out. After several fights and two major battles, nearly 800 Nez Perce Indians took their tepees and 2,000 horses over the trail as they fled from General Oliver O. Howard and his Army troops in Idaho. Captain Charles Rawn from newly established Fort Missoula was ordered to delay the Nez Perce and built log breastworks near the eastern end of the trail. The Indians simply used an "impassable" ridge to avoid the place, which was dubbed Fort Fizzle.

In the 1930s, the narrow, rocky Lolo "Motorway" was built by the Civilian Conservation Corps along the ridge trail in Idaho. It was not until 1962 that U.S. 12 was completed, providing a reliable transportation link across these rugged mountains.

The fun

Begin by stopping at a Forest Service office to pick up a map of the area and a U.S. 12 self-guided driving-tour cassette and guidebook. Start your tour on U.S. 93 just south of Lolo at the Traveler's Rest sign marking Lewis and Clark's camp of September 9–10, 1805. The land is now one of Montana's newest state parks. Then follow U.S. 12 west up Lolo Canyon, watching for

The outdoor pool at Lolo Hot Springs is a welcome treat during the winter.

roadside interpretive signs. Five miles west of Lolo near milepost 28, watch for the Fort Fizzle sign. Besides viewing the reconstructed log breastworks here, you can take a break at the Forest Service picnic area. At Howard Creek, 18.5 miles west of Lolo, you can follow a 0.4-mile loop that includes part of the original trail.

Lolo Hot Springs, 25 miles west of Lolo, is one of the hubs for activities. Here you'll find a lodge, restaurant, RV park, campground, snowmobile rentals, gift shop, a Lewis and Clark exhibit, and hot springs pools. During the winter you can explore hundreds of miles of snow trails by snowmobile or on cross-country skis, or you can just soak in the indoor 103-degree hot pool while the kids enjoy the outdoor 94-degree swimming pool. Forest Service campgrounds nearby are open during the summer.

Thirty-two miles west of Lolo is Lolo Pass (5,233 feet) and the border of Idaho. The scenery is superb during the winter and the snow is deep, making this a winter mecca for outdoor enthusiasts. There are more than 80 miles of marked snowmobile trails, 30 miles of marked ski trails, and 8 miles of groomed ski trails radiating from here. Be sure to stop at the new Visitor and Interpretive Center (opening scheduled for 2002) for information on this portion of the trail and the latest snowmobile and ski trail conditions.

Continue west on U.S. 12 into Idaho. Look for the sign marking the

Lolo Trail crossing, 3.2 miles west of Lolo Pass. Ten miles west of the pass is the Bernard DeVoto Memorial Cedar Grove where the ashes of the author of *The Journals of Lewis and Clark* were scattered at his final request. This stop provides picnic tables, rest rooms, a garbage receptacle, and a pleasant interpretive trail through the giant western red cedar grove during the summer months. Thirteen miles west of the pass at milepost 163, take the turnoff to Lochsa Lodge. A rustic hand-hewn log hunting lodge that was built here in 1929 burned down in March 2001. Stop here for refreshments and check out the rebuilt lodge, gift shop, gas pump, and cabins.

Powell Ranger Station is just beyond the lodge. Stop here for information on this portion of the trail and to see the wild and beautiful Lochsa River and the Lewis and Clark campsite of September 14, 1805. Picnic areas and campgrounds nearby are open during the summer. From here you can either return to Lolo (45 miles east on U.S. 12) or strap on your skis for a trip to one of the natural hot springs in the area.

Next best

If you visit between mid-June and mid-September, you will find all of the tourist facilities and campgrounds open. If you have the time and are the adventurous type, you can ask at the Powell Ranger Station for information on following the Lolo Trail across the Bitterroot Mountains via the old Lolo Motorway. This is a one-day trip in itself, and the primitive road is closed by deep snow in the winter.

Unique food and lodging

The newly rebuilt **Lochsa Lodge** near the Powell Ranger Station offers rustic wood- and propane-heated cabins (the wood is provided), and the restaurant specializes in homemade soups, wild huckleberry pie, and apple-huckleberry cobbler. For even more rustic accommodations, during the summer try any of the four tepees at the **Lolo Hot Springs Campground.**

Practical information

Site: Lolo Trail National Historic Landmark; Lewis and Clark National Historic Trail, Nez Perce National Historic Trail, west of Lolo.

Recommended time: Late March.

Minimum time commitment: One or two days. Because of its remoteness and the many sights to see and things to do, it is best to devote an entire weekend.

What to bring: Warm clothes, sturdy waterproof winter boots, hat, gloves, sunblock, sunglasses, swimsuit, camera, and binoculars. Cross-country skis or snowshoes are also fun accessories. Although there are interpretive signs and self-guided driving tours, for the full effect bring along a copy of *The Journals of Lewis and Clark* and *Following The Nez Perce Trail: A Guide to the Nee-Mee-Poo National Historic Trail.*

Admission fee: None for most activities. Lolo Hot Springs pool rates are $6.00 adults, $5.00 seniors, $4.00 ages 5 to 12, and $3.00 for children under 4. A parking permit is required for the Lolo Pass parking lot during the winter snowmobile and cross-country ski season. You can purchase a day pass for $5.00 or a season pass for $25.00 at the visitor center, at Lolo Hot Springs, or from Missoula outdoor shops. Travel on the primitive Lolo Motorway in Idaho may require a $6.00 lottery permit application and a $25.00 permit from the Clearwater National Forest between July 1 and October 1 during the Lewis and Clark Bicentennial Observance from 2002 to 2007.

Hours: The Lolo Pass Visitor Center is open daily from Memorial Day through September, and Friday through Monday during the winter. Hours are 8:30 A.M. to 4:00 P.M. Lolo Hot Springs is open 10:00 A.M. to 10:00 P.M. daily year-round.

Directions: From Missoula, go south on U.S. 93 12 miles to Lolo. Follow the Lolo Trail west on U.S. 12 over Lolo Pass into Idaho and down to the Lochsa River.

For more information

Powell Ranger Station
Clearwater National Forest, Lolo, MT 59847
(208) 942–3113
www.fs.fed.us/r1/clearwater

Superintendent, Nez Perce National Historical Park
Route 1, P.O. Box 100, Spalding, ID 83540
(208) 843–2261
www.nps.gov/nepe

Lochsa Lodge
Powell Ranger Station, Lolo, MT 59847
(208) 942–3405

The First American Horse Breed

The first European explorers brought horses with them to America. By the early 1700s the Shoshone Indians had brought the horse to the northern tribes. When Lewis and Clark reached the Rocky Mountains in 1805, they noticed the Nez Perce Indians' spotted horses were different from all of the others they had seen. As the only Native Americans known to selectively breed their horses, the Nez Perce desired only the strongest, fastest, and most sure-footed of mounts. In doing so they ended up with a breed of distinctive, colorful spotted horses with mottled skin, striped hooves, and thirteen coat patterns.

The influx of white settlers to the Northwest changed the Nez Perce's destiny and nearly destroyed the legacy of their horse-breeding efforts. War ensued when some of the Nez Perce rebelled against imposed treaties. Over several months and across 1,300 miles, the Appaloosa horses helped the nontreaty Nez Perce elude the U.S. Cavalry in 1877. At the time of Chief Joseph's surrender in Montana, the Army confiscated most of their horses, including Appaloosas. The prized characteristics of the distinctive horse then became lost or severely diluted due to indiscriminate breeding. Claude Thompson, an Oregon wheat farmer, realized the importance of preserving the spotted horse breed. In 1938 he established the Appaloosa Horse Club to promote the Appaloosa's return from the brink of obscurity.

Although the Nez Perce never called their spotted horses "Appaloosas," the breed's name comes from either the Palouse River in eastern Washington and northern Idaho, where the horses were known to be plentiful, or from the Palouse tribe, whose main village was situated on the Palouse River. White settlers first described the colorful native mounts as "a Palouse horse," which was soon slurred to "Appalousey." Today, more than a half million Appaloosas are registered with the Appaloosa Horse Club.

Lolo Hot Springs
38500 West Highway 12, Lolo, MT 59847
(800) 273–2290
www.lolohotsprings.net

Lolo Trail Center
P.O. Box 386, Stevensville, MT 59870
(406) 273–2201
www.lolotrailcenter.com

13

Captain Clark Leaves His Mark
Pompeys Pillar National Monument

"... at 4 P.M. I arrived at a remarkable rock ... I marked my name and the day of the month & year July 25th, 1806." Walk in William Clark's footsteps to the top of the sandstone rock that reads like a history book of the western frontier.

The history

On July 25, 1806, Captain William Clark of the Lewis and Clark Expedition noticed a 200-foot rock outcropping on his way down the Yellowstone River to St. Louis. He climbed the pillar and carved his name and date in the sandstone. Clark's inscription remains the only physical evidence of the Lewis and Clark Expedition in Montana. Clark wrote in his journal, "This rock I ascended and from its top had a most extensive view in every direction ... on the northerly side of the river high romantic clifts approach & jut over the water for some distance both above and below."

Clark named the pillar "Pomp's Tower," a reference to his nickname for little Jean Baptiste Charbonneau, infant son of Sacagawea, the expedition's Shoshone interpreter and guide who contributed so much to its success. An image of Sacagawea carrying young Pompy adorns the new United States golden dollar coin. Pomp means "little chief" in the Shoshone language. The landmark's name was changed to Pompeys Pillar when Nicolas Biddle published an account of the Expedition in 1814.

Pompeys Pillar is at a natural ford in the Yellowstone River. As a crossroads in history, the sandstone is marked with literally hundreds of etchings and drawings. The Crow Indians knew the rock as the place "where the mountain lion lies." Indians, fur trappers, military expeditions, railroad workers, and early settlers also used the sandstone as a register. In fact, a year

Pompeys Pillar is an imposing landmark on the Yellowstone River.

before the Expedition stopped here, fur trapper Francois Antoine Larocque described it as "a whitish perpendicular rock." The rock was also a haven for wildlife, as Clark noted, "For me to mention or give an estimate of the different Species of . . . Elk, Antelopes and Wolves would be incredible."

The tower was later the scene of a minor skirmish between Custer's 7th Cavalry and the Sioux in 1873 when the Army was protecting the Stanley Expedition's railroad survey crew. The pillar still typifies the Yellowstone Valley as Clark saw it in 1806.

The fun

A great time to visit is in late March when you can visit the rock the way Clark did—on foot and without the hustle and bustle of the tourist season. You can call the BLM Billings Field Office for an off-season tour or take your own self-guided tour. Park at the gate and walk up the gravel road to the rock. You can still see Clark's inscription today. The first effort to preserve it came from the Northern Pacific Railroad, which placed an iron grating over the signature in 1882. The Foote family, who owned and preserved the site for many years, replaced the grate with a shatterproof glass case.

After you have seen the signature, climb the stairway to the overlook on top of the rock. From here, you have the same view that Clark did in 1806, and it hasn't changed much. Listen to the wind and the water and imagine what you would have seen here if you were with the Expedition. Return down the stairway to the cottonwood grove below. Stop to see the replicas of the canoes the Expedition used, then walk to the edge of the river. The cavalry was camped on the other side in 1873 when they were ambushed by the Sioux war party.

If the weather is nice, the grove is a good place for a picnic; there are also rest rooms here. If you called to get a tour, or during the summer, stop by the visitor center to pick up brochures, see the mock-up of Clark's signature and other exhibits, and visit the gift shop and bookstore.

Next best

If you like reenactments, the last weekend in July is "Clark Day" at the monument. Food, entertainment, and interpretive activities are scheduled, including the arrival of the Expedition in canoes and Sergeant Pryor embarking on a bullboat. During the summer months, the monument also sponsors Friday evening programs on Expedition and local history topics at 7:00 P.M.

If you want the complete western experience, come on the third weekend in June for the Montana Reenactment on the Russell Peery Ranch, 7 miles east of Pompeys Pillar on the old highway. You can participate or just watch the three-day Army-Indian reenactment in period dress, complete with a re-created Army fort, barracks, and Indian camp.

Practical information

Site: Pompeys Pillar National Monument and National Historic Landmark, 28 miles east of Billings.

Recommended time: Late March.

Minimum time commitment: Two hours, plus driving time.

What to bring: Warm clothes, water, sunglasses, binoculars, camera, and picnic lunch.

Admission fee: $3.00 per vehicle; $25.00 per bus or group. No fee for walk-ins.

Hours: Open daily 8:00 A.M. to 8:00 P.M. from Memorial Day weekend through September. Walk-in access only (1 mile round-trip) from October through Memorial Day weekend.

Directions: Take I–94 28 miles east of Billings to Pompeys Pillar exit 23, then follow signs 0.8 mile to the park entrance.

For more information

Pompeys Pillar Visitor Contact Station
(406) 875–2233
www.mt.blm.gov/pillarmon

Bureau of Land Management Billings Field Office
P.O. Box 36800, Billings, MT 59107-6800
(406) 896–5004

Pompeys Pillar Historical Association
P.O. Box 213, Worden, MT 59088
(406) 967–3281

14

The Cradle of Montana Civilization
Fort Owen and St. Mary's Mission

As "the cradle of Montana civilization," St. Mary's Mission and Fort Owen have a lot to tell you about the men and women who brought Christianity, medicine, agriculture, and trade to Montana. Here you'll see customer service, 1860s style.

The history

The histories of St. Mary's Mission and the pioneer trading post of Fort Owen are closely intertwined. It was here, at the present site of Fort Owen, that the first Roman Catholic mission in Montana was established, followed shortly by a number of other "firsts": the first permanent white settlement, gristmill, sawmill, agriculture, irrigation, and school. Father Pierre Jean DeSmet arrived here in 1841 and built a cottonwood chapel for more than 700 Salish (Flathead) Indians, who had long been asking for the "blackrobes." Before the end of the year, Father DeSmet had imported wheat, oats, potatoes, and garden seeds for the first crops. In 1842 he brought the first cattle, pigs, and chickens to Montana before leaving for Europe to seek recruits and funding. One of those recruits was Father Anthony Ravalli, who taught classes to the Salish and started the first gristmill and sawmill.

Despite these achievements, lack of funds, harassment by the Blackfeet tribe, and a dwindling number of converts forced the church to close the mission. In 1850 John Owen, a former Army sutler from Fort Hall, bought the mission for $250 in the first recorded land transaction in Montana. Soon Fort Owen boomed as a trading post for traders, trappers, and immigrants. A good host and an honest trader, Owen was appointed acting Indian Agent in 1856, and in 1860 replaced the wood stockade with adobe walls. But business

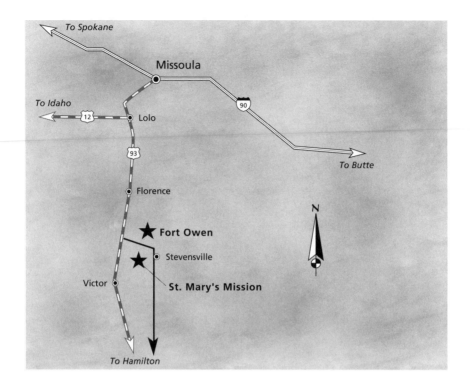

faltered as the Mullan Road bypassed the fort to the north, and Owen's health declined after his Shoshone wife, Nancy, died in 1868. The fort was auctioned off in 1872.

Meanwhile, in 1866 Father Ravalli was called back to reestablish St. Mary's Mission at its present location, about a mile south of Fort Owen. It became the headquarters for the Rocky Mountain province and ministered to the Salish Indians until 1891 when Chief Charlo's band was forced to move to the Flathead Reservation.

The fun

Springtime comes early to Montana's Bitterroot Valley. The weather is often sunny and the views of snow-clad St. Mary's Peak from Fort Owen and St. Mary's Mission are breathtaking. You will enjoy a guided tour of the mission, but stop first at Fort Owen State Park. The site is unstaffed and nothing is left of the first mission, sawmill, or gristmill, which was a landmark until it burned in 1890. But you can start your tour in the well-preserved adobe east

Brother William Cloessens built St. Mary's Mission Chapel in 1866.

barracks where John and his wife lived and entertained. Look at the interpretive displays, drawings, photos, and samples of entries from his ledger. Visit each room and imagine the life of an early day trader on the fringe of civilization. Make a small donation and pick up a park brochure to use as your guide to the remaining structures and foundations, including the west barracks, well house, and main gate. Also pick up the brochure listing the flora of Fort Owen. In it you will find descriptions of native shrubs, wildflowers, and plants the pioneers brought with them that still grow at the fort.

Next drive to St. Mary's Mission, where you can eat your picnic lunch at DeSmet Park. Stop at the visitor center first and see the museum, gift shop, and library. Ask to take the tour of the mission, which will take you through the mission chapel, Father Ravalli's log house and pharmacy, and Chief Victor's log house. The chapel altar and statue were hand-carved by Father Ravalli. Finish up your tour with a visit to the Indian cemetery, Father Ravalli's grave, and the last living apple tree he planted, which are behind the mission chapel.

Next best

If you visit on the second weekend in July, you can also take in the Chief Victor Days in nearby Victor.

Unique food and lodging

For local color, stop by the **Stevi Cafe,** 202 Main Street in Stevensville. The **Stevi Hotel,** 107 East Third Street, offers accommodations amid vintage decor. If that doesn't "move" you, try **The Country Caboose Bed and Breakfast,** 852 Willoughby Road, about 4 miles south and east of Stevensville, where you can sleep in a wooden 1923 Chicago, Burlington & Quincy caboose.

Practical information

Site: Fort Owen State Park and St. Mary's Mission, Stevensville.

Recommended time: Mid-April.

Minimum time commitment: Three hours, plus driving time.

What to bring: Sunglasses, camera, and binoculars.

Admission fee: St. Mary's Mission: $3.00 adults, $1.00 students, children under 6 free for tours. Fort Owen: free, but donations are accepted.

Hours: St. Mary's Mission tour hours are 10:00 A.M. to 4:00 P.M. April 15 through October 15, or by appointment. Fort Owen is open year-round during daylight hours.

Directions: From Missoula, go south on U.S. 93 for 24 miles. Take the Stevensville turnoff and go 0.8 mile on Secondary Road 269 to the state park entrance. To get to St. Mary's Mission, continue down Stevensville's Main Street. Turn right on Fourth Street and go 3 blocks.

For more information

Park Manager, Fort Owen State Park
3201 Spurgin Road, Missoula, MT 59804
(406) 542–5500
www.fwp.state.mt.us/parks

St. Mary's Mission
P.O. Box 211, Stevensville, MT 59870
(406) 777–5734

Father Ravalli

The Flathead, or Salish, Indians learned from other tribes about the "blackrobes," the Jesuit Priests who could talk to the Great Spirit. One of these was Father Anthony Ravalli. He was born in Italy in 1812 and entered the Jesuit order when he was fifteen years old. He was an eager learner; by the time he was thirty-one he had knowledge of surgery, pharmacology, medicine, and mechanics. He was also well versed in literature, the natural sciences, and many other fields.

In 1843 Ravalli was recruited by Father DeSmet to serve as a missionary in America. The two millstones given to him by a Belgian merchant were sent ahead to the newly established St. Mary's Mission in the Bitterroot Valley. When Father Ravalli arrived at the mission in November 1845, the millstones became part of the first gristmill in Montana. He also constructed the first sawmill, and the first still (for extracting medicinal alcohol from camas roots).

The church closed the mission in 1850 and transferred Father Ravalli as the Salish ranged farther from the mission and threats from the Blackfeet tribe worsened. Sixteen years later, Father Ravalli was assigned to reestablish St. Mary's Mission, and it still stands today. Not only did he rebuild the church, but also a blacksmith shop and a hospital-pharmacy that became his home. As Montana's first physician, surgeon, and pharmacist, his fame was so widespread that the pharmacy had a window for dispensing medicine, and was in fact, Montana's first "drive-up" pharmacy. Also an accomplished architect, artist, and sculptor, Father Ravalli made most of the furnishings in the pharmacy and chapel himself.

He also taught classes in religion, reading, writing, and mathematics—in the Salish language. Father Ravalli taught the Salish how to plow, plant, cultivate, irrigate, and harvest crops. One of the crab apple trees he planted still stands behind the mission church. Father Ravalli died and was buried in the mission cemetery in October 1884. Bitterroot Valley's Ravalli County and the town of Ravalli farther north are both named in his honor.

Bitterroot Valley Chamber of Commerce
105 East Main Street, Hamilton, MT 59840
(406) 363–2400
www.bvchamber.com

15

Raising the Fastest Horses in the World
Marcus Daly Mansion

Copper King Marcus Daly's Bitterroot Valley horse empire rivaled his Anaconda mining empire. Daly even had to build a town to house all the employees he needed to build and maintain his racetracks, stables, and agricultural businesses. Be a guest in Daly's home while you learn about his many enterprises.

The history

The Daly Mansion, also known as "Riverside" and "The Bitterroot Stock Farm," was a summer retreat for Butte's "Copper King" family, Margaret and Marcus Daly. Daly immigrated to the United States from Ireland when he was fifteen, and through ingenuity, skill, good luck, and great timing made a fortune in the copper mines. He was a huge influence on the Montana economy and politics for many years.

In 1886 Marcus Daly purchased the Anthony Chaffin homestead and 22,000 acres for his summer home, where he raised prized Thoroughbred racing horses. He remodeled the farmhouse in 1889 and by 1890 he was busy platting the town of Hamilton. He remodeled the house again in 1897, creating a Queen Anne–style Victorian home for entertaining. When completed, it reminded him of a church, so he planned to change it again but died in 1900 before the project could be started. In 1910 Daly's widow, Margaret, had A. J. Gibson of Missoula finish remodeling the house into a Georgian Revival–style mansion.

The 24,000-square-foot mansion has three floors, twenty-four bedrooms, fourteen bathrooms, and seven fireplaces, five of which are faced with Italian

A tree-lined lane brings you to the Georgian Revival–style Daly Mansion.

marble. Outside are formal gardens, a greenhouse, orchards, a lake, a tennis court, and a heated pool. On a hill three-quarters of a mile to the south on private property is Tammany Castle, the barn that housed Daly's famous racing horses. After Margaret Daly died in 1941, the mansion was boarded up until it came into public ownership and was restored in 1987.

The fun

A great time to visit is in mid-April when the mansion opens for the summer season and the signs of spring have come to the Bitterroot Valley. The Daly Mansion Preservation Trust manages the remaining fifty-acre property and provides tours, cultural programs, community events, exhibits, and other associated activities to pay for the mansion's operation and maintenance.

Drive in the main gate and park in the parking lot on the left, then stroll along the tree-lined drive to the front of the mansion. The entrance is on the north side, where you'll find a small gift shop and bookstore. Take a tour of the mansion and ask for a walking tour guide to the mansion grounds. As you stroll through the grounds, imagine that you are Daly's guest as he points out the sights. Take a moment to read the identification plaques on the many exotic trees and shrubs he had planted.

Also request a *Walking Tour of Historic Downtown Hamilton* brochure. On your return trip to town, take some time to look up at the buildings as you cruise down Main Street and stop to see the antique kitchen in the Ravalli County Museum at South Third Street and Bedford Avenue. Finish the day with dinner in what used to be Haigh's Pool Hall and Bar in the Drinkenberg block.

Next best

Another good time to visit the Daly Mansion is on the third weekend in July for the annual Marcus Daly Days, featuring a Saturday Microbrew Festival in Hamilton and a Sunday Daly Mansion Yard and Garden Tour from 1:00 to 4:00 P.M.

Unique food and lodging

At Hamilton's **Spice of Life** cafe in the 1909 Drinkenberg block, 163 South Second Street, you can have lunch on weekdays and dinner Wednesday through Saturday.

Practical information

Site: Marcus Daly Mansion, 45 miles south of Missoula.

Recommended time: Mid-April.

Minimum time commitment: Two hours, plus driving time.

What to bring: Camera with flash attachment.

Admission fee: $6.00 adults, $5.00 seniors, $4.00 ages 12 to 17, $3.00 ages 6 to 11, free for children under 6.

Hours: Open daily from 11:00 A.M. to 4:00 P.M. April 15 to October 15. Tours begin on the hour. Open by appointment during the winter.

Directions: Take U.S. 93 south from Missoula 45 miles to the town of Hamilton. Turn left off of U.S. 93 onto Fairgrounds Road at the stoplight. Go 1 mile beyond the fairgrounds to the Eastside Highway (Secondary Road 269). Turn left and drive 0.6 mile to the mansion entrance on your left.

For more information

Daly Mansion Preservation Trust
P.O. Box 223, Hamilton, MT 59840
(406) 363–6004
www.ohwy.com/mt/d/dalymans.htm

Tammany

In the 1890s, copper king Marcus Daly's Bitterroot Stock Farm produced many trotters and Thoroughbreds that were winning at all the big East Coast racetracks—horses with names like Bathhampton, Scottish Chieftain, and Montana. But his finest and favorite horse had the New York name of Tammany. Foaled in Tennessee in 1889, Tammany was sold to Daly in 1891 for $2,500, more than the cost of a house at that time.

Daly was determined to prove that racehorses raised in a cold climate at a high elevation would have more endurance. Tammany finished first in eight out of fourteen races, and became a legend to the people back in Butte and Anaconda. Tammany once lost to Charade in the Tidal Stakes at Coney Island, and for the next month his trainer worked on eliminating any remaining weaknesses. At the next race, Tammany beat Charade by three lengths.

In 1893 when Tammany had won more than $100,000, a rival challenged Daly to a match. A race between Tammany and Lamplighter, the favorite horse of the East Coast, was held in Guttenberg, New Jersey, and Daly promised, "If Tammany beats Lamplighter, I'll build him a castle." Fifty thousand people watched as Tammany came from behind and won by four lengths. On the train ride back to Montana, Tammany nearly died of pneumonia but was reportedly nursed back to health with doses of champagne and port ale.

Daly kept his word and built a brick stable called Tammany Castle on a hill about a mile east of Hamilton. The stable had carpeted floors, brass rails, and modern plumbing. Daly also had a replica of his beloved horse's head inlaid into the hardwood floor of the Montana Hotel in Anaconda. It is said that anyone found standing on it was obliged to buy drinks for the house.

All of Marcus Daly's horses were auctioned off in Madison Square Garden when he died in 1900. The offspring from these Thoroughbreds resulted in four Kentucky Derby winners: Regret, Paul Jones, Zev, and Flying Ebony.

Ravalli County Museum
205 Bedford Street, Hamilton, MT 59840
(406) 363–3338
www.cybernet1.com/rcmuseum

Bitterroot Valley Chamber of Commerce
105 East Main Street, Hamilton, MT 59840
(406) 363–2400
www.bvchamber.com

16

Pioneers in Forestry
Savenac Tree Nursery

Travel through conservation and transportation history, learn how a German immigrant's homestead along the Mullan Road became a focal point in creating the image of the Forest Service, then take a bicycle trip "through" the mountains on the old Milwaukee Railroad.

The history

In 1907 Elers Koch established Savenac Tree Nursery for a new government agency called the U.S. Forest Service. A Yale graduate of 1902, Koch was one of Gifford Pinchot's "young men" and one of the first professional foresters in America. In addition to being in the forest, the nursery needed to be on a well-established transportation route. The Mullan Road, built by the military here in 1862, ran right in front. The Yellowstone Trail, U.S. 10, and finally Interstate 90 followed it.

By 1909 Savenac had two bunkhouses, a cookhouse, a storehouse, and sixteen acres planted with seedlings. Then in August 1910 the "Great Burn" struck; in two days, a firestorm of biblical proportions killed eighty-five people and burned three million forested acres in western Montana and northern Idaho. Whole towns were incinerated. Smoke drifted across the country, reportedly darkening the skies so much that streetlights remained on all day in Watertown, New York. At Savenac, only the seedbeds survived, but they were enlarged and the nursery was rebuilt to restock the burned acres.

Electricity came in 1928, followed by a Civilian Conservation Corps (CCC) camp from 1935 to 1942. The CCC quadrupled the nursery's capacity to 12 million trees annually and added many of the buildings, including the administration building, that remain today. The nursery was transferred to the new Coeur d'Alene Nursery in 1969. It was used as a Young Adult

CCC stonemasons did fine work at Savenac Nursery.

Conservation Corps (YACC) camp from 1979 to 1982 and continues to be used as an environmental education camp for area schools.

The fun

Savenac illustrates the role and philosophy of the Forest Service and early professional foresters, as well as the importance of the CCC in the restoration of the nation's natural resources. This beautifully landscaped historic site contains buildings built by the Civilian Conservation Corps, a pond, a small arboretum, a creek, and a section of the Mullan Road. If you come in the early spring, the visitor center in the administration building is closed, but the grounds are open, the cabins are usually available, and you will avoid the summer crowds. Stop at the Superior Ranger Station and pick up a *Savenac Historical Interpretive Trail* guide. You can sign up for a cabin here too if you like.

When you get to the nursery, be sure to walk the old Mullan Road across Savenac Creek on the Yellowstone Trail concrete arch bridge. Look for swallows, cinnamon teal, and mallards at the pond, and forest birds along Savenac Creek. Continue the tour through the arboretum to the Big Burn Memorial Rock, dedicated in 1996. If you've brought your mountain bike, don't miss the Hiawatha Bike Trail on the old Milwaukee Railroad right-of-way. You can ride the 13-mile trail with a 2 percent grade through ten tunnels and seven trestles. Then retrace your ride or, during the summer, return by shuttle. The tunnels are dark, wet, and cold (36 degrees F) but fun. St. Paul's Pass tunnel is almost 2 miles long, so don't forget your helmet and flashlight. There is a trailhead parking lot at the east portal. To get there take Taft exit 5 off Interstate 90 and go 2 miles south on Forest Road 506. The summer shuttle returns you from the Idaho side of the trail and bike rentals are available at Lookout Pass (exit 0).

Next best

If you'd like to meet some of the men who worked in the Civilian Conservation Corps here, time your visit to coincide with the annual Savenac Days, a reunion of former employees and CCC workers on the third Friday in July.

Unique food and lodging

Those who like rustic accommodations can stay right at Savenac Nursery. Three historic oil- and wood-heated cabins are available (the wood and the ax are provided). The **Savenac Bunkhouse** sleeps thirty-five people and has showers; the smaller **Savenac Cookhouse** sleeps up to ten people and also has a dining room and showers; and the **West Cottage** has a kitchen, bath, and two bedrooms, and sleeps six. They can be reserved by contacting the Superior Ranger District. If you don't want to make your own breakfast but still want the atmosphere of Old Montana, try the nicely renovated 1911 **Hotel Albert** bed-and-breakfast, DeBorgia exit 18 off Interstate 90.

Practical information

Site: Savenac Tree Nursery, 17 miles west of St. Regis.

Recommended time: Late April.

Minimum time commitment: One day.

What to bring: Warm clothes, water bottle, and camera. A mountain bike, helmet, and light are also fun accessories for the nearby Hiawatha Trail.

Admission fee: None for nursery. Hiawatha Trail fees are $7.00 adults, $3.00 ages 3 to 13.

Hours: The site is open year-round; the visitor center is closed from September through May, then open daily from 9:00 A.M. to 6:00 P.M. from

Memorial Day to Labor Day.

Directions: From St. Regis, take Interstate 90 17 miles west to Haugan exit 16, then look for the nursery's entrance sign on the north side of the frontage road.

For more information

Lolo National Forest, Superior Ranger District
P.O. Box 460, Superior, MT 59872
(406) 822–4233

Mineral County Chamber of Commerce
P.O. Box 483, Superior, MT 59872
(406) 822–4891
www.thebigsky.net/MineralChamber/

Hotel Albert Bed and Breakfast
P.O. Box 300186, DeBorgia, MT 59830
(406) 678–4303, (800) 678–4303
www.rusticweb.com/hotelalbert

Route of the Hiawatha
Lookout Pass Ski and Recreation Area
P.O. Box 108, Wallace, ID 83873
(208) 744–1301
www.silvercountry.com, www.skilookout.com

17

The Valley of the Mission
St. Ignatius Mission

Visit the mission to the Indians that a town, a valley, and a mountain range take their names from, and see the miracle of the mission inside. Then drive among the shaggy beasts that formed the basis of the Indian economy until they were nearly exterminated.

The history

St. Ignatius Mission was founded in 1854 by Jesuit Father Adrian Hoecken, who moved the mission here from eastern Washington to be closer to the Indians. The Salish name for the location, which was a popular rendezvous for area tribes, was *Sinyalemin,* the "place of encirclement."

The chapel was built of whipsawed lumber held together with wooden pins. A log cabin was built nearby to house the fathers. The Flathead Indian Reservation was established the following year, and soon more than a thousand Indians had settled in the area. A frame cabin was built to house the first Catholic nuns to arrive in Montana in 1864. Between 1875 and 1900, the mission grew to include a flour mill, sawmill, hospital, blacksmith shop, an agricultural and industrial school for boys, and a boarding school for girls. The fathers also printed *Narratives from the Holy Scripture in Kalispell* and a *Kalispell Dictionary* on their own printing press.

The beautiful brick church was begun in 1891 and completed in 1894. The missionaries and the Indian people built it together, using bricks made of local clay and trees cut nearby. The walls and ceiling are covered with fifty-eight colorful frescoes painted during the early twentieth century. Unallotted land on the Flathead Reservation was opened to settlement in 1910, and the last mission school closed in 1972. Today the only buildings left are the red-brick church, the rectory, and two of the original cabins. A chapel built for

Brother Carignano's *The Three Visions of St. Ignatius Loyola* adorns the church altar.

the Jesuit priests in the 1880s was moved in 1961 to the Jocko Valley and is still used as a church.

The fun

Start your tour at the church, which is beautiful in the spring with the snow-clad Mission Mountains behind it, and even more spectacular inside. The murals that were painted by the mission cook and handyman depict scenes from the Old and New Testaments, as well as scenes from the life of St. Ignatius Loyola, the founder of the Jesuits. Brother Joseph Carignano (1853–1919), an Italian Jesuit who had no formal training in art, painted during what little time he could spare from his duties as cook and custodian. Some say that if there is a miracle at this church, it is the fact that this artwork was done by an "amateur."

On the north side of the church is the original log home of the Jesuits, built in 1854. It is now the mission museum and includes a photographic history, Indian artifacts from several Northwest tribes, and a copy of the *Kalispell Dictionary*. A statue of Christ hand-carved by Father Anthony Ravalli is also on display here. Nearby are the stones used in the mission's flour mill, and adjacent to the cabin is the home of the first Catholic nuns in Montana, now a museum of their work at the mission.

After your visit to the mission, take a drive to see the only reason the Indians would travel out of these beautiful mountains: the buffalo. To get to the National Bison Range go south 5 miles on U.S. 93 to Ravalli, then turn west on Montana Highway 200 and go 6 miles to Dixon. Turn north on Secondary Road 212 and go about 3 miles to the entrance.

Here, 300 to 500 of these shaggy beasts roam nearly 19,000 acres. When you get to the refuge, stop at the visitor center to learn about the Native Americans' bison-based economy and their traditions. Exhibits also tell the history of the bison range, one of the first wildlife refuges in America. Don't miss the two-hour Red Sleep Mountain self-guided drive. It is a gravel one-way road, but the views and wildlife make the trip worthwhile. Besides the bison, the range also has whitetail and mule deer, elk, bighorn sheep, prong-horns, and even a few Rocky Mountain goats. Finish up your trip with a pic-nic at the range's day-use area on Mission Creek, where the deer often linger long enough to have their pictures taken.

Next best

If you visit St. Ignatius Mission on May 23, you can also explore the National Bison Range for free during the annual celebration of its establishment on May 23,1908. Also included are lemonade and cookies, free poster giveaways, special coloring pages for children, and presentations of historic film footage and newspaper articles.

Unique food and lodging

In St. Ignatius, the **Stoneheart Inn Bed and Breakfast,** 26 North Main Street, is a remodeled historic hotel that offers four rooms and appropriate decor to suit your fancy, including the Sweetheart, Wildlife Wilderness, Dream Catcher, and Bunkhouse rooms.

Practical information

Site: St. Ignatius Mission, 40 miles north of Missoula.

Recommended time: Late April.

Minimum time commitment: Four hours, plus driving time.

What to bring: Jacket, sturdy walking shoes, binoculars, and camera with flash and telephoto lens.

Admission fee: None for the mission. $4.00 per vehicle for the National Bison Range.

Hours: The mission is open daily from 8:00 A.M. to 7:00 P.M. The National Bison Range is open daily from 7:00 A.M. to 9:30 P.M.

Directions: Take U.S. 93 to St. Ignatius, turn at the St. Ignatius Mission sign, and go a half mile to the mission at 102 Taelman Drive.

For more information

St. Ignatius Mission Church
P.O. Box 667, St. Ignatius, MT 59865
(406) 745–2768

National Bison Range
132 Bison Range Road, Moiese, MT 59824
(406) 644–2211
www.r6.fws.gov/bisonrange

Stoneheart Inn Bed and Breakfast
P.O. Box 236, St. Ignatius, MT 59865
(406) 745–4999, (800) 866–9197
www.stoneheart.com

18

Steamboat's a Comin'
Upper Missouri River Breaks National Monument

Think of what it must have been like to travel 2,000 miles by river from St. Louis to Fort Benton on a stern-wheeler full of whiskey, gold pans, salt, bacon, and boots as you retrace Lewis and Clark's journey through "seens of visionary inchantment" on the Upper Missouri.

The history

The Upper Missouri River is one of the nation's oldest rivers of commerce and one of its newest national monuments. The Upper Missouri was the homeland of Indians, the pathway for Lewis and Clark, the road of trappers and traders, the highway of steamboats, and later the homestead of ranchers and settlers willing to bet their lives that they could adapt and overcome its fickle ways. The beauty and wildness of the river were the subjects of writers like Meriwether Lewis, William Clark, Prince Maximilian of Weid, Charles Larpenteur, Hiram Chittenden, and James Willard Schultz. Artists including Karl Bodmer and Charles M. Russell tried to capture its character in their work.

In the two centuries since it was first explored, the Upper Missouri has remained virtually unchanged, and that is what makes it so attractive. Many of the landmarks named by Lewis and Clark and later by steamboat pilots remain untouched. The wildlife species indigenous to the area are nearly as abundant as they were in centuries past. Remnants of Indian villages, trading posts, and Army forts can still be seen along the river. The White Cliffs section of the Upper Missouri is the most scenic and popular part of the entire river for floaters wishing to capture the feeling that Lewis had when he

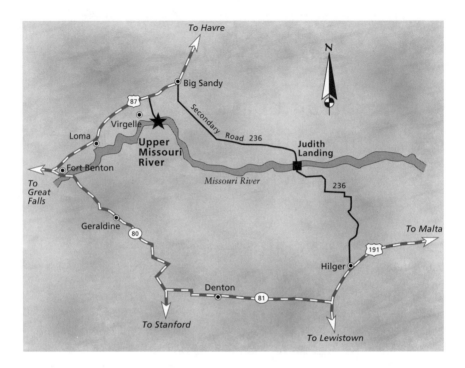

wrote on May 31, 1805, "The hills and river Clifts which we passed today exhibit a most romantic appearance. The bluffs of the river rise to the hight of from 2 to 300 feet and in most places nearly perpendicular; they are formed of remarkable white sandstone . . . it seemed as if those seens of visionary inchantment would never have an end."

The fun

One of the best times to see this river of history is in the spring when the prairies are green and the summer crowds have not arrived. For those with limited time, it is possible to see the Virgelle ferry crossing, Coal Banks Landing, and Judith Landing by road in a few hours. But the best way—some would say the only way—to see the Upper Missouri is the way Lewis and Clark did: by boat. Many bring their own boats, camping gear, and drinking water. The campsites are primitive, with vault toilets nearby. It is a three-day 48-mile trip from Coal Banks Landing to Judith Landing, the two most popular access points. At a leisurely pace of 3 miles per hour, you can expect to go about 15 miles a day, with time for some hikes. Don't forget your snakebite kit, because this is rattlesnake country.

Most people camp at Coal Banks Landing on Thursday night after the

Hole-in-the-Wall Trail provides an unusual view of the Missouri River.

two-hour 100-mile round-trip vehicle shuttle to Judith Landing from Big Sandy by way of Secondary Road 236, first 16 miles of which are paved. Friday's float takes you to the Lewis and Clark campsite of May 31, 1805, on Eagle Creek, one of the most beautiful camps on the river. Saturday's float through the White Cliffs takes you to the Lewis and Clark campsite of May 29, 1805, and July 29, 1806, at Slaughter River. Sunday's float takes you past homesteads, prairie dog towns, and steamboat wrecks to the takeout point at the bridge at Judith Landing. Your speed will depend on the flow of the river and the direction of the wind. You can also take your fishing pole and catch your dinner if you like as there are forty-eight species of fish in this section of the river.

Next best

Another good but more crowded time to see the Upper Missouri River is the first weekend in June when Virgelle hosts its Touch the Trail of Lewis and Clark event and the James Kipp Recreation Area conducts Lewis and Clark living-history encampment activities.

Unique food and lodging

The 1912 **Virgelle Mercantile** offers meals and rustic accommodations in restored homestead cabins or in the mercantile itself. In addition, there are many guided float trip outfitters, canoe rentals, and shuttle services available on the river. The Fort Benton chamber of commerce has a list of these services.

Practical information

Site: Upper Missouri River Breaks National Monument, 27 miles north of Fort Benton.

Recommended time: Early May.

Minimum time commitment: Three hours to three days.

What to bring: Sunglasses with polarizing lenses to cut glare on the water, warm jacket, sturdy walking shoes and water shoes, insect repellent, first-aid and snakebite kit, binoculars, and camera with telephoto lens and polarizing filter. A boat, food, sleeping bag, and tent are also needed if you float the river. Bring along a copy of *The Journals of Lewis and Clark* and the two Bureau of Land Management river maps of the route.

Admission fee: None, but floaters must register at the visitor registration sign.

Riverboats

The Missouri River is the longest river in the United States, joining the Mississippi near St. Louis after flowing 2,466 miles. The "mighty Mo" has served as an important artery of commerce since the beginning of history, beckoning the explorer, trapper, and trader as well as serving the Indians. Thus many types of riverboats were used on the Missouri, including bullboats, canoes, pirogues, Mackinawboats, keelboats, and steamboats.

Probably the earliest type of boat was the bullboat. The Indians were adept at making bullboats by fastening together a framework of willows and stretching the hide of a buffalo bull over it, giving it the appearance of an inverted mushroom. Canoes were made from a shell of wood, often hewn from a large cottonwood tree. They were 15 to 20 feet long and strengthened by partitions left crosswise in the shell. Both bullboats and canoes were used for shorter trips. Canoes were often used in pairs joined by a platform, and sometimes a sail was even used. A pirogue was simply a canoe with a square end.

To float men and freight downriver, many traders built Mackinaws, which were flat-bottomed, high at each end, and built of hand-sawed planks fastened together with dowels. A crew of four oarsmen and a fifth at the rudder could float a load of fifteen tons of freight downriver. Keelboats were 60 to 70 feet long and were also made of sawed planks, but they had a keel from bow to stern, a 30-foot mast, and a square sail to use when the winds were right. In unfavorable winds or when the current was strong, they could be pulled upstream or "warped" by a long line called a cordella. The cordella was attached to the top of the mast and to the shore, and men on the deck would pull the boat in. Oars could be used as well as long poles to push the boat.

Probably the best-known riverboat was the steamboat. Although the steamboat Independence had gone 200 miles upriver by 1819, early side-wheel steamboats were not designed for the shallow water and fast currents of the Upper Missouri. Newer "mountain" boats had broad beams and shallow drafts, some as little as 18 inches, and were propelled by a huge stern wheel driven by two steam engines. Wood or coal was used to heat the boilers. Smaller boats were also used to transfer freight during low water. The first steamboat reached the Fort Benton area in 1859, but within thirty years they were rendered obsolete by the railroad.

Hours: The river is accessible from approximately April to November.

Directions: From Fort Benton, go 27 miles north on U.S. 87 to the Virgelle turnoff, then go 7 miles south on the gravel Virgelle Road. Pass under the old railroad, then either turn right and go about a mile to the Virgelle ferry crossing, or turn left and go about a mile to Coal Banks Landing Campground and boat ramp.

For more information

Bureau of Land Management, Lewistown District Office
P.O. Box 1160, Lewistown, MT 59457-1160
(406) 538–7461
www.mt.blm.gov/ido

Fort Benton Chamber of Commerce
P.O. Box 12, Fort Benton, MT 59442
(406) 622–3864
www.fortbenton.com

Virgelle Mercantile–Missouri River Canoe Company
HC 67 Box 50, Loma, MT 59460
(406) 378–3110, (800) 426–2926
www.canoemontana.com

19

If Cattle Were Kings, Sheep Were Queens
Charles M. Bair Family Museum and Ranch

Take a drive along the remote and beautiful Upper Musselshell River Valley and see the mansion of the Montana millionaire who claimed to be the biggest sheep rancher in all of North America and filled forty-seven freight cars with wool from a single shearing.

The history

Here at Martinsdale is the ranch of Charles M. Bair, the most famous sheep rancher in Montana. In 1883 Bair ran away from home as a teenager and ended up working as a brakeman on the Northern Pacific Railroad in Montana. By 1890 he had saved enough money to buy a sheep ranch near Billings and within five years had 40,000 Spanish merino sheep. In 1898 he went north to seek his fortune in the Alaska gold rush, quickly becoming a millionaire by selling machinery to miners.

When Bair came back to Montana, he invested in mining, oil, and real estate. Counted among his many friends were Will Rogers, Charlie Russell, Tom Mix, Chief Plenty Coups, and several U.S. presidents. Bair became one of the most successful sheep ranchers in the world. In 1900 there were 6 million sheep in Montana and by 1910 Charles Bair owned 300,000 of them.

In 1913 Bair bought the John Grant ranch after he lost his grazing lease on the Crow Reservation. He expanded his acreage during the dry years of the 1920s and 1930s as homesteaders sold out. The family remodeled and added to the ranch house until it had twenty-six rooms. Charles Bair died in 1943, about the time many sheep operations were falling victim to labor shortages caused by World War II.

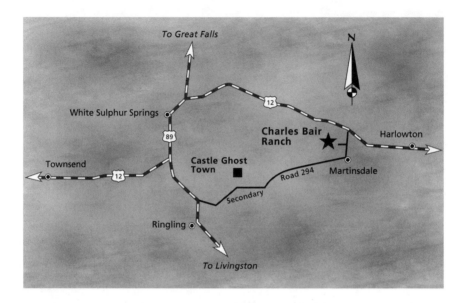

The fun

An early May visit to the Bair Ranch will reward you with the sights and sounds of spring on the prairie as you drive through this Montana ranch country. Charles Bair's daughters, Alberta and Marguerite, were the last to live in the house, filling it with antiques and works of art purchased during their frequent trips to Europe. Alberta Bair was as charitable as she was flamboyant; she donated much of her fortune to charities. The sisters agreed to leave the house to the people of Montana as a museum.

The white frame house is unmistakable with its red shingle roof and blue shutters. Stop first at the barn that has been remodeled into a visitor center. Admission is free, and you can tour the exhibits, learn more about Charles Bair, and get a glimpse of some of the Louis XV furniture brought back from London and Paris. The visitor center also has books and a pleasant gift shop with sheepskin gloves, wool sweaters, goblets, and T-shirts.

The one-hour tour of the house is the highlight of the trip. Formal and informal rooms are nicely furnished with eighteenth- and nineteenth-century antiques. A collection of Indian artifacts is displayed in the Pine Room, the Bairs' favorite, which includes a small beaded vest given to Alberta Bair at about age six by Chief Plenty Coups. Throughout the house are original paintings by C. M. Russell, Joseph Henry Sharp, and other world-renowned artists.

Charles Bair's red-roofed ranch house on the prairie near Martinsdale.

After the tour, ask for the *Welcome to the Upper Musselshell Valley* brochure, which contains a walking tour of the nearby town of Martinsdale. If you want to spend a day in the area, the brochure also has a great driving tour of many other historic sites in the area, including a prehistoric buffalo jump and the 1880s ghost town of Castle. Be sure to ask about road conditions in Martinsdale before taking any side roads.

Next best

Another good time to visit the Bair Ranch is during late September when the cottonwoods and aspen trees along the highways and canyons are yellow and gold and the air is crisp and clear.

Unique food and lodging

If you want some small-town atmosphere, have lunch or dinner at the **Crazy Mountain Inn** in downtown Martinsdale where there is always an empty room to rent for overnight guests. Built in 1920, the **Checkerboard Inn,** 16 miles west on U.S. 12, also serves meals to hungry travelers.

Practical information

Site: Charles M. Bair Family Museum and Ranch, Martinsdale.

Recommended time: Early May.

Minimum time commitment: Two hours, plus driving time.

What to bring: Camera with flash attachment.

Admission fee: None for the visitor center. Tours are $3.00 adults, $1.50 ages 6 to 16.

Hours: Open Wednesday to Sunday from 10:00 A.M. to 5:00 P.M. during May and September; open daily from 10:00 A.M. to 5:00 P.M. Memorial Day to Labor Day; open by appointment during the winter.

Directions: From White Sulphur Springs, take U.S. 89 north 3 miles, then take U.S. 12 east 31 miles to the Martinsdale turnoff. Continue 1.5 miles south on Secondary Road 294 to the ranch.

For more information

C. M. Russell Museum
400 13th Street North, Great Falls, MT 59401
(406) 727–8787
www.bairmuseum.org

White Sulphur Springs Chamber of Commerce
P.O. Box 356, White Sulphur Springs, MT 59645
(406) 547–3928, (406) 547–3911

Crazy Mountain Inn
Martinsdale, MT 59053
(406) 572–3307

20

General Miles's Frontier Outpost
Miles City Historic District

Take a trip back in time to where the west is still wild, where cattle and horses roam the open range, and where cowboys show their stuff at the "cowboy Mardi Gras" known as the Miles City Bucking Horse Sale.

The history

In the heart of the open-range country of the 1880s, Miles City became known as the "cow capital" of Montana. Captain William Clark camped on an island just downstream from here on July 29, 1806. The 7th Cavalry had its first fight with the Sioux just west of here while protecting railroad surveyors in 1873.

After Custer's defeat at the Little Bighorn in 1876, Colonel Nelson Miles was ordered here. He built Tongue River Cantonment while pursuing the Sioux, Cheyenne, and Nez Perce Indians. A year later, Milestown was named after the newly promoted general and moved to its current location and Fort Keogh was built nearby. Named after an officer killed with Custer, the fort became the largest Army post in Montana and later served as a horse remount station during World War I. The soldiers used Signal Butte, east of Miles City, to send messages to the Black Hills 175 miles away by flashing sun mirrors.

In the 1880s, Miles City consisted of general stores, gambling dens, dance halls, bordellos, boardinghouses, and twenty-three saloons. It was a wild town of soldiers, buffalo hunters, bullwhackers, mule skinners, cowboys, and Indians. Judge D. S. Waide described it as "utterly demoralized and lawless." In fact, the 1882 election tallied 1,700 ballots out of a population of only 1,200.

The Northern Pacific Railroad arrived in 1881, and the livestock market boomed as cattle and sheep grazed the open range. By 1884 the Montana

The Range Riders Museum preserves one of Fort Keogh's officers' quarters.

Stockgrowers Association had been established, with the county woolhouse handling 2 million pounds of sheep wool. Despite the harsh stock-killing winter of 1886, Miles City grew, and soon a new livestock industry developed. The first wild horse roundup, rodeo, and sale was held in 1914. The tradition continues today with the annual Bucking Horse Sale.

The fun

The best time to sample the traditions and history of the cow capital of Montana is the third weekend in May, during the world famous Miles City Bucking Horse Sale. More than 300 horses and bulls are bucked out and sold to rodeo buyers from every state west of the Mississippi at prices up to $4,500. If you go, get your room reservations early, or plan to sleep outdoors.

Start your day on Saturday with a special breakfast at the Range Riders Museum. Go early so you have time to see the many exhibits, including an officer's quarters from Fort Keogh. Unfortunately, the site of old Fort Keogh has been methodically destroyed by the U.S. Department of Agriculture over the years. Don't miss the old Milestown exhibit, Old West photographs, and the Bert Clark gun collection, then pick up a *Miles City Walking Tour* brochure and get down to Main Street to learn about the historical buildings as you wait for the parade.

After Saturday's parade, head to the fairgrounds for the cowboy luncheon, Bucking Horse Sale, and horse races. If you're not tired yet, you can spend the rest of the night at the street dance. Main Street is closed to traffic and the whole town is invited to whoop it up, with live bands playing until the wee hours of the morning. If you're the quiet type, you can also visit the Custer County Art Center, located in the old city water plant, or Pirogue Island, where the Lewis and Clark Expedition reportedly camped.

Next best

Miles City has a lot going on year-round. Sample the local culture and history at the annual Beef Breeders Show on the first Friday in February, when sixty pens of cattle stretch the length of the central business district on Main Street. Or try the Highland Festival on the third Saturday in June. You can also see historical demonstrations at the Fort Keogh Days 5th Infantry Encampment, Pioneer Day, and Ghost Tour, all during the second weekend in July.

Unique food and lodging

If you want to see the antique room Gus McRae stayed in on the ABC miniseries *Lonesome Dove,* stay at the 1898 **Olive Hotel,** 501 Main Street, one of the oldest in town. The hotel also has dining facilities and J. K. Ralston's mural of Custer's Last Stand in the lounge.

Practical information

Site: Miles City Historic District.

Recommended time: Third weekend in May.

Minimum time commitment: One day.

What to bring: Sunglasses, hat, sunblock, camera, and binoculars.

Admission fee: None for most activities. Bucking Horse Sale admission is $8.00 adults, $5.00 for children under 12. Range Riders Museum admission is $5.00 adults, $4.00 seniors, $1.00 students, and 50 cents for children, under 6 free.

Hours: The Range Riders Museum is open daily from April through October. Hours are 8:00 A.M. to 6:00 P.M. Custer County Art Center is open Tuesday through Sunday from February through December. Hours are 1:00 to 5:00 P.M.

Directions: Miles City is located 145 miles east of Billings. Take Interstate 94 to Miles City exit 135, then go 1 mile east on U.S. 10/12 to town.

For more information

Miles City Area Chamber of Commerce
315 Main Street, Miles City, MT 59301
(406) 232–2890
www.mcchamber.com
www.buckinghorsesale.com

Range Riders Museum
West Main Street, Miles City, MT 59301
(406) 232–4483

The Olive Hotel
501 Main Street, Miles City, MT 59301
(406) 232–2450

21

Guarding the Whoop-Up Trail
Fort Assinniboine

Visit the last and largest military fort on Montana's northern frontier, where whites, blacks, and Indians lived and worked together to protect the American frontier. Break bread with real pioneers, smell the black powder, and listen to the crack of pistols of days gone by.

The history

Fort Assinniboine was established in 1879 to protect the country's northern border after the Sioux fled to Canada in 1876 and the Nez Perce tried to in 1877. The largest military reservation in Montana at the time, it included 104 brick, stone, and frame buildings and was designed to house ten companies of infantry and cavalry soldiers. The military reservation was 15 miles wide by 40 miles long and included Beaver Creek and the Bear Paw Mountains. The fort is named after the Assiniboine or "stone boiler" Indians, but the post office put an extra "n" in the spelling.

By the 1880s the soldiers were busy chasing bootleggers and gunrunners on the Whoop-Up Trail from Fort Benton to Fort Walsh and chasing Chippewa and Cree Indians back to Canada after the 1885 Riel Rebellion. In 1896 the famous "buffalo soldiers" of the all-black 10th Cavalry Regiment were assigned to the post, as well as Indian scouts and volunteer white officers, one of whom was Lieutenant John J. "Blackjack" Pershing.

In 1898 most of the troops left for the Spanish-American War. By 1911 the frontier was disappearing rapidly, so the post was closed and turned into an Agricultural Experiment Station. Many Chippewa and Cree Indians under Chief Stone Child, whom the whites called Rocky Boy, continued to slip across the border, camping on cattle ranches and scavenging for food. Finally, in 1916 the Rocky Boy Indian Reservation was created out of 56,000 acres

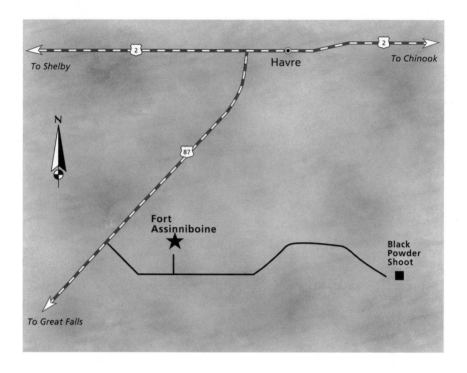

of the former military reservation by an Executive Order. Over the years more land was added and the reservation now includes 121,000 acres. Today the State Agricultural Experiment Station occupies the grounds and some of the remaining buildings.

The fun

The best time to visit is on Memorial Day weekend when a number of activities are going on. If you want to get up early, go on Memorial Day so you can stop in Big Sandy and meet some Montana pioneers at the annual Historical Society Breakfast. Visit the open house at the museum and learn about the history of this part of Montana, then drive north on U.S. 87 through Box Elder and the Rocky Boy Reservation to Fort Assinniboine. Stop first at Highway Historical Marker 78 just north of the turnoff to the fort, then go back and turn onto the gravel road leading to the Agricultural Experiment Station entrance. Before stopping at the fort, continue on the gravel road, following the signs another 2 miles to the annual black powder shoot. This three-day event is open to the public, and primitive dress is encouraged. Contestants of all ages compete in rifle and pistol events with

Some of the root cellars at Fort Assinniboine are still being used.

period weapons. Other events include tomahawk-, knife-, and frying-pan-throwing competitions and a pancake race.

Return to Fort Assinniboine for an afternoon tour. Although the fort is a working experiment station not open to the public, the Fort Assinniboine Preservation Association is allowed to conduct regular tours of the site during the summer months. So call ahead for an appointment, then get ready for an interesting look at the remaining bachelor officer's quarters, guardhouse, post library, stables, carriage houses, and post trader building.

Next best

Another good time to visit is on the fourth Saturday in June during the annual Old Forts Trail Rendezvous, which celebrates the Old Forts International Historic Trail from Fort Benton to Fort Assinniboine and on to Fort Walsh in Saskatchewan, Canada.

Practical information

Site: Fort Assinniboine, 5 miles south of Havre.

Recommended time: Memorial Day weekend.

Minimum time commitment: Four hours, plus driving time.

General "Blackjack" Pershing

John J. Pershing is one of America's most famous Army officers, serving in the Spanish-American War, the Philippine Insurrection, the Mexican Expedition, and as the overall American Commander in Europe during World War I. He earned his nickname, however, chasing Indians on the northern prairies of Montana.

Pershing was born in Missouri on September 13, 1860, and graduated from West Point in 1886. He served in the Apache campaign in 1886, and the Sioux campaign in 1890 and 1891.

By 1895 he was a First Lieutenant with the all-black 10th Cavalry Regiment, called the Buffalo Soldiers by the Cheyenne Indians because their fearlessness and their dark curly hair reminded the Cheyenne of the buffalo. In October, Pershing was ordered to join his unit and the 24th and 25th Infantries, also black regiments, at Fort Assinniboine, the state's military headquarters at that time. Pershing's H Troop patrolled the Whoop-Up Trail to Canada and was involved with the forced repatriation of a large band of Cree Indians to Canada.

In 1897, Pershing became a tactical officer at West Point. This dour and remote Missouri-born German was a stickler for spit and polish and did not win much affection from the cadets. Because he had led the 10th Cavalry, the cadets began calling him "Nigger Jack." When softened to "Black Jack," the nickname stuck because it seemed to fit his temperament as well.

Blackjack Pershing went on to serve in several wars. In 1917 he was appointed commander-in-chief of the Allied Expeditionary Force in France during World War I. For his contribution to the Allied victory, he was made General of the Armies of the United States, a rank he shares only with George Washington. As Chief of Staff of the U.S. Army in 1921, it was Blackjack Pershing who finally combined the Army, the National Guard, and the Army Reserve to work as one cohesive military organization, just as he had done with blacks, Indian scouts, and white officers so many years earlier at Fort Assinniboine.

What to bring: Sunglasses, hat, sunblock, camera, binoculars, and earmuffs or plugs for watching the black powder shooting events.

Admission fee: $4.00 adults, $1.50 students, under 6 free.

Hours: Tours are offered from 4:00 P.M. to sunset daily from June through August, at other times by request.

Directions: Take U.S. 87 south 5 miles from Havre (28 miles north of Big Sandy), turn on gravel entrance road, and go 0.5 mile east to the headquarters of the Agricultural Experiment Station.

For more information

H. Earl Clack Museum, The Heritage Center
306 Third Avenue, Havre, MT 59501
(406) 265–4000
www.theheritagecenter.com

Havre Area Chamber of Commerce
518 First Avenue, Havre, MT 59501
(406) 265–4383
www.havremt.com

Fort Assinniboine Preservation Association
P.O. Box 308, Havre, MT 59501
(406) 265–8336, (406) 265–6233

Big Sandy Area Chamber of Commerce
P.O. Box 411, Big Sandy, MT 59520
(406) 378–2492, (406) 378–2176

Bullhook Bottoms Blackpowder Club
8976 Highway 2 West, Havre, MT 59501
(406) 265–2483, (406) 265–7431

22

Bear's Tooth Meets Sleeping Giant
The Gates of the Mountains

Take a boat ride on the "Pirogue" through the Gates of the Rocky Mountains and see the wild country and the wildlife that were first described by Lewis and Clark, then learn about the tragedy that led to the Ten Standard Fire Orders now used by firefighters everywhere.

The history

On July 19, 1805, Captain Meriwether Lewis of the Lewis and Clark Expedition wrote in his diary, "this evening we entered much the most remarkable clifts that we have yet seen. these clifts rise from the waters edge on either side perpendicularly to the hight of 1200 feet. . . . from the singular appearance of this place I called it the gates of the rocky mounatins." The name stuck, and the towering limestone cliffs and rock formations, with names such as the Sleeping Giant and the Bear's Tooth have inspired travelers for two centuries.

In 1886 Nicholas Hilger started giving tours of the river with a paddle-wheeled steamboat he named the *Rose of Helena*. The paddle wheel is still on display at the Gates of the Mountains marina. The canyons also proved to be a good place for hydroelectric dams; over the years Holter, Hauser, and Canyon Ferry dams were built.

The country is steep and rugged and can also be dangerous. On August 5, 1949, the Mann Gulch fire here killed thirteen Forest Service smoke jumpers in one of the worst firefighting tragedies in smoke jumper history. The investigation of the tragedy led to new and safer firefighting methods nationwide. Although much of the "Gates" are slack water lakes now, the scenery is no less spectacular, and the tour boat rides continue today.

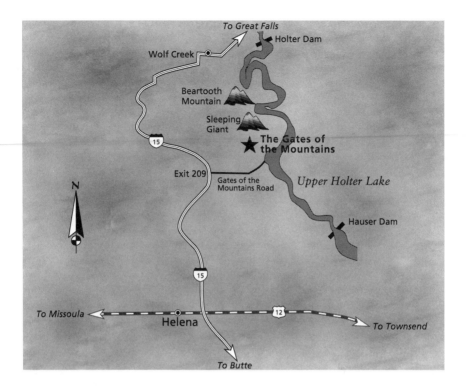

The fun

The Gates of the Mountains are accessible by foot, horseback, canoe, and motorboat, but by far the best way to get acquainted with them is by taking a 105-minute tour boat trip from the Gates of the Mountains marina. On the trip the scenery is only surpassed by the abundant wildlife, including ospreys, eagles, bighorn sheep, mountain goats, deer, elk, and an occasional black bear. The narrated trip also allows you to view the Mann Gulch Smokejumper Memorial and Indian pictographs as the Gates of the Mountains appear to open and close behind you.

Get to the marina early so you have plenty of time to see the exhibits on the Lewis and Clark Expedition, local history, and a video on the wildlife of the area. There is also a gift shop and a snack bar. Pick up a boat tour brochure and a Mann Gulch guide, then decide how long you want your trip to be. You can take the boat tour and be back within two hours, but it's a lot more fun to get there early and bring a picnic lunch. You can take the early boat to the beautiful boat-in Meriwether picnic area, one of the places the Expedition camped. Here you can picnic, swim, fish, hike to Mann Gulch, or even don your pack for a trip through the Gates of the Mountains

The Hilger Ranch appears much as it did when steamboat tours began in 1886.

Wilderness, then catch a later boat for a ride back.

If you like minerals as well as rocks, bring your garden trowel and tweezers. On your trip back to Helena you can mine Montana sapphires at the Spokane Bar Sapphire Mine at Hauser Lake. You can buy buckets of sapphire concentrate, or for faster results, get a sapphire or garnet already faceted.

Next best

If you like festivals, another good time to visit is during the fourth week in July during Helena's Last Chance Stampede parade, rodeo, and fair. In fact, it was during this week that Meriwether Lewis discovered the Gates of the Mountains.

Practical information

Site: Gates of the Mountains, 20 miles north of Helena.

Recommended time: Early June.

Minimum time commitment: Two hours, plus driving time.

What to bring: Sturdy boots, hat, sunblock, sunglasses, windbreaker for lake breezes, camera, and binoculars.

Admission fee: Boat tour fees are $8.50 adults, $7.50 age 60 and over, $5.50 ages 4 to 17.

Hours: The area is accessible year-round. Boat tours leave weekdays at 11:00 A.M. and 2:00 P.M. and weekends at 10:00 A.M., noon, 2:00 and 4:00 P.M. in June; weekdays at 11:00 A.M. and 1:00 and 3:00 P.M. and weekends and holidays hourly from 10:00 A.M. to 4:00 P.M. in July and August; weekends at 11:00 A.M. and 2:00 P.M. and weekends and holidays at 11:00 A.M. and 1:00 and 3:00 P.M. in September.

Directions: Go north on Interstate 15 from Helena 17 miles to Gates of the Mountains exit 209. Follow the signs on the paved Gates of the Mountains Road east 2.8 miles to the Gates of the Mountains marina.

For more information

Gates of the Mountains Boat Tours
P.O. Box 478, Helena, MT 59624
(406) 458–5241
www.gatesofthemountains.com

Helena National Forest, Helena Ranger District
2001 Poplar Street, Helena, MT 59601
(406) 449–5490

Spokane Bar Sapphire Mine
5360 Castles Drive, Helena, MT 59602
(406) 227–8989, (877) 344–4367
www.sapphiremine.com

23

Where the Sister Saved Her Brother
Rosebud Battlefield State Park

Savor the aroma of the wild rose and lupine that carpet the sacred ground of the Rosebud Valley, where Sioux and Cheyenne warriors fought to save their vanishing way of life, and where the sister saved her brother.

The history

On June 17, 1876, eight days before Custer's column breathed its last, the Battle of the Rosebud was fought here. The largest battle of the Indian Wars to take place on the Northern Plains, it involved 2,000 to 3,000 fighters. The Indian campaign of 1876 began in May, with General George Crook's Big Horn and Yellowstone Expedition playing a key role in the Army's three-pronged pincer movement to round up the Indian tribes that refused to move onto reservations. Crook marched north from Fort Phil Kearney, Colonel John Gibbon marched east from Fort Ellis, and General Alfred Terry with Lieutenant Colonel George Custer's 7th Cavalry marched west from Fort Abraham Lincoln.

As Crook's column of more than 1,300 men stopped for coffee on their march down the Rosebud Valley, thousands of hostile Sioux and Cheyenne attacked from their camps in the Little Bighorn and lower Rosebud Valleys. Crook was saved from annihilation by his scouts, who held off the first attack. During the attack, Cheyenne Chief Comes-in-Sight's horse was shot, leaving him helpless. His sister, Buffalo Calf Road Woman, braved the withering fire to ride to his rescue. The battle became known to the Cheyenne as "where the sister saved her brother." Cavalry officer Captain Anson Mills later wrote that the Indians "proved then and there that they were the best cavalry soldiers on earth."

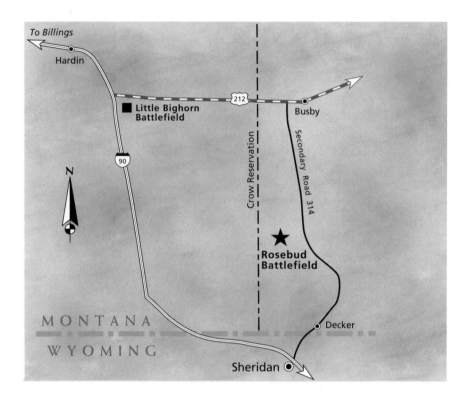

After six bloody hours, during which Crook could make no maneuvers without his men being cut to pieces, the Indians broke off the attack and left him to bury nine dead soldiers and take the wounded back to his base camp in Wyoming. This attack effectively nullified the Army's campaign strategy and set the stage for the Custer massacre the following week.

The fun

Stop first at the interpretive signs just north of the park entrance road to pick up a park brochure and other information, then take the main road along Rosebud Creek to the next cattle guard at the park boundary to get a feel for the size of the cavalry camp. Turn around and take the loop road from Rosebud creek north toward Crook's Hill. To comprehend just how large the battle was, park at the gate and walk a mile up the ridge to the top of the hill, where much of the fighting took place. A beautiful view of the snow-clad Bighorn Mountains awaits you at the top of the hill.

Return to the road, drive down to Mills coulee, and walk a half mile north up the coulee to the 2,000-year-old Slim Kobold Buffalo Jump. This buffalo-killing method was used long before Indians acquired horses. Unfortunately, vandals have also left their etchings in the soft sandstone, obliterating ancient petroglyphs.

Although the park is open year-round, the high plains (elevation 4,100 feet) are subject to temperature extremes. Snow can pile up into deep drifts at any time from November through March. Be prepared for cool, windy weather and muddy roads in the spring and fall, and for midday temperatures in the 90s during July and August, with occasional rain or even hailstorms. Stay on roads, paths, and ridges where the grass is sparse and you can see the ground, as this is also the home of the prairie rattlesnake.

Next best

If you can't visit the battlefield during the June 17 battle anniversary, join the activities at the June 25 Little Bighorn Battle commemoration, or visit anytime from mid-May to early September when the weather is likely to be warm and the roads are dry.

Unique food and lodging

In Sheridan, Wyoming, 30 miles south via Decker, you can have a meal at the historic 1893 **Sheridan Inn,** where Buffalo Bill Cody used to hang out. His signature is still on the hotel register.

Practical information

Site: Rosebud Battlefield State Park, 23 miles south of Busby.

Recommended time: Second weekend in June.

Minimum time commitment: Four hours, plus driving time.

What to bring: Sturdy hiking boots, daypack, hat, rain poncho, water, sunglasses, sunblock, binoculars, and camera.

Admission fee: None.

Hours: The Rosebud Battlefield is open daily during daylight hours and is accessible year-round, depending on snow conditions.

Directions: From Interstate 90 take the Little Bighorn Battlefield exit 510 and go 24 miles east on U.S. 212. Turn right and go 20 miles south on Secondary Road 314, then go 1.5 miles west on a gravel county road to the park entrance. From Sheridan, Wyoming, drive north 18 miles on State Highway 338 to Decker, Montana, then go 10 miles north on Secondary Road 314 to the gravel county road.

Both the U.S. Army and the Indians fought bitterly for control of Crook's Hill.

For more information

Park Manager, Rosebud Battlefield State Park
P.O. Box 1630, Miles City, MT 59301
(406) 232–0900
www.fwp.state.mt.us/parks

Little Bighorn Battlefield National Monument
P.O. Box 39, Crow Agency, MT 59022-0039
(406) 638–2621
www.nps.gov/libi

Southwest Parks and Monuments Association
P.O. Box 190, Crow Agency, MT 59022-0039
(406) 638–2465, (888) 569–7762
www.spma.org

24

—

Fur Traders and Free Trappers
Fort Union National Historic Site

> Summer is rendezvous time on the Northern Plains. Join
> trappers, traders, clerks, and Indians for a glimpse of a
> not-so-long-ago time when fashion was fur, beaver was king,
> and Fort Union was the greatest fur trading post on
> the Upper Missouri.

The history

In 1828 John Jacob Astor of the American Fur Company sent the proud,
competent Scottish-born Kenneth McKenzie up the remote Missouri River
with orders to build a trading post that would dominate the Upper Missouri
fur trade. The post he built nearly 1,800 miles from St. Louis at the confluence of the Yellowstone and Missouri Rivers did just that for thirty-nine
years. It was a handsome post, with a gate facing south toward the Missouri
and vertical log walls surrounding stores, storerooms, employee quarters, and
the imposing headman or "bourgeois" house.

Northern Plains Indians, including Assiniboine, Cree, Crow, Ojibway
Blackfeet, and Sioux, traded beaver pelts and buffalo robes for salt, sugar, blan-
kets, steel knives, gunpowder, lead, kettles, beads, and other manufactured
goods. Trade dropped sharply for a while after the 1837 smallpox epidemic
decimated the Indian tribes, but then continued unabated until the 1860s.
Fort Union hosted a "Who's Who" of the American frontier, including
Prince Maximillian, George Catlin, Father DeSmet, John James Audubon,
Karl Bodmer, and Sitting Bull.

In its heyday, up to one hundred traders, hunters, interpreters, clerks, and
laborers lived and worked at the post. But advancing civilization, another
Sioux territorial expansion, a smallpox epidemic, and the outbreak of the

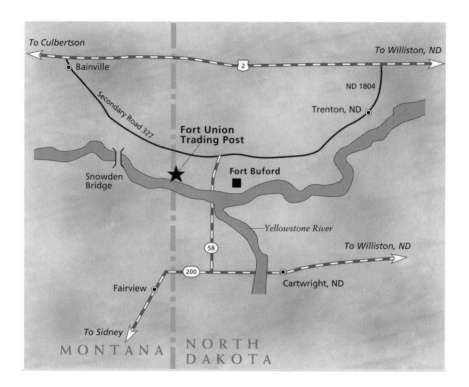

Civil War put an end to the fur trade business. In 1867 the post was sold to the U.S. Army and dismantled to build Fort Buford, 2 miles downstream.

The fun

The National Park Service has partially reconstructed Fort Union to its appearance in 1851. You can climb the stone bastions or look out the river gate just like Alexander Culbertson did when he was the bourgeois. For the "total immersion" experience, be there on the third weekend in June for the Fort Union Rendezvous. The scene is right out of the 1850s, as trappers, traders, and Indians come from both the United States and Canada for four days of fun and games. Tomahawk throwing, kettle cooking, fur trading, period crafts and music, as well as some good old-fashioned storytelling are the order of the day.

Enter the fort by the river gate the way that Prince Maximillian did, and go past the flagpole to the Bourgeois House. First visit the museum displays and see how the bourgeois lived, then walk the inside perimeter past wayside exhibits that explain the purpose of each building. Return to the trade room at the front gate where, for a few "skins," you can buy a blanket, a steel arrowhead, or some beads just like the Indians did. Wander through the camp on the prairie outside the fort, watch the tomahawk contest, see what's in the kettle for dinner, and check out the many furs, beads, robes, blankets, and tents that are on display. Finally, rest a spell while you listen to the fiddlers and the storytellers.

While you're here, don't miss Fort Buford, only 2 miles east. At the visitor center you can pick up a tour guide to the remaining buildings and the cemetery of this Army post where Sitting Bull surrendered in 1881. If you're even more adventurous, ask how to get to Snowden Bridge, 3 miles west of Fort Union, originally built for both cars and trains.

Next best

Some other great celebrations and reenactments to visit include the Fort Buford Encampment during the second weekend in July, the Indian Arts Showcase in August, and the Fort Union Living History Weekend during the Labor Day weekend.

Unique food and lodging

If you're not into roughing it with the free trappers, you can float the river, sleep in rustic elegance in a not-so-old log cabin, and get a home-cooked breakfast at the **Montana River Ranch Inn,** 10 miles west of Fort Union near Bainville. On Fairview's Main Street, **Hotel Albert,** built in 1915, no longer offers rooms but offers noon buffets and dinners until 2:00 A.M. daily.

Practical information

Site: Fort Union Trading Post National Historic Site, 24 miles north of Sidney.

Recommended time: Third weekend in June.

Minimum time commitment: One day.

What to bring: Sunglasses, hat, water, rain poncho, sunblock, binoculars, and camera.

Admission fee: None at Fort Union or Fort Buford.

Hours: Open daily 8:00 A.M. to 8:00 P.M. Memorial Day weekend through Labor Day, 9:00 A.M. to 5:30 P.M. the rest of the year. Closed on Thanksgiving, Christmas, and New Year's Day.

Directions: Fort Union is 24 miles north of Sidney and 25 miles southwest of Williston, North Dakota. From Sidney, go 13 miles north on Montana Highway 200 to the North Dakota state line. Turn left on North Dakota

The reconstructed Bourgeois House dominates Fort Union's skyline.

Highway 58, go 11 miles, and cross the Missouri River. Turn left on North Dakota Highway 1804 and go 2 miles to the park entrance.

From Williston, go 7 miles west on U.S. 2, then turn left on North Dakota Highway 1804 and go 18 miles to the park entrance.

From Culbertson, go 15 miles east on U.S. 2, turn right at Bainville and go 15.5 miles south on gravel Secondary Road 327 to the park entrance.

For more information

Superintendent, Fort Union Trading Post NHS
15550 Highway 1804, Williston, ND 58801-8680
(701) 572–9083
www.nps.gov/fous

Fort Buford State Historic Site
15349 39th Lane NW, Williston, ND 58801
(701) 572–9034
www.discoverND.com/hist

More Deadly Than Bullets

During the first half of the nineteenth century, a number of fur trading posts similar to Fort Union were built on the Upper Missouri and Yellowstone Rivers to sell the Indians trade goods from St. Louis in exchange for beaver pelts and buffalo robes. Unfortunately, not only were manufactured goods imported, but also virulent European diseases that the Indians were extremely susceptible to. By far the worst was smallpox. In the summer of 1837, the American Fur Company steamboat St. Peter, laden with trade goods, arrived at Fort Union. Smallpox broke out among the crew as they steamed upriver to Fort McKenzie. They stopped at the mouth of the Judith River, but the Blackfeet were anxious to trade and the boat continued upriver.

Contact with the crew during the distribution of the trade goods exposed the Blackfeet and two months later the traders at Fort McKenzie had still not seen any Indians. A party sent to look for them found a village of sixty abandoned lodges and hundreds of dead bodies. By the winter of 1838, when the smallpox epidemic had run its course, it is estimated that more than 6,000 Blackfoot Indians had died of this dreaded disease.

Many other tribes suffered the same fate. Among the Assinniboine, 94 percent of the Wichiyabina band was wiped out, leaving only eighty survivors. The Crow tell the story of two young warriors who returned to their village after a war expedition to find their loved ones dying or dead. Deciding to sacrifice themselves, they dressed in their finest clothes and rode a blindfolded white horse over a cliff to their deaths. The twelve survivors who witnessed the event buried them and left the camp.

The disease attacked swiftly, striking down the young and vigorous as well as the old and feeble. It spread so fast that it was often impossible to bury so many victims. In 1857 smallpox struck again, causing the Plains tribes to break into even smaller bands and scatter to escape its effects. Even in the early 1900s, a smallpox epidemic decimated the Metis people who were living near the Dearborn River near Great Falls. The discovery of a smallpox vaccine came too late to save these vanishing cultures.

Montana River Ranch Inn
HC 58 Box 9, Bainville, MT 59212
(406) 769–2404, (877) 277–4084
www.montanariverranch.com

25

Custer's Last Stand
Little Bighorn Battlefield
National Monument

Relive the defining moment of America's western experience here on Montana's prairie as you ponder the heroism and suffering, the brashness and humiliation, the triumph and tragedy, the victory and defeat of that fateful day.

The history

On June 25, 1876, a week before the nation's centennial celebration and a week after a large force of Sioux and Cheyenne Indians stopped General Crook, Lieutenant Colonel George Armstrong Custer's 7th Cavalry attacked the largest Indian village his scouts had ever seen. When the guns fell silent and the dust cleared, 263 soldiers and scouts, including Custer and his immediate command, were dead. The battle had such a stunning and unexpected outcome that it has been studied by military historians around the world and has captured the imagination of generations of western history buffs. Many books and articles have been written to explain the circumstances and reasons for the battle and its consequences. Although the Indians won a stunning victory, the battle was a turning point in their war against the white man's efforts to end their independent, nomadic ways.

The 7th Cavalry was anxious for victory. Custer thought his 600 men were enough for any contingency he might face, but he underestimated the size and fighting power of his adversaries, the Sioux and Cheyenne. Custer divided his forces for the attack and ordered his second in command, Major Marcus Reno, to attack the Indian village from the south while he attacked from the north. Reno was routed in his attack, withdrew to defensive positions, and successfully survived the following siege. After defeating Reno, the

A gravestone marks where one of Custer's cavalrymen fell.

Indians were free to counterattack and annihilate Custer's command. The Indians then scattered before General Terry's column arrived. Some say that never before or since has there been an Indian village as large as the one on the Little Bighorn that day.

The fun

There is no substitute for visiting the battlefield during Little Big Horn Days, on the fourth weekend in June. If you come early, it's easier to find lodging, and if you wear period dress you can dance at the 1876 Grand Ball on Thursday evening.

Weekend festivities begin with the mock trial of General Custer on Friday afternoon. On Saturday take a tour of the battlefield, visitor center, and museum during the cooler morning hours. There is a National Veterans Cemetery on the battlefield, and a private museum in the nearby town of Garryowen.

Your next decision is which reenactment to go to. Custer's Last Stand Reenactment, 6 miles west of Hardin, is held at 1:30 P.M. on Friday, 1:30 and 5:00 P.M. on Saturday, and 1:30 P.M. on Sunday. The Real Bird Reenactment, at Garryowen, is held at 2:00 P.M. on Friday, Saturday, and Sunday. For real history buffs, I would suggest doing one on Saturday and the other on Sunday. On Saturday there is also an annual memorial service at 4:00 P.M. on Last Stand Hill. Finally, don't miss the Big Horn County Historical Museum's pioneer village, shady picnic area, museum, and gift shop.

Next best

If you absolutely can't be there for Little Bighorn Days, or if you don't like crowds, you can visit anytime from June to early September when the weather is warm and the tours, talks, museums, and tourist facilities are still operating. Or visit on the third weekend of August for the Crow Fair at nearby Crow Agency. All-Indian parades and rodeos highlight this premier powwow of the Plains Indian.

Unique food and lodging

You can get a gigantic Indian taco or homemade pie made by native Crow Indian cooks at the **Crow's Nest Cafe** across from the entrance to the battlefield. Accommodations in Hardin include the 1904 three-story brick **Historic Hotel Becker** bed-and-breakfast, 200 North Center Street. You can stay in a restored 1915 boardinghouse at the **Kendrick House Inn** bed-and-breakfast, 206 North Custer Avenue. If you want to sleep in a tepee, **The**

Graham Ranch, 22 miles southwest of Lodge Grass, can provide one, and a horseback ride to go with it.

Practical information

Site: Little Bighorn Battlefield National Monument, 15 miles east of Hardin.

Recommended time: Fourth weekend in June.

Minimum time commitment: Two days.

What to bring: Sunglasses, hat, water, sunblock, binoculars, and camera.

Admission fee: $10.00 per vehicle, $5.00 per bus passenger, motorcycle, or walk-in (free on June 25 and August 25). Grand Ball participant admission is $10. Reenactment admissions vary from $10 to $15. The Big Horn County Historical Museum is free.

Hours: Open daily 8:00 A.M. to 9:00 P.M. Memorial Day through Labor Day, 8:00 A.M. to 6:00 P.M. during April, May, September, and October, and 8:00 A.M. to 4:30 P.M. the rest of the year.

Directions: From Hardin, go 17 miles south on Interstate 90. From Sheridan, Wyoming, go 72 miles north on Interstate 90. Take U.S. 212/Battlefield exit 510 and go 0.5 mile east on U.S. 212 to the park entrance.

For more information

Little Bighorn Battlefield National Monument
P.O. Box 39, Crow Agency, MT 59022-0039
(406) 638–2621
www.nps.gov/libi

Big Horn County Historical Museum
Rt. 1, Box 1206A, Hardin, MT 59034
(406) 665–1671

Custer's Last Stand Reenactment
P.O. Box 300, Hardin, MT 59034
(406) 665–3577, (888) 450–3577
www.custerslaststand.org

Historic Hotel Becker
200 North Center, Hardin, MT 59034
(406) 665–3074

Kendrick House Inn
206 North Custer Avenue, Hardin, MT 59034
(406) 665–3035

The Graham Ranch
P.O. Box 135, Lodge Grass, MT 59050
(406) 639–8903

26

Homesteading the Medicine Line
Scobey Pioneer Town

During Pioneer Days you can relive the lives and times of turn-of-the-twentieth-century homesteaders, moguls, and moonshiners who transformed the last frontier of the American West into the breadbasket of the world.

The history

Scobey was named after Major Charles Scobey, an army officer who served at Camp Poplar and helped the town get its first post office. The town was established on the Poplar River near the junction of two historic trails to Canada: the Wood Mountain Indian Trail and the Outlaw Trail. Indians used the Wood Mountain trail for centuries to pursue migrating buffalo along the Poplar River to Wood Mountain, Saskatchewan. After the Battle of the Little Bighorn, Sitting Bull and 5,000 Sioux used the trail to flee from the U.S. Army across the border or "medicine line" into Canada. The infamous Outlaw Trail was used from the 1880s into the 1900s by some of Montana's most notorious criminals to escape to Saskatchewan where frontier justice or vigilante "stranglers" could not find them.

One of the first settlers in this area was Mansfield Daniels, who established a ranch here in 1901 and started the town of Scobey as a stopover for travelers. In 1912 he built a twenty-room mansion in anticipation of the coming of the railroad. The railroad spur, however, stopped 1.5 miles east and the whole town had to be moved. By 1920 "county splitters" had created Daniels County and by 1924 Scobey had become the largest primary wheat shipping point in North America. Over the years as the town grew, instead of demolishing their past, the people of Scobey painstakingly moved the older buildings to the outskirts of town, creating the largest homestead museum park in the northwest.

The Great Northern red caboose greets visitors to Scobey Pioneer Town.

The fun

Make your first stop historical highway marker 140 on Montana Highway 13 about a mile south of Scobey. Near here you can still see travois ruts on the old Wood Mountain Indian Trail up the Poplar River Valley. Once you reach town, check out the unique square-posted Daniels County Courthouse at 213 Main Street. It was once a hotel called One-eyed Molly's House of Pleasure. Head for Pioneer Town at the west end of Second Street where an entire old west "main street" of more than fifty homestead-era buildings from Scobey and nearby towns have been rescued, renovated, and furnished. The town even has a general store and operating blacksmith shop, as well as a restored car and tractor exhibit, museum, archives, and gift shop.

The best time to visit is during the annual Pioneer Days celebration on the last weekend in June. The town opens at 9:00 A.M. with a "thresherman's" breakfast in restored railway cook cars. After breakfast, visit the museum and then walk the streets and boardwalks past St. Michael's Ukrainian Orthodox Church. Stop for some entertainment and refreshments at the Dirty Shame Saloon and check out the blacksmith and equipment demonstrations. Don't miss the Dirty Shame Dancers vaudeville show and Dixieland band in the restored Rex Theatre (a converted granary from Scobey's first townsite). Complete your tour by watching some of the historical reenactments and the

The County Splitters

Montana didn't always have fifty-six counties. In fact, when Montana became a state in 1889 there were only sixteen counties, with Custer and Dawson Counties comprising all of eastern Montana. The homestead boom of the early 1900s brought in thousands of rural citizens and new voters, yet weather, geography, and technology limited their access to local government. Farmers wanted government closer to the farm. By 1904 the number of Montana's counties had increased to twenty-six, but it took an act of the state legislature to create a new county, and that was not good enough for some progressive-era reformers of the time. In 1911 they mustered enough votes to enable citizens to petition their county commission to force a popular election on creating a new county.

To one American entrepreneur, this looked like a potential growth industry. Scottish immigrant bricklayer Dan McKay of Glasgow decided to become a professional county splitter. For a fee, McKay would get the petition signed and filed, and then use his gift of gab to hobnob and promote the establishment of the new county until the vote was taken. By 1918 the number of Montana's counties had increased to forty-three and by 1925 to fifty-six. McKay was the key person behind the establishment of probably ten or more of these new counties. As a bricklayer, he often got the job of building the new courthouses. Some say that government could be streamlined and taxes reduced if some of Montana's smaller counties were consolidated; others say that would put too many county commissioners out of work.

afternoon antique car and tractor parade with its colorful costumed characters.

If you're a serious history buff, inquire about driving the 2.5 miles to old Scobey, where Mansfield Daniels's mansion still stands not far from what remains of the old outlaw hangout known as the Dugout Saloon.

Next best

Another great time to visit is the second week in August during the three-day Daniels County Fair and Rodeo, which features entertainment, exhibits, booths, carnival rides, and a demolition derby.

Unique food and lodging

A friendly meal is always available in the restaurant at **MJ's Bar,** 17 Main Street, or you can sit on a bar stool and admire the 1900 antique back bar as you eat.

Practical information

Site: Scobey Pioneer Town, at the west end of Second Avenue in Scobey.

Recommended time: Last weekend in June.

Minimum time commitment: One day.

What to bring: Sunglasses, hat, sunblock, binoculars, and camera.

Admission fee: $5.00 adults, $2.50 children, free for preschoolers. Dirty Shame Show tickets start at $6.00.

Hours: Open daily 12:30 to 4:30 P.M. from Memorial Day through Labor Day; open at 9:00 A.M. during Pioneer Days.

Directions: Scobey is 55 miles north of Wolf Point and 41 miles west of Plentywood. From U.S. 2 east of Wolf Point, go 48 miles north on Montana Highway 13 to Scobey. Continue north on Main Street (Montana Highway 13) to Second Avenue. Turn left on Second Avenue and go west a half mile to the entrance.

For more information

Pioneer Town and Museum
P.O. Box 133, Scobey, MT 59263
(406) 487–5965
www.scobey.org/museum.html

Daniels County Chamber of Commerce
P.O. Box 91, Scobey, MT 59263
(406) 487–2061
www.scobey.org

27

The Wild Bunch Goes Shopping
The Great Train Robbery

On a hot July afternoon in 1901, 5 miles west of Malta on the Great Northern Railroad, Kid Curry executed one of the greatest train robberies in history. Relive the life and times of Curry's "Wild Bunch" at the annual Outlaw Days celebration.

The history

On the afternoon of July 3, 1901, Harvey Logan (alias "Kid Curry"), Ben Kilpatrick, Camilla Hanks, and Laura Bullion—The Wild Bunch—blew up the safe on the express car of the Great Northern No. 3 passenger train and made off with $41,500 in unsigned banknotes. Despite years of work by the best Pinkerton detectives, the money was never recovered and Kid Curry was never apprehended. The event went down in the history books as "The Great Train Robbery."

It seems that Harvey Logan and his three brothers changed their names to Curry when they showed up as ranch hands near the town of Landusky in the 1890s. The area was a haven for outlaws. The Sundance Kid got away with only $18 when he robbed the train here in 1892. In 1894 Kid Curry shot and killed Pike Landusky, then fled on the Outlaw Trail to Wyoming where he joined the Hole-in-the-Wall Gang with Butch Cassidy and the Sundance Kid.

The Great Train Robbery of 1901 was well planned by the Wild Bunch, which did not include Butch or Sundance because they had fled to Argentina by this time. Previous robberies taught them to enlist the aid of someone on the "inside." In this case it was reported to be fireman Mike O'Neil, who often worked in the locomotive with the engineer. The train was stopped at gunpoint as it neared the bridge on the west branch of Exeter Creek. Kid

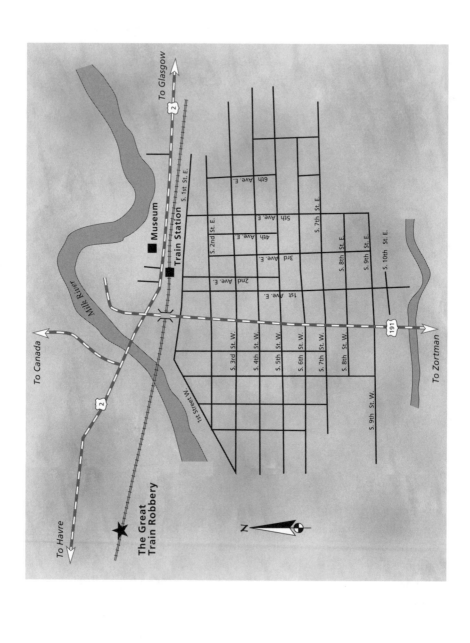

To Havre

To Canada

To Glasgow

2

2

191

To Zortman

Milk River

Museum

Train Station

The Great
Train Robbery

1st Street W.

S. 1st St. E.

S. 2nd St. E.

S. 3rd St. W.

S. 4th St. W.

S. 5th St. W.

S. 6th St. W.

S. 7th St. W.

S. 8th St. W.

S. 9th St. W.

6th Ave. E.

5th Ave. E.

4th Ave. E.

3rd Ave. E.

2nd Ave. E.

1st Ave. E.

S. 7th St. E.

S. 8th St. E.

S. 9th St. E.

S. 10th St. E.

N

Curry had to use three charges of dynamite to open the safe. When it blew, banknotes, $5.00 silver pieces, and gold watchcases filled the air. The gang escaped to the south, crossing the Milk River on a raft they had made to get to their waiting horses. Some say the Kid later joined Butch and Sundance in Argentina, while others say he died of pneumonia in a Denver hospital in 1911.

The fun

Start your visit at the Phillips County Museum in Malta on the north side of U.S. 2 east of its intersection with U.S. 191. The museum has an excellent outlaw exhibit, which includes the Colt .45-caliber pistol Kid Curry used to kill Pike Landusky and Dutch Henry's ivory-handled Colt. Don't miss the stagecoach display and the museum's paleontology lab and dinosaur exhibits, including a tyrannosaur skeleton. The museum gift shop also has an excellent selection of books on turn-of-the-century outlaw gangs.

Next drive (or take the train!) west on U.S. 2 to the "Early Day Outlaws" historical highway marker 126 pullout where you can see Exeter Creek and the railroad tracks to the south. You can board an Amtrak passenger train at the Malta station and follow the route of the Great Northern No. 3, but it doesn't stop at Exeter Creek. The actual holdup site was the railroad bridge on the west branch of Exeter Creek, another 0.9 mile west near what was fireman Mike O'Neil's family ranch. Then head back to Malta for the annual Outlaw Days events and Kid Curry Symposium. You can enjoy cowboy poetry, the world fast-draw competition, a sidewalk festival with Old West reenactments, the arts-and-crafts fair, and a campfire dinner. If this isn't enough for one day, stop back by the Phillips County Museum and sign up for a family dinosaur expedition, or get directions to Kid Curry's hideout in the Missouri Breaks.

Next best

If you can't make it to Malta's Outlaw Days, visit during the Lewis and Clark Bicentennial Encampment on the first weekend in June. The encampment is at the James Kipp Recreation Area on the Missouri River 70 miles south of Malta and features two days of Lewis and Clark and Native American camp life demonstrations, plant use, storytelling, and a buffalo feed lunch. Another good time to visit is during the Milk River Wagon Train and Parade on Labor Day.

The Phillips County Museum's Outlaw Exhibit features Kid Curry's Colt pistol.

Unique food and lodging

The **Milk River Inn** bed-and-breakfast, U.S. 2 East, is a restored 1898 farm-house on the Milk River with four double rooms and one single. For a "total immersion" cowboy experience, try **Beaver Creek Trail Rides,** 30 miles east of Malta, where you can sleep in a cabin and sample a bunkhouse breakfast on a working cattle ranch.

Practical information

Site: The Great Train Robbery, 5 miles west of Malta.

Recommended time: First weekend in July.

Minimum time commitment: One day.

What to bring: Sunglasses, hat, sunblock, binoculars, and camera.

Admission fee: None.

Hours: The Great Train Robbery site can be viewed daily year-round. The Phillips County Museum hours are Monday through Saturday 10:00 A.M. to 5:00 P.M. and Sunday 12:30 to 5:00 P.M. from June through August.

Directions: To visit the site, from the Milk River Bridge in Malta, go west

The Outlaw Trail

During the late 1880s and 1890s, jobless cowboys drifted north due to a drought in the western United States. A number of them formed outlaw gangs that rustled cattle and horses, robbed trains, and generally upset local ranchers. When chased by a posse of vigilantes, the outlaws would often escape using a number of rough trails that led into areas either unsafe or unknown to their pursuers. Butch Cassidy and others organized these routes from Canada to Mexico into one of the most amazing escape systems in history.

The "Outlaw Trail" had way stations every 15 miles or so where fresh horses and supplies were available. The trail began at the Outlaw Caves near Big Beaver, Saskatchewan, passed through Montana's Big Muddy Valley, the Little Rockies, and Kid Curry's hideout in the Missouri Breaks, then down to the Hole-in-the-Wall and Brown's Park country in Wyoming, Robber's Roost in Utah, and Alma, New Mexico, terminating in Juarez, Mexico.

The trail was used by some of the most elusive outlaws in the West, including Butch Cassidy, the Sundance Kid, Kid Curry, Dutch Henry, Coyote Pete, and Kid Trailor. One stock inspector during this time wrote in his report that "Valley County Montana is the most lawless and crookedest county in the Union. . . ." On January 15, 1910, the Yellowstone News reported "Dutch Henry, the scourge of the cattle country for many years, was killed yesterday in a desperate gunfight with a mounted policeman in the badlands south of here. . . ." The Outlaw Trail was soon fenced off and plowed up.

on U.S. 2 for 4.5 miles to the "Early Day Outlaws" historical highway marker 126 pullout on the south side of the highway near milepost 467. To visit the museum, from the Milk River Bridge, go east on U.S. 2 past Central Avenue (U.S. 191). The museum is on the left (north) side of the highway.

For more information

Phillips County Museum
431 U.S. 2 East, Malta, MT 59538
(406) 654–1037

Malta Area Chamber of Commerce
P.O. Box GG/MR, Malta, MT 59538
(406) 654–1776
www.maltachamber.com

Milk River Inn
Highway 2 East, Malta, MT 59538
(406) 654–2352

Beaver Creek Trail Rides
HC 65 Box 6180, Malta, MT 59538
(406) 658–2111
www.beavercreektrailrides.com

28

Nation of the Plains Indian
North American Indian Days

> Return to a time when the prairie east of Glacier National Park was home to the most powerful Indian nation on the Northern Plains; experience the culture and traditions of the Blackfoot Nation.

The history

The Blackfeet have played a significant role in Montana history as the largest and most dominant Indian tribe in the state. Their name comes from the blackened moccasins they traditionally wore. The Blackfoot Nation is actually a loose confederacy of three tribes. The southern tribe, which today lives in Montana, is called the Piegan or Pikuni. The other two tribes—the Northern Blackfeet or Siksika, and the Bloods or Kainah—live in Alberta, Canada. While anthropologists prefer the name Blackfoot, the Indians prefer the name Blackfeet when referring to the individual tribes. Like most of the Great Plains tribes, the Blackfeet came from the east, possibly north of the Great Lakes, and were pushed westward in the 1600s by the arrival of the Europeans.

They quickly shed the life of woodland hunters and gatherers and adopted the nomadic life of the Plains Indian, originally using dogs as their beasts of burden. They traveled in bands of twenty to thirty, coming together only for ceremonies, rituals, and trade. But the introduction of the horse, by either the Shoshone, Kootenai, or Nez Perce, combined with guns from French fur traders, soon changed their entire culture. Within a century, the Blackfeet became the best horsemen and most feared tribe on the Northern Plains and aggressively expanded their territory.

The Fort Laramie Treaty of 1851 required that the tribe live on a Blackfoot Reservation, but by the winter of 1883 the buffalo were gone and government rations were short, causing 25 percent of the tribe to starve to

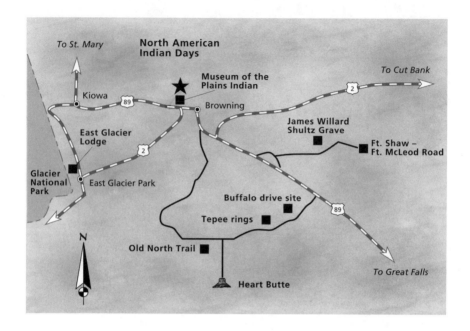

To St. Mary

North American Indian Days

To Cut Bank

Kiowa

89

2

Museum of the Plains Indian

Browning

James Willard Shultz Grave

Ft. Shaw – Ft. McLeod Road

East Glacier Lodge

2

Glacier National Park

East Glacier Park

Buffalo drive site

89

Tepee rings

N

Old North Trail

Heart Butte

To Great Falls

death. Today the tribal headquarters are in Browning and about half of the 14,750 enrolled tribal members live on the reservation. Nearly 27 percent of enrolled members are of three-fourths or greater Indian blood.

The fun

The best time to see Blackfoot culture in full splendor is during the annual North American Indian Days celebration in Browning during the second week of July. Come on Saturday so you can enjoy the parade. Begin your tour at the Museum of the Plains Indian to see the creative achievements of Native American artists and craftspeople. Look at the displays of Northern Plains Indians artifacts and two special galleries featuring changing presentations. The museum also sells native crafts and has a great selection of books on Native Americans. Don't miss the five-screen multimedia presentation or the authentic re-creation of an encampment next to the museum. Before you leave, get an *Indian Days* program and a *Blackfeet Trail Tour* map and guide prepared by the museum and the Browning Lions Club.

Find a place on Main Street to watch the pageantry of the North American Indian Days parade, then try some authentic Indian fry bread at one of the tribal fairgrounds food concessions. After lunch, take the "Blackfeet Trail Tour," a four-hour 70-mile drive through the heart of the reservation. The loop drive goes south toward Heart Butte and "Ghost Ridge," where the 600

North American Indian Days participants make camp the traditional way.

people who died in the starvation winter of 1883 were buried. It passes by tepee rings and buffalo drive sites before returning via U.S. 89.

After the drive, return to the tribal fairgrounds for a dinner of "Indian tacos" and get ready for entertainment. There is always something going on, and the grand entry and intertribal dance contests begin at 7:00 P.M. If one day isn't enough for you, come early and stay for the full four days!

Next best

If you can't make it to the celebration, come on the first weekend in August for the smaller but more traditional Heart Butte Indian Days in the tiny town of Heart Butte, about 30 miles south of Browning.

Unique food and lodging

If you want to stay where presidents, kings, and princes have stayed, drive 13 miles west of Browning on U.S. 2 to **Glacier Park Lodge** on the eastern edge of Glacier National Park. Sixty immense 40-foot-tall timbers support the lobby of this early luxury hotel, which was completed in 1913. The restaurant's specialties are trout, steak, ribs, and chicken. At the other end of the spectrum is the **Lodgepole Gallery and Tipi Village,** 2.5 miles west of Browning on U.S. 89. Here you can camp in a traditional tepee, complete with fire ring, and eat traditional cuisine while learning about the Blackfoot culture.

Practical information

Site: North American Indian Days, Browning.

Recommended time: Second weekend in July.

Minimum time commitment: One day.

What to bring: Sunglasses, hat, sunblock, and camera.

Admission fee: None for most activities. Museum of the Plains Indian admission is $4.00 adults, $1.00 ages 6 to 12.

Hours: Open daily daylight to dusk; museum hours are 9:00 A.M. to 4:45 P.M., until 6:00 P.M. during North American Indian Days

Directions: Browning is 33 miles west of Cut Bank and 13 miles east of East Glacier Park. The celebration is held at the Blackfeet Tribal Fairgrounds behind the Museum of the Plains Indian at the west end of town at the junction of U.S. 2 and U.S. 89.

For more information

Museum of the Plains Indians
P.O. Box 410, Browning, MT 59417
(406) 338–2230

Blackfeet Nation
P.O. Box 850, Browning, MT 59417
(406) 338–7276

Glacier Park Lodge, East Glacier Park
P.O. Box 2025, Columbia Falls, MT 59912
(406) 892–2525
www.glacierparkinc.com

Lodgepole Gallery and Tipi Village
P.O. Box 1832, Browning, MT 59417
(406) 338–2787
www.blackfeetculturecamp.com

29

The Sheriff Was a Road Agent
Bannack Ghost Town State Park

During Bannack Days, you can relive an 1860s rip-roaring gold-mining camp, walk the dusty streets and boardwalks, and explore the buildings that were home to some of Montana Territory's most respected and most despised citizens.

The history

The ghost town of Bannack is the site of Montana's first major gold strike, territorial capital, jail, hotel, hard rock mine, and electric gold dredge. On July 28, 1862, John White and William Eads found "color" here in Grasshopper Creek, and a swarm of prospectors soon followed. By 1863 the town, named after the Bannock tribe of local Indians and misspelled by the post office, swelled to more than 3,000 inhabitants. As the town grew, lode mining quickly followed placer mining, which was later replaced by dredging and hydraulic mining.

The rich gold strike attracted not only miners, but also a number of other, more sinister desperadoes. The eloquent, well-educated Henry Plummer arrived on Christmas in 1862 and shot a man to death the same day. Some say the man deserved it, and the citizens elected Plummer sheriff. Sheriff Plummer quickly proceeded to keep the law by day, but others said he trampled it by night. Some blamed Plummer (spelled Plumer in his younger days) for organizing an assortment of cutthroats and highwaymen into a gang of road agents that preyed on travelers between Bannack and Alder Gulch, 90 miles to the east. Finally, a victim recognized an old wound on Plummer's hand during a holdup. A posse of vigilantes was organized to bring him to justice, and Plummer was hanged from a gallows in Bannack's Hangman's Gulch in 1864.

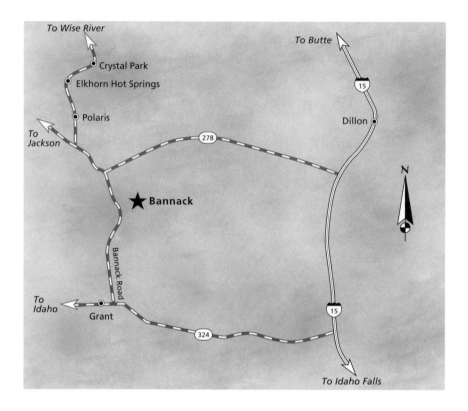

In 1862 Bannack was part of Oregon Territory, becoming the first capital of the newly created Montana Territory in 1864. But the first meeting of the legislature in Bannack on December 12, 1864, was also the last, as miners scurried to the new bonanza springing up in Alder Gulch. By 1880 Bannack's population had dwindled to 232, but several mines and quartz mills were still active. Between 1895 and 1904, a number of gold dredges operated on Grasshopper Creek, digging out the deep gravel that placer mining could not reach. Finally, by 1939, only hydraulic mining with high-pressure hoses worked the hillsides around Bannack. In its day, Bannack coughed up more than $12 million worth of high-grade gold ore.

The fun

More than fifty structures have survived the elements in Bannack, from the two-story brick Hotel Meade to the sod-roofed log jails that Henry Plummer built. If you want to experience what life on the frontier was like, be there for the annual two-day Bannack Days celebration. Plan to arrive

Horse-drawn wagons rumble down Main Street during Bannack Days.

early and stop at the visitor center, where you can see some of the historical artifacts and pick up a walking tour guide and a list of events. Stop at the Hotel Meade for hotcakes and coffee, and then walk the streets using the walking guide. When you get tired, just flag down a passing wagon and hop aboard for a ride to your next destination—the buffalo burger lunch at Hotel Meade. After lunch watch the debates, "shoot-outs," and mule-packing demonstrations, join the mine tours, and listen to old-time fiddle music. For the young at heart, there are frontier games, gold panning, and candle making. You can even try your hand at ringing the gong with a bullet from a .50-caliber black powder rifle. If you arrive on Sunday, you can attend a service in the 1877 church.

Take a walk up Hangman's Gulch to where Henry Plummer gave his last eloquent speech, and then to "Boot Hill" where the grave markers attest to the rough life. You can finish up the day in one of the hot pools at Elkhorn Hot Springs north of Polaris. If you want to do a little hard-rock mining of your own, go another 5 miles past the hot springs to Crystal Park, set aside by the Forest Service for anyone wishing to prospect for amethyst and smoky quartz crystals.

Next best

If you don't like crowds and want to see Bannack as a ghost town, one of the best times is mid-September when the leaves of the aspens and cottonwoods are a bright yellow. For a unique winter outing, try the skating pond at Bannack.

Unique food and lodging

Twenty miles south of Bannack near the town of Grant is the **Centennial Livestock Cross Ranch Cookhouse and Bunkhouse.** The cookhouse seats twenty-five and specializes in family-style ranch cooking in a working ranch atmosphere. Accommodations include a ranch-style bunkhouse and a family apartment. Twenty miles north of Bannack is **Elkhorn Hot Springs,** which offers rooms, cabins, and hot pools.

Practical information

Site: Bannack State Park, 26 miles southwest of Dillon.
Recommended time: Third weekend in July.
Minimum time commitment: One day.
What to bring: Clothes for warm weather plus a warm jacket for the cool evenings, water, swimsuit, towel, rain poncho, sturdy boots, shovel, pick, gold pan, hat, sunblock, sunglasses, camera, and binoculars.
Admission fee: $2.00 for adults, $1.00 for children ages 6 to 12, or $24.00 for an annual state park passport.
Hours: The park and visitor center are open daily 7:00 A.M. to 9:00 P.M. during the summer, 8:00 A.M. to 5:00 P.M. during the winter.
Directions: Bannack is located 26 miles southwest of Dillon. Take Interstate 15 south of Dillon to Secondary Highway 278 exit 59. Go west on Highway 278 for 20 miles. Turn south onto the paved Bannack Road, go 4 miles, and turn left onto the gravel park entrance road.

For more information

Park Manager, Bannack State Park
4200 Bannack Road, Dillon, MT 59725
(406) 834–3413
www.fwp.state.mt.us/parks

Dillon/Beaverhead Chamber of Commerce
P.O. Box 425, Dillon, MT 59725
(406) 683–5511

Codes of the Vigilantes

The tale of the vigilantes is one of Montana's most famous stories and is rich in folklore. It is said that the figures 3-7-77 were written below a skull and crossbones on a card and pinned on a tent or cabin when the "Vigilance Committee" wanted to warn the dweller that his presence in the community would no longer be tolerated. Some say it meant he had 3 hours, 7 minutes, and 77 seconds to leave town. Others said it meant he should prepare to occupy a grave 3 feet wide, 7 feet long, and 77 inches deep.

A more likely explanation is that the first Vigilance Committee was familiar with the procedures the California vigilantes used during the '49 gold rush and simply adopted those. The organizer of the California vigilantes, William T. Colman, was referred to only as "No. 1." Orders from No. 1 were final and obedience was mandatory. As new members were enrolled each was given a number and eventually No. 3, No. 7, and No. 77 came to hold executive positions. They soon became feared by the lawless elements of San Francisco as they signed notices of banishment with 3-7-77.

There were a number of Masons among the vigilantes and as with the Masons, rituals and passwords were used to keep the organization a tight one. The password for their secret meetings was an ironic "I am innocent," and they also adopted a special knot for their neckerchiefs. Even the hanging of their victims was preceded by a special signal to the guard: "Men, do your duty." Years later, the Montana National Guard adopted the phrase "Men, do your duty" as their motto. Montana Highway Patrol uniforms and vehicles also carry on the folklore by displaying the numbers 3-7-77.

Centennial Livestock Cross Ranch Cookhouse
16925 Highway 324, Dillon, MT 59725
(406) 681–3173
horseprairie.com

Elkhorn Hot Springs Resort
P.O. Box 514, Polaris, MT 59746
(406) 834–3434
www.butteamerica.com/hotsprings.htm

30

The Golden Gulch
Virginia City and Nevada City

Alder Gulch, road agents, vigilantes, Boot Hill. These are the names that make Virginia City the best-known 1860s boom-town in America. See where Jack Slade met his end as Mark Twain tells in his 1871 book, Roughing It.

The history

Alder Gulch was the second major gold discovery in Montana Territory. It all began when William Fairweather and his party of six prospectors discovered one of the richest placer deposits in the world on May 26, 1863. By fall, a string of mining camps containing 35,000 people lined Alder Gulch for 14 miles. Varina City was the name chosen by Southern sympathizers for the largest town, after the wife of Confederate president Jefferson Davis. It was changed to Virginia City by the pro-Union territorial judge.

Robbery and murder were not uncommon in this lawless town. A gang of "road agents" soon began terrorizing the country. By December 1863 a "Vigilance Committee" was formed and within three weeks nearly two dozen criminals had been hanged, which tamed the town considerably. In less than three years, prospectors lifted $30 million in gold from Alder Gulch. The territorial capital quickly moved from the depopulated town of Bannack, and the first newspaper was established. Never a ghost town, Virginia City became the county seat of Madison County and remained prosperous into the twentieth century. Over the years the placers, dredges, and mines have yielded more than $100 million in gold.

Unlike most other towns of that era, many of the original buildings were not destroyed by fire. In the 1940s, Charles and Sue Bovey of Great Falls began buying and restoring buildings and furnishings. The Boveys even

Couples promenade for Virginia's City's "Grand Ball."

reconstructed Nevada City, which had completely disappeared. They moved in more than one hundred historic buildings from around Montana and made the town an open-air museum. The state of Montana purchased the Boveys' legacy from their heirs in 1997.

The fun

The placer mining towns of Virginia City and Nevada City arguably have more Wild West history and original buildings than any other boomtowns in the American West. One of the best times to visit is the fourth weekend in July during Victorian Weekend and Heritage Days. Residents and visitors are encouraged to wear period dress. Local craftspeople demonstrate dressmaking, blacksmithing, woodworking, tinsmithing, and much more. If you're coming from the west, stop at Nevada City and pick up a walking tour guide. Play the music machines at the Music Hall and leave the twenty-first century behind. From here, you can ride to Virginia City on a narrow gauge railroad behind a 1910 steam locomotive, moved here in 1999.

When you reach the Virginia City Depot, pick up a walking tour brochure and begin your tour on Wallace Street, the main street, where nineteenth century blacksmith shops, saloons, cafes, mercantiles, and boardinghouses still occupy their original sites. If you want to get even further into the spirit, pan for gold or take the Overland Stage, a fire engine, or a carriage tour of the city. Don't miss Boot Hill on the north edge of town, the final resting place of the road agents hanged by the Vigilantes.

The Sanders–Vanderbeck Center provides a constant flow of events, some period and some contemporary. Nearby, you can stop at one of Montana's first breweries not for a beer, but for a Saturday matinee of the *Brewery Follies,* Victorian style. Then take the train back to Nevada City to pick up your car, grab some "grub" at a local eatery, and visit the Virginia City Opera House for an evening of Victorian theater and vaudeville. If you haven't had enough for one day, the Bale of Hay Saloon stays open late and the Fairweather Inn is just across the street.

Next best

If you don't like crowds but you like living history, a great time to visit is the last Saturday in August. The tourists are not quite as plentiful, and you can watch or take part in the customs and costumes of "The Grand Ball of 1864."

Unique food and lodging

Virginia City has a number of historic places where you can eat, including **Bob's Place** in the 1864 Content Corner building, and the **Roadmaster Grille** in the 1864 Stone Creighton Block where you can reserve a car booth. If you want to sample a restored boardinghouse, try the **Fairweather Inn** on Wallace Street. Other accommodations include **The Bennett House,** 115 East Idaho Street, an 1879 Queen Anne Victorian home; and the 1884 **Stonehouse Inn** bed-and-breakfast, 306 East Idaho Street.

In Nevada City you can eat at the **Star Bakery,** or stay at the **Nevada City Hotel and Cabins,** a restored stage station and miners' cabins.

Practical information

Site: Virginia City and Nevada City, 13 miles west of Ennis.

Recommended time: Fourth weekend in July.

Minimum time commitment: One day.

What to bring: Clothes for warm weather plus a warm jacket for the cool evenings, water, rain poncho, sturdy walking shoes, hat, sunblock, sunglasses, camera, and binoculars.

Admission fee: None.

Hours: The towns are open year-round. Tourist attractions are open June through August.

The Fate of the Chinese

In 1870, 10 percent of Montana's population was Chinese. The first Chinese came in 1865 and worked as domestic servants and laundry workers. Soon a few started reworking mining claims. Although the Chinese were very good miners, many whites were frightened by Chinese food, dress, customs, clannishness, and religious beliefs. This resulted in name-calling, obstruction of their legal rights, anti-Chinese laws, and even violence. One Westerner, A. K. McClure, wrote in 1867 "the popular prejudice against them is very strong" and they are "compelled to subordinate themselves in all respects to the interests of the mining population. They are not allowed to work placer diggings until the whites desert them; and then they must avoid all disputes with the ruling race."

The Chinese did not have equal rights. Many towns passed laws requiring them to live in segregated "Chinatowns." Virginia City's ordinance confined them to the western end of town, "owing to immoral and filthy habits and also the extreme carelessness with fire." The Chinese were law-abiding, taxpaying citizens, and appealed to the courts to live with full rights and liberties. Early Montana court cases allowed that the Chinese did have rights equal to the white population, but in 1882 the U.S. Congress enacted the first Chinese Exclusion Act to prohibit Chinese labor immigration for ten years. Soon Montana courts also began reflecting the popular prejudices of the white population, stripping away the civil rights of Montana's Chinese population. By the 1920s, most of Montana's Chinese had left the state for greener pastures.

Directions: From Ennis, go 13 miles west on Montana Highway 287. From Twin Bridges, go 30 miles east on Montana Highway 287.

For more information

Virginia City Chamber of Commerce
P.O. Box 218, Virginia City, MT 59755
(800) 829–2969
www.virginiacitychamber.com

The Virginia City Preservation Alliance
P.O. Box 55, Virginia City, MT 59755
(406) 843–5300
www.virginiacity.com

Montana Heritage Commission
P.O. Box 201204, Helena, MT 59620-1204
(406) 841–4014
www.virginiacity.com/state

The Bennett House
115 East Idaho Street, Virginia City, MT 59755
(877) 843–5220
www.bennetthouseinn.com

Stonehouse Inn
306 East Idaho Street, Virginia City, MT 59755
(406) 843–5504

Historic Experience Company
Fairweather Inn, Nevada City Hotel and Cabins
P.O. Box 57, Virginia City, MT 59755
(406) 843–5377, (800) 829–2969

31

Liver Eatin' Johnston Slept Here
Red Lodge Historic District

It's been a frontier stage stop full of desperadoes, a coal mining town split by ethnic enclaves, a depression-era city living off bootleggers, and a city rocked by the greatest mine disaster in Montana history. Learn how this small western town survived its several transformations to become today the city of the Festival of Nations.

The history

According to legend, a band of Crow Indians many years ago painted its council tepee with red clay here, creating the first "red lodge." The discovery of high-grade coal and the coming of hungry Northern Pacific steam engines to southern Montana in the 1880s brought prosperity and the first brick buildings to Red Lodge. Twenty saloons, hundreds of immigrant miners, and the likes of Kid Curry and the Wild Bunch also came to share in the wealth. In 1894 the town hired as constable one John Johnston. He was better known as "Liver Eatin' Johnston," for an earlier episode involving the killing of a Sioux warrior whose liver he pretended to pluck out and eat.

Although these immigrants found their way into mines, farms, and town activities, they kept to themselves. Red Lodge had its Little Italy, Finn Town, and Slavic side, where language and customs were familiar to these displaced Europeans. Each group built its own meeting halls and festival grounds based on nationality, and any intermingling resulted in fistfights and brawls. Only the onset of the Great Depression brought them together, as they stood in the same bread lines, worked on the same WPA projects, and lived in the same CCC camps. Afterward, when they turned to community cultural activities to enrich their lives, they did it together. Over the years, the Festival of Nations was born.

Red Lodge's Main Street still retains the flavor of 1890s architecture.

The fun

On the first weekend in August, you can usually visit two major festivals at the same time. The ten-day Mountain Man Rendezvous is just wrapping up, and the eight-day Festival of Nations is just beginning. Start your day at the Mountain Man Rendezvous about 5 miles north of Red Lodge of off U.S. 212. This reenactment of the pre-1840 Rocky Mountain fur trade era offers something for all ages. Activities include black powder shoots, knife throws, children's games, authentic cooking, trade goods for sale, seminars, gunfighter shootouts, and pageants.

Your next stop should be downtown Red Lodge for the Festival of Nations parade, which begins at noon. After the parade, stop in at the Peaks to Plains Museum to learn more about the history of the area, explore a coal mine, and see the special Festival of Nations exhibits. While you're here, get directions to Liver Eatin' Johnston's cabin and pick up a brochure for a self-guided walking tour of the downtown area.

During your walking tour, visit the colorful Festival of Nations programs. A different nationality is featured each day, with shops selling a variety of ethnic specialties. For dinner, try the national food of the day, and don't miss the free horse-drawn wagon rides through town from 7:00 to 9:00 P.M. "Finnish" up the evening with festival performances and evening dances.

On Sunday morning you can return to the Mountain Man Rendezvous for the final day, or rest up for the afternoon's Festival of Nations activities. At the end of the day, head for the town of Bear Creek, 7 miles east of Red Lodge, for an unforgettable evening at the Bear Creek Pig Races. Families are welcome, and half of all wagers on your favorite porker will go to local scholarships. If you haven't had enough yet, head back to Red Lodge where you can dance to the music of a Finnish band until midnight.

Next best

If you can't get to Red Lodge in the summer, come during the first weekend in March for the Winter Carnival. Activities include an opening parade, snow painting, a fire hose ski race, fireworks, a spaghetti feed, and a torchlight parade.

Unique food and lodging

If you like interesting places to find a meal, try the **Red Box Car,** near the creek in Red Lodge. In the **Round Barn Restaurant and Theater,** 2 miles north of town on U.S. 212, you can have a homestyle buffet and enjoy a show in a converted dairy barn that also had a past life as a building in Bear Creek. Seven miles east of Red Lodge, the **Bear Creek Saloon** has steaks and shrimp as well as pig races from 5:00 to 10:00 P.M. The 1893 **Pollard Hotel,** 2 North Broadway, has a restaurant as well as rooms, and has been restored considerably since the likes of Calamity Jane and Liver Eatin' Johnston last visited there.

Practical information

Site: Red Lodge Historic District, 60 miles southwest of Billings.

Recommended time: First weekend in August.

Minimum time commitment: Two days.

What to bring: Light jacket for cool nights, sunglasses, hat, sunblock, binoculars, and camera.

Admission fee: None for most activities. Peaks to Plains Museum is $3.00 adults, $2.00 ages 6 to 17. Mountain Man Rendezvous is $3.00 adults, $1.00 ages 6 to 12, free for those in costume.

Hours: The town is accessible year-round.

Directions: From Interstate 90 at Laurel take the Red Lodge exit and fol-

Explosion at Smith Number Three

During the early 1900s, the Bear Creek coalfield near Red Lodge was found to contain a dozen workable beds of clean, high-grade subbituminous coal with seams up to 8 feet thick. Coal continued to be in high demand by railroads and industry during World War II. The Smith Mine Number 3 seam had a reputation for being a "gassy" mine because small amounts of methane were seeping from the coal faces. Although methane can be highly explosive when mixed with air, the company considered the amounts too small to be significant. The Smith Number 3 had a good safety record and had been inspected in early 1943, but safety precautions were terribly deficient. Smoking was permitted, open-flame lamps were used, fuses were lit with open flames, and no rescue equipment was on hand.

On the morning of February 27, 1943, smoke came pouring out of the mine entrance. The hoist operator heard a muffled explosion, felt a tremendous wind, and nervously called up, "There's something wrong down here. I'm getting out." Then the phone went dead. Rescuers worked around the clock in six-hour shifts to clear debris and search for survivors. By March 1, more than one hundred rescue workers had been treated for methane and carbon monoxide poisoning; one died. The first bodies were found on March 4, and the death toll mounted until a total of seventy-four bodies had been found, making the Smith Mine the worst coal mining disaster in Montana's history.

An investigation found that thirty of the miners probably died from the explosion, and the remainder from poisonous gas and lack of oxygen. Five miners in a small shop tried to barricade the area from the deadly gas but failed. Just before they died, two of them wrote a message in chalk on a dynamite box: "Walter & Johnny. Goodbye wives and daughters. We died an easy death. Love from us both. Be good."

low U.S. 212 south 44 miles to Red Lodge. For a more scenic and less traveled route, take the Columbus exit from Interstate 90 and follow Montana Highway 78 south to Red Lodge.

For more information

Red Lodge Area Chamber of Commerce
601 North Broadway, Red Lodge, MT 59068
(406) 446–1718, (888) 281–0625
www.redlodge.com

Carbon County Historical Society/Peaks to Plains Museum
224 North Broadway, Red Lodge, MT 59068
(406) 446–3667

Red Lodge Mountain Man Rendezvous
P.O. Box 461, Red Lodge, MT 59068
(406) 446–2806

Pollard Hotel and Restaurant
2 North Broadway, Red Lodge, MT 59068
(406) 446–0001, (800) 765–5273
www.pollardhotel.com

32

Surprise Attack on the Nez Perce
Big Hole National Battlefield

When cultures clash, the results can be tragic. Walk the sacred ground where more than a hundred men, women, and children lost their lives as a surprise attack turned into a two-day siege for Colonel Gibbon's 7th U.S. Infantry.

The history

In 1877, after confrontations with miners, settlers, and stockmen, five bands of Nez Perce Indians led by Chief Looking Glass fled their homelands in Idaho and Oregon under threat of confinement to reservations. Numbering about 800 people, including 125–150 warriors, they were pursued 1,300 miles across parts of Idaho, Montana, and Wyoming. The Nez Perce fought numerous pitched battles with U.S. Army troops under General Oliver Howard, Colonel John Gibbon, and later Colonel Nelson Miles, who had orders to return them to the reservation.

After a peaceful journey through settlements in the Bitterroot Valley, on August 7 the Nez Perce set up camp here in the Big Hole Valley. August 9 marked a tragic turning point in the Nez Perce War. Just before dawn, 7th U.S. Infantry troops and thirty-four civilian volunteers under the command of Colonel John Gibbon attacked the Nez Perce encampment here, firing indiscriminately into the village, killing men, women, and children. But Nez Perce snipers rallied, using deadly accuracy to force the soldiers back across the river. After two days of fighting, the battle was over. Thirty Indian warriors lay dead, along with more than eighty other tribal members. Military losses included twenty-nine dead and forty wounded. Although victory belonged to the Nez Perce, they realized that they did not leave the war behind them in Idaho and would have to flee for their lives. The chiefs

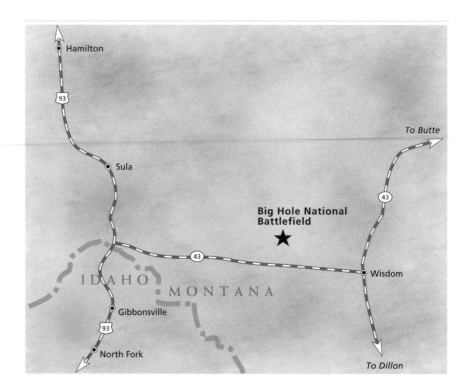

decided to head for Canada, eventually surrendering in October, only 40 miles from their goal.

The fun

In order to better understand why the Nez Perce felt they had left their troubles behind, you need to visit the battlefield during the second weekend in August when the grass is tall and the skies are blue. If you arrive on Saturday, you can also join in the annual battle Commemoration Day. Activities start at 9:00 A.M. and include the pipe ceremony, empty saddle ceremony, and traditional song and prayer by the Nez Perce.

Make your first stop the visitor center to see the eighteen-minute video overview of the battle. Check out the bookstore, and then browse through the center's photos and quotations, and see the personal belongings of some of the battle participants.

After the ceremony, pick up a self-guided tour booklet and head for the battlefield. Stop first at the Nez Perce Camp Trail, a 1.2-mile ninety-minute walk that takes you through the battle from the perspective of the Indians as they were awakened by the sound of gunfire. Then walk the Siege Area Trail on the hillside for a soldier's perspective of the fight. This 0.8-mile trail, which climbs about 50 feet among trees and rifle pits still visible from the battle, takes about forty-five minutes to walk. You can also make the twenty-minute climb to the site where the Indians captured a howitzer. If you've brought a picnic lunch, the parking area has tables where you can sit and reflect on the bravery of the participants in this tragic battle.

Next best

Another good time to visit the battlefield is August 25 during Founders' Day. Activities start at 9:00 A.M. with talks by noted authors and historians.

Unique food and lodging

This is hot springs country. You can soak in the hot pool and get a meal or a rustic cabin at **Lost Trail Hot Springs Resort,** 25 miles west of the battlefield on U.S. 93 near Sula. Or try the panfried trout and marinated ostrich steak at **Jackson Hot Springs Lodge** in Jackson, 19 miles south of Wisdom on Secondary Road 278. The lodge also offers hot pools and accommodations.

Practical information

Site: Big Hole National Battlefield, Nez Perce National Historical Park, Nez Perce National Historic Trail, 10 miles west of Wisdom.

Recommended time: Second Saturday in August.

Minimum time commitment: Four hours, plus driving time.

What to bring: Sunglasses, hat, water, sunblock, binoculars, camera, and mosquito repellent.

Admission fee: $5.00 per vehicle; free on Commemoration Day and Founders' Day.

Hours: Open daily 9:00 A.M. to 5:00 P.M. April through October and 9:00 A.M. to 5:00 P.M. November through March.

Directions: The battlefield is located 10 miles west of Wisdom on Montana Highway 43, 17 miles east of the junction of U.S. 93 at Lost Trail Pass.

Tepee poles mark the location of the 1877 Nez Perce campsite.

For more information

Superintendent, Big Hole National Battlefield
P.O. Box 237, Wisdom, MT 59761
(406) 689–3155
www.nps.gov/biho

Gold West Country Regional Tourism Office
1155 Main Street, Deer Lodge, MT 59722
(406) 846–1943, (800) 879–1159
www.goldwest.visitmt.com

Jackson Hot Springs Lodge
P.O. Box 808, Jackson, MT 59736
(406) 834–3151
www.jacksonhotsprings.com

Lost Trail Hot Springs Resort
8321 Highway 93 South, Sula, MT 59871
(406) 821–3574, (800) 825–3574
www.losttrailhotsprings.com

33

They Call Them the Apsaalooke
Crow Indian Fair

> *"Crow country is a good country. The Great Spirit has put it exactly in the right place; while you are in it you fare well; whenever you go out of it, whichever way you travel, you will fare worse."*
> —Crow Chief Arapooish

The history

The ancestors of the present Crow Indians probably came from the headwaters of the Mississippi near Lake Winnipeg in the latter part of the 1300s, migrating west of the Mississippi River in search of buffalo. They settled in semipermanent villages along the Missouri River in what is now North and South Dakota and were known as the "people who lived in earthen lodges."

Around 1625 they split into two bands, one of which became nomadic and migrated west, inhabiting a region that extended from the Wind River *(Hutchaashe)* in Wyoming north to the confluence of the Musselshell *(Bishoochaashe)* and Missouri *(Aashisee)* Rivers, and from the headwaters of the Yellowstone *(Iichiilikaashaashe)* east to the Black Hills.

In the Hidatsa language they were known as the *Apsaalooke* people, meaning "children of the long-beaked bird." The large-beaked bird they referred to was probably a raven. In sign language, other tribes would simulate the flapping of bird wings in flight. The white men interpreted this to mean "crow" and thus called the tribe the "Crow Indians."

The Crow were widely known for their horse-stealing raids on other tribes, and their first encounter with the Lewis and Clark Expedition on the Yellowstone River relieved Captain Clark of his mounts. Despite this, the Crow tried to establish and maintain friendly relations with the white man, as they sought allies against their perpetual enemies, the Blackfeet and the

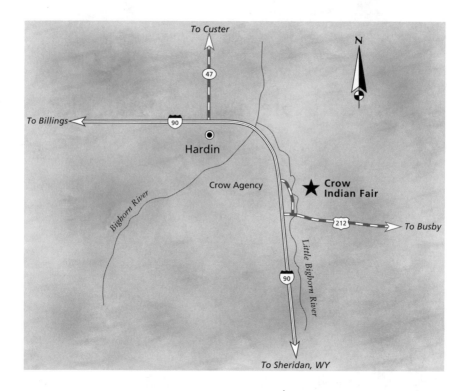

Sioux. Crow scouts took part in many of the U.S. Army battles against the Sioux, Cheyenne, Blackfeet, and Nez Perce.

Despite the tribe's friendliness to the white invaders, between 1868 and 1882 the U.S. government took 30 million acres from Crow "Indian Country" treaties, resulting in today's 2.2-million-acre Crow Reservation. Today the nomadic life is gone, but Crow culture and ties to the land remain strong. Their society is a tightly knit matrilineal clan system. About 90 percent of the tribe still speaks the native language, and 85 percent of tribal members live on or near the reservation.

The fun

The best time to experience the culture of the Apsaalooke is during the third weekend of August (the moon of heat waves on the grass). Crow Agency hosts the annual Crow Fair, the premier powwow of the Plains Indian, becoming the tepee capitol of the world as Indians from every western state and Canada set up their tepees along the Little Bighorn River. Come early,

Tepees dot the banks of the Little Bighorn River during the Crow Fair.

pick up a fair program with events and times, and join the fun at the Crow Fairgrounds.

Each morning a parade is held highlighting the best traditional regalia and beaded native dress, followed by an all-Indian rodeo, horse races, and a wild horse race. Some of the best events are the traditional dances, a few of which you can join in. Be sure to see the other cultural games as well, including the hand games and arrow throw. Walk the grounds and inspect the tepees, beaded clothing, accessories, and art made by the best artisans of the tribe using traditional methods. Some are for sale, but you'd better have enough "skins" because they are in great demand by collectors.

Finish the day with an Indian taco made with traditional Indian fry bread from one of the food concessions. If you have time, you can even consider extending your trip to include a visit to the nearby Little Bighorn Battlefield, where six of Custer's scouts were Crow Indians.

Next best

Other cultural celebrations you can enjoy are the Valley of Chiefs Powwow and Rodeo during the first weekend in July, and Native American Day on the last Friday in September.

Unique food and lodging

You can get Indian tacos and other homemade native Crow Indian foods at the fair, or nearby at the **Crow's Nest Cafe** across from the entrance to the Little Bighorn Battlefield. Accommodations in Hardin include the 1904 three-story brick **Historic Hotel Becker** bed-and-breakfast, 200 North Center Street. Or you can stay in a restored 1915 boardinghouse at the **Kendrick House Inn** bed-and-breakfast, 206 North Custer Avenue. If you want to sleep in a tepee, **The Graham Ranch,** 22 miles southwest of Lodge Grass, can provide one, and a horseback ride to go with it.

Practical information

Site: Crow Indian Fair, Crow Agency.

Recommended time: Third weekend in August.

Minimum time commitment: One day.

What to bring: Sunglasses, hat, water, sunblock, binoculars, and camera.

Admission fee: None.

Hours: Open daily daylight to dusk.

Directions: From Hardin, go 12 miles south on Interstate 90. From Sheridan, Wyoming, go 72 miles north on Interstate 90. Take Crow Agency exit 509 and go 1 mile south to Crow Fairgrounds.

For more information

Crow Tribal Office
P.O. Box 159, Crow Agency, MT 59022
(406) 638–2601

Big Horn Canyon National Recreation Area
P.O. Box 458, Fort Smith, MT 59035
(406) 666–2412
www.nps.gov/bica

Historic Hotel Becker
200 North Center Street, Hardin, MT 59034
(406) 665–2707

Kendrick House Inn
206 North Custer Avenue, Hardin, MT 59034
(406) 665–3035

The Graham Ranch
P.O. Box 135, Lodge Grass, MT 59050
(406) 639–8903

34

The Frenchman Becomes a Cowboy
Pierre Wibaux House

Learn how a young French cavalry dragoon who was searching
for fame and fortune found the American dream, western
style, and built the largest cattle shipping point on the
Northern Pacific Railroad.

The history

Pierre Wibaux *(wee-bo)* was born in Roubaix, France, in 1858 into a wealthy
textile industry family. He was trained in technical subjects and literature,
then enlisted in the French cavalry for a time. He later traveled widely while
working for his father. After visiting England, where he met his future wife
and heard tales of the American "beef bonanza," he borrowed $10,000 from
his father and came to America. In 1883 he took the new Northern Pacific
Railroad route to a small siding named Mingusville. On nearby Beaver Creek
he established the W–Bar Ranch, which soon became one of the largest
open-range cattle operations on the Northern Plains.

Wibaux had a knack for turning a profit. Now that the Indians and buffalo had been cleared from the range, he stocked it with 10,000 cattle, buying
them for one cent on the dollar. By 1885, Mingusville was shipping 17,000
cattle (the equivalent of 792 railroad cars full) by rail to eastern markets. After
the brutal winter of 1886–1887 decimated cattle herds, Wibaux bought cows
for $18 per head, selling them for $40 after pioneering the cutting and stor-
ing of hay for winter feed. In 1903 he bought 36,000 acres for less than $1.00
per acre and sold it the next year for $16 per acre.

By the 1890s the W–Bar Ranch had 65,000 cattle ranging from Wyoming
to the Killdeer Mountains in North Dakota. In 1892 Wibaux and his new
partner, Henry Boice, built a house and office building near the railroad
tracks in Mingusville. In 1895 he successfully petitioned to have the town

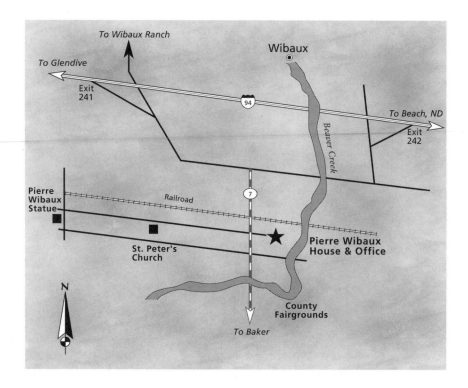

renamed Wibaux. By 1907 he was a banker in Miles City and his wife and son had returned to France. Before he died of liver cancer in 1913, he provided the money for his ashes to be buried under a heroic-size statue of himself in the town "overlooking the land I loved so well."

The fun

During the last weekend of August, the Wibaux County Fair and Parade brings everyone in from the ranches. Your first stop should be Pierre Wibaux's House and Office at the museum complex. Here you can get a free tour of his town headquarters and learn more about him. You can also tour a 1900s barbershop, livery stable, and the Centennial Car that was part of Montana's 1964 World's Fair Exhibit in New York. Next pick up a *Wibaux Historical Walking Tour* brochure and take a stroll through a real western cow town. Don't miss the antique bit and spur collection in the Orgain Building, the Antiques and Ice Cream Parlour in the 1911 Chappell block, the 1895 St. Peter's Church faced with native stone, and Pierre Wibaux's statue, which still stands on the western edge of town.

Pierre Wibaux's bronze statue faces toward his old ranch.

You can return to the shade of the cottonwoods at the Wibaux Museum for a picnic, check out the jewelry at Montana Pewter on 110 South Wibaux Street, or even ask for directions to Wibaux's ranch on Beaver Creek. His house burned long ago, but remnants of the stone horse barn are still visible on private land. Finish your visit by taking in the events at the Wibaux County Fairgrounds, off of Montana Highway 7 on the south edge of town. You'll meet some very friendly people and learn why Pierre Wibaux never returned to France.

Next best

If you like the sights and sounds of the prairie coming alive, one of the most beautiful times of the year to visit Wibaux is in the springtime during May and June.

Unique food and lodging

Steak and potatoes lovers will like the nightly specials at the **Shamrock Club** in the 1905 Orgain Building, 101 South Wibaux Street. Here in cow country you won't see a salad bar, but you will see cakes, cookies, and ten different kinds of pie. Seven miles south of Wibaux on Montana Highway 7, **Nunberg's Ranch** bed-and-breakfast offers four guest rooms decorated with antiques in a 1913 two-story ranch house. If you are driving to Glendive, the **Charley Montana** bed-and-breakfast, 103 North Douglas Avenue, offers seven guest rooms amid the vintage decor of the 1907 home built by railroad and cattle tycoon Charles Krug.

Practical information

Site: Pierre Wibaux House and Office, on the block between First Avenue South and Orgain Avenue, Wibaux.

Recommended time: Late August.

Minimum time commitment: Four hours, plus driving time.

What to bring: Sunglasses, hat, sunblock, and camera.

Admission fee: None.

Hours: The Pierre Wibaux Museum Complex is open daily from May through September, 9:00 A.M. to 5:00 P.M.

Directions: From Glendive, go 29 miles east on Interstate 94 and take the Wibaux exit 241; from Beach, North Dakota, go 9 miles west on Interstate

94 and take the Wibaux exit 242. Follow signs to Montana Highway 7 south on Wibaux Street into the town of Wibaux. Cross under the railroad tracks, then turn left onto Orgain Avenue and go 1 block to the museum complex.

For more information

Wibaux County Museum
P.O. Box 74, Wibaux, MT 59353
(406) 796–9969, (406) 796–2381

Wibaux County Chamber of Commerce
P.O. Box 159, Wibaux, MT 59353
(406) 796–2412

Nunberg's Ranch
HC 71 Box 7315, Wibaux, MT 59353
(406) 795–2345

Charley Montana
103 North Douglas Avenue, Glendive, MT 59330
(406) 365–3207
www.bbonline.com/mt/charley

35

The Last Chief of the Crows
Chief Plenty Coups State Park

Here in the shadow of the sacred mountain of the Crows
stands the last home of their last chief. Chief Plenty Coups
came here to adopt the white man's lifestyle, and he was
buried here. Feel his presence as you drink from the sacred
Medicine Spring.

The history

On the remote western end of the Crow Indian Reservation north of the Pryor
Mountains is the site of the last home and burial place of the last—and some say
the greatest—of the Crow war chiefs, Plenty Coups. He was born in 1848 not
far from where the city of Billings is today. As a boy he journeyed to the Crazy
Mountains of central Montana for a "vision quest" to receive guidance for his
life. His vision advised him to be like a chickadee and develop his mind and lis-
tening skills. His vision also foretold of the disappearance of the buffalo and the
appearance of cattle.

But his prowess as a warrior eventually gained him chief status. His many
honors or "coups" earned him the name *Aleek-chea-ahoosh*, or Plenty Coups.
He was one of the Crow scouts that fought with General Crook against the
Sioux and Cheyenne at the Rosebud Battlefield and was responsible for saving a number of soldiers from annihilation by the Sioux that day. His influence with his people caused them to cooperate with the white man ". . . not
because we loved the white man . . . but because we plainly saw that this
course was the only one which might save our beautiful country for us."

Plenty Coups proved to be a wise and able leader. Although he could
not read or write, Plenty Coups learned the English language well enough
to represent the Crow people on several trips to Washington, D.C. He repre-
sented all the Indian nations at the dedication of the Tomb of the Unknown

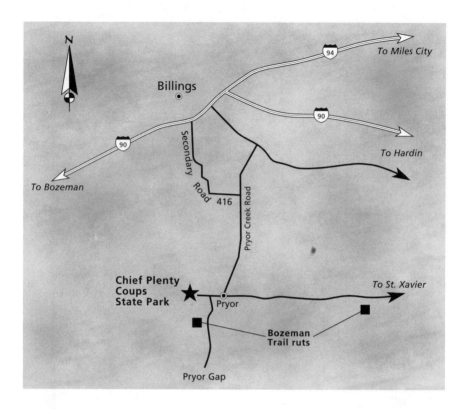

Soldier in 1921. His short speech on war and peace is still regarded as a masterpiece.

Plenty Coups built a two-story log house and farm on upper Pryor Creek, living there until his death in 1932 at the age of eighty-four. Before he died, he willed his property to the public as a "nations park." Plenty Coups is still revered as the greatest chief of the Crow, who never again elected another chief.

The fun

A great time to visit Chief Plenty Coups State Park is in early September after the heat of the summer has passed, the tourists are gone, and the wild plums are ripening. Stop at the museum and visitor center first to learn about the chief and the history of the Crow tribe and culture, then ask for a tour of his two-story home and log trading post. Some say the chief preferred living in a tepee outside and never could get used to the "white man's" house. Take a stroll down to the Medicine Spring, which has its own legends, and then stop at the grave of the chief and his wives. From here you can see Pryor Gap

A bust of Chief Plenty Coups watches over the museum
and visitor center entrance.

The Vision Quest

The Indians used many of Montana's mountain ranges for "vision quests," and the remains of their sacred rock piles remain today. Intertribal wars necessitated that each tribe develop warriors with superb physical, mental, and spiritual abilities. They believed that by fasting, young men could receive supernatural powers from animal emissaries of the Great Spirit, such as a chickadee or an eagle. They believed this power, which they sometimes carried with them as "medicine bundles," would make them better warriors and eventually great chiefs. Suffering through thirst, hunger, exposure, and sacrifice brought on the spiritual experience. Sometimes pain was induced by cutting off a finger at the first joint and bleeding into unconsciousness in order to receive an early visit from the animal spirits. Dreams and instructional visions were sure signs of receiving the sacred power.

For a vision quest, rows of stones were piled into oblong rings from a few inches to more than a foot high to make a symbolic "fasting bed." The circle of stones might be oriented toward the east, with that end left open so that the blessings of the morning sun would fall directly on the seeker. A closed circle could be oriented in any direction. Sometimes several men would build vision quest sites and fast together. The famous Medicine Wheel in the Bighorn Mountains may have been a mass vision quest site.

Each individual chose where to put his vision quest site. They have been found on open hilltops, under trees, on high cliffs, and on river islands—wherever the spirits were most likely to be. Sometimes the same site was used again and again if someone had had a good vision there. One thing is certain: No warrior ever attained great wealth, high prestige, or became a great chief without a vision.

to the south. If you take a short drive south from the park, past the 1891 St. Charles mission school on the gravel road, you will cross the Bozeman Trail. A small sign marks the spot. Pryor Gap is still sacred to the Crow tribe. A few miles east and south of the town of Pryor you can see more Bozeman Trail ruts. Also near here is the Will James Ranch where the famous cowboy author-artist worked. Return to the park for a picnic and listen closely for the call of the chickadee.

Next best

If you prefer a more festive occasion, come for the Chief Plenty Coups Day of Honor. It has recently been held on the first Saturday in August and includes traditional dance and drum groups, a buffalo feast, presentations by historians, and a craft fair. Another option is to visit on a weekend in July or August when Crow elders and historians offer interpretive programs on Crow traditions, beadwork, crafts, war bonnets, legends, herbal medicine, tepee raising, and history.

Practical information

Site: Chief Plenty Coups State Park, 35 miles south of Billings.

Recommended time: Early September.

Minimum time commitment: Three hours, plus driving time.

What to bring: Sunglasses, hat, sunblock, binoculars, camera, and picnic lunch.

Admission fee: $1.00 per person or $24.00 state park passport; free for Native Americans.

Hours: Open daily from May through September 8:00 A.M. to 5:00 P.M. Visitor center hours are 10:00 A.M. to 5:00 P.M. from May through September, by appointment from October through April.

Directions: From Interstate 90 in Billings, take Blue Creek Road exit 447, then go 14.5 miles south on Secondary Road 416 to Pryor Creek Road. Turn right and go 17 miles to the town of Pryor. Turn right at the stop sign and go 0.75 mile on the county road to the park entrance.

For more information

Park Manager, Chief Plenty Coups State Park
P.O. Box 100, Pryor, MT 59066
(406) 252–1289
www.plentycoups.org
www.fwp.state.mt.us/parks

Friends of Chief Plenty Coups Association
P.O. Box 100, Pryor, MT 59066
(406) 252–1289

36

The Steel Rail Crosses the West
The Charlie Russell Railroad

On the first Saturday after Labor Day, you can experience the bygone days of the first-class passenger train, view the landscape that inspired the famous western artist Charlie Russell, and try some homesteader recipes for the wild chokecherry.

The history

The dinner train's route follows the old Milwaukee Railroad line through the landscape that inspired much of the artwork of Charlie Russell, the western cowboy artist. Along the way, you travel through the hills and valleys of central Montana, viewing wildlife, flowers, and farms. The train also passes by the homesteader towns of Ware, Danvers, and Hoosac, going through a tunnel and crossing three 150-foot-high trestles. The thirty-three-span 1,953-foot-long Judith River Trestle is the longest. The Sage Creek/Hoosac Tunnel is more than 2,000 feet long and was completed in 1913. Initially, Lewistown was served by two railroads, Milwaukee Road and Great Northern. The Great Northern became the Burlington Northern through a merger in 1970. The Milwaukee Road later abandoned its lines in the area and the Burlington Northern took over. A private railroad, Central Montana Rail, was established in 1985.

The Charlie Russell Chew-Choo is a 1950s-era five-car passenger train pulled by a Detroit and Perkins Diesel locomotive. The cars include up to three passenger cars, a kitchen car, and a gift shop car. The train only operates as a dinner train and can carry up to 220 passengers. The round-trip from Lewistown to Denton and back, a distance of 56 miles, takes about three and a half hours.

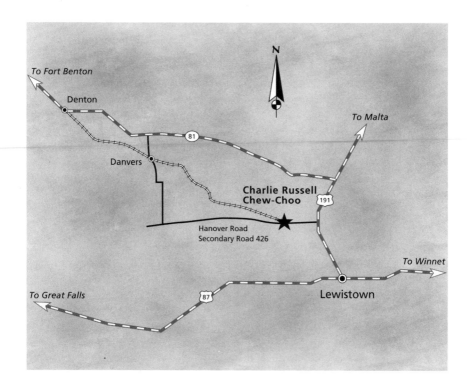

The fun

Plan to arrive early so you can take in the Annual Chokecherry Festival on your way to the train. The chokecherry is a small maroon fruit with a taste so tart it makes your mouth pucker. It grows wild in Montana, and in Lewistown it reigns supreme on the first Saturday after Labor Day each year. The festival is held about the time the fruit ripens, and there is fun for everyone from tots to grandparents. You may see thousands of people at the Chokecherry Festival, which grows in popularity each year. The big day gets under way at 7:00 A.M. when the Lewistown Kiwanis Club begins serving an outdoor breakfast at Main Street and Second Avenue. On the menu are pancakes, served with—what else?—chokecherry syrup. At 8:00 A.M. the Farmers Market opens and local craftspeople open their arts-and-crafts booths. At 9:00 A.M. a fun run begins at the city park. Then there are the events, including a chokecherry pit-spitting contest and a chokecherry culinary contest (on Chokecherry Lane, of course). Other activities include a supervised Kids'

The Charlie Russell Chew-Choo dinner train crosses a 150-foot high trestle.

Corner, and free entertainment.

You can begin boarding the train at the boarding ramp at 3:00 P.M., one hour before departure. Don't be late; the train pulls out promptly at 4:00 P.M. Like the song "The City of New Orleans," the Charlie Russell Chew-Choo commemorates the heyday of the first-class passenger train. But unlike the song, you won't be singing the "dissappearin' railroad blues." Instead, you'll be watching the scenery, buying engineer hats in the gift shop car, eating a full-course prime rib dinner, and having a truly "moving" experience in the cash bar. And by the way, don't be surprised if you get "robbed" by The Denton Gang.

Next best

If you can't get there during the regular season, there are three special trains during the winter season: a Valentine's Day train on the second Saturday in February, a Christmas train on the second Saturday in December, and a New Year's Eve train on December 31. The New Year's Eve train includes a cash bar and hors d'oeuvres, with dinner back in Lewistown at the Yogo Inn and live entertainment to welcome in the New Year.

Unique food and lodging

The 1909 shingle-style Arts and Crafts **Symmes/Wicks House** bed-and-breakfast is located in Lewistown's historic Silk Stocking District. The three-story sandstone house offers three guest rooms.

Practical information

Site: Charlie Russell Chew-Choo Dinner Train, north of Lewistown.

Recommended time: First weekend in September.

Minimum time commitment: One day.

What to bring: Camera with flash attachment, binoculars.

Admission fee: $85 adults, $50 children under 12; $120 for New Year's Eve Train. Call Main Connection Travel for reservations and information packet.

Hours: Saturday trains depart at 6:00 P.M. from the last weekend in May through July, 5:00 P.M. in August, and 4:00 P.M. in September. Special trains are also run for Christmas, New Year's, and Valentine's Day.

Directions: Lewistown is 105 miles east of Great Falls on U.S. 87. To get to the Charlie Russell Chew-Choo boarding ramp, take U.S. 191 north of Lewistown and turn west on Hanover Road (Secondary Road 426). Go 8 miles to the boarding ramp at the underpass.

For more information

Lewistown Area Chamber of Commerce
P.O. Box 818, Lewistown, MT 59457
(800) 216–5436
www.lewistownchamber.com

Main Connection Travel
P.O. Box 1123, Lewistown, MT 59457
(406) 538–2527

Symmes/Wicks House
220 West Boulevard, Lewistown, MT 59457
(406) 538–9068

37

Where Low Rent Means High Spirits
Havre Beneath the Streets

> Visit one of the newest historic sites in Montana, restored
> from the dust and dirt of Havre's secret underground
> past when the town was full of bootleggers, rum runners,
> wolfers, saloons, opium dens, and bordellos, and known as
> the blood bucket of the west.

The history

They first called it Bullhook Bottoms, but James J. Hill didn't like the name when his Great Northern Railroad reached here in 1890. So when he decided to make the town a division point and locomotive maintenance center, the locals renamed it Havre after Le Havre in France. But the name was the only thing pretty about the town. With the coming of the railroad, Havre became a melting pot of races, but racism was also prevalent. Soon this railroading, whiskey drinking, bootlegging, wolfer hangout with eighteen bordellos, no fewer saloons, and several opium dens gained a reputation as one of the toughest towns west of the Mississippi.

In January 1904 a fire destroyed much of the downtown area, and as building supplies were short, many businesses simply reopened in their basements until they could afford to rebuild. They were connected with underground passages and used glass blocks in the sidewalks to let light in. Even though most businesses soon moved above ground, the Chinese kept a number of businesses underground where they wouldn't be harassed by the whites. One of the best hotels also kept a passage under the street to an underground bordello. When Prohibition came to Montana in 1918, one of

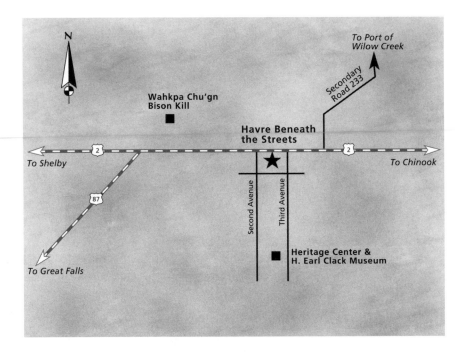

Havre's infamous characters, cigar-smoking Shorty Young, used the underground passages along with a couple dozen other saloon operators to operate three liquor distilleries and a brewery, keeping the town in high "spirits." When Prohibition ended in 1933, so did Havre's underground city.

The fun

If you want the full load, come to Havre during the third weekend in September for the Havre Festival Days celebration of music, parades, and fun. Start at the Havre Railroad Museum at 120 Third Avenue for the underground tour of Havre Beneath the Streets. The underground city was restored entirely by volunteers. Here you can get a glimpse of Havre's early years in the Sporting Eagle Saloon, a century-old honky-tonk, an opium den, a Chinese laundry, a post office, bakery, dentist office, meat market, drugstore, barbershop, blacksmith shop, mercantile, an ethnic restaurant, and of course, a bordello.

After you're above ground again, don't miss the H. Earl Clack Memorial Museum and Heritage Center's exhibits just down the street. The center is also the place to ask for a tour of the 2,000-year-old buffalo jump just behind the Holiday Village Mall on the west end of town. Known as the Wahkpa Chu'gn (*wock-pa-jew-kon*) bison kill site, it was given the Assinniboine Indian name for the Milk River just below. The extensive bone bed displays give a unique view of the extent of the site. If you pick up a *Havre Visitors' Guide,* you can also take the walking tour of the downtown area while you wait for the festival parade to begin.

Next best

Another good time to visit is the second weekend in August during the Great Northern Fair. This old-fashioned county fair is held at the Hill County Fairgrounds in Havre and features everything from rides, arts and crafts, and 4-H projects to nightly rodeos and concerts.

Unique food and lodging

For a light snack you can try the **Palace Bar,** 228 First Street, just above Havre Beneath the Streets. Of note is the ornately carved 1883 back bar that was made in St. Louis and spent its first fifty years in the small town of Chinook.

Practical information

Site: Havre Beneath the Streets, Havre.

Recommended time: Third weekend in September.

Minimum time commitment: Four hours, plus driving time.

What to bring: Camera with flash attachment.

Admission fee: $6.00 adults, $5.00 seniors, $4.00 ages 6 to 12, $4.00 per person for conventions and class reunions, $3.00 per person for school-sponsored functions.

Hours: Winter hours are 10:00 A.M. to 4:00 P.M. Monday through Saturday; summer hours (mid-May through Labor Day) are 9:00 A.M. to 5:00 P.M. daily.

Directions: Havre is located 115 miles north of Great Falls east of the junction of U.S. 2 and U.S. 87. Havre Beneath the Streets is at the corner of First Street (U.S. 2) and Third Avenue.

For more information

Havre Beneath the Streets and the Havre Railroad Museum
120 Third Avenue, Havre, MT 59501
(406) 265–8888, (406) 265–2644

H. Earl Clack Museum, The Heritage Center
306 Third Avenue, Havre, MT 59501
(406) 265–4000
www.theheritagecenter.com, www.buffalojump.org

Havre Area Chamber of Commerce
518 First Avenue, Havre, MT 59501
(406) 265–4383
www.havremt.com

38

Reflections of Glaciers
Lake McDonald Lodge

When the Great Northern Railroad developed "America's Little Switzerland" the idea of "Seeing America First" was one of classic luxury that included every sort of transportation and accommodation available in that day. You can still experience this at the Lake McDonald Lodge, Glacier's first resort hotel.

The history

When James J. Hill's Great Northern Railroad began passenger service on its new transcontinental route through Marias Pass in 1893, there was no Glacier Park. But word of the Glacier country's beauty spread quickly and local entrepreneurs soon recognized the tourism potential of Lake McDonald. George Snyder obtained a homestead patent and built the first hotel in Glacier at the head of the lake in 1895. Because there was no road, he also purchased a 40-foot steamboat and hauled it to the lake. In 1906 John Lewis of Columbia Falls bought Snyder's hotel and built thirteen cabins that are still being used today on the north side of the hotel.

By 1910 Glacier National Park had been created and the Great Northern Railroad began its own building program with a series of grand lodges, tent camps, and mountain chalets, including Belton and Sperry Chalets. Not to be outdone, Lewis contracted with Spokane architect Kirtland Cutter, who also designed the Conrad Mansion in Kalispell, to design a new hotel. Lewis's Glacier Hotel opened for business in 1914. When the Going-to-the-Sun Road reached the hotel in 1922, Lewis had to redesign the lobby because the front of the hotel faces the lake. In 1930, during the Great Depression, Lewis sold his hotel to the railroad, which renamed it the Lake McDonald Hotel. That same year a new excursion boat, the *DeSmet,* was brought to the lake and has operated there ever since. In 1932 the Going-to-the-Sun Road was

Trees provide dramatic scenery along the shoreline near Lake McDonald Lodge.

completed over Logan Pass and today the Lake McDonald Lodge remains one of the park's most popular establishments.

The fun

Early fall brings the best weather, prettiest colors, and least crowds of any season at Glacier. Start your trip by picking up a *Waterton-Glacier Guide* at the West Glacier park entrance, then take the scenic 11-mile drive along the shore of Lake McDonald to the lodge. As you enter, the lobby provides a taste of the old times, with John Lewis hunting trophies still on display. The vernacular Swiss-style architecture is highlighted by gnarled log posts, beams, and steps made of quarter-cut logs. Among the hotel's regular guests were movie stars such as Clark Gable and artists such as Charlie Russell, who, it is rumored, drew the native-style pictographs surrounding the massive fireplace. Ask at the lobby desk for a translation of the Kootenai Indian phrases carved into the floor and see if you can find all nine of them.

The hotel is still a hub for Glacier activities. If you come early enough in September, you can take a half-day or full-day tour of the park by van or soon-to-be restored 1930s era "jammer" red bus, then hop on the *DeSmet* and take a one-hour boat trip to see the lake and the lodge the way the first guests did. Just a few miles up the road along Avalanche Creek is the Trail of the Cedars, a handicapped-accessible nature trail. For the more adventurous, the trail to Avalanche Lake starts there also. If you return to the lodge, you can also rent a horse or hike the trail from here to Sperry Chalet and Sperry Glacier. Complete your day in the lodge's dining room before heading back to town or bedding down for the night.

Next best

If you like the sights and sounds of spring in the Rockies, visit during late May when the trees are leafing out, the bears are out of their dens, and the last of the snowpack comes roaring down the avalanche chutes.

Unique food and lodging

There are several other incredibly beautiful and historic lodges in and near Glacier that have both restaurants and accommodations. They include the restored 1910 **Belton Chalets** in West Glacier, **Glacier Park Lodge** at East Glacier Park, the **Many Glacier Hotel** on Swiftcurrent Lake, and the **Prince of Wales Hotel** in Waterton Park. If you want to get to your room the old-fashioned way, by foot or horseback, try the 1914 **Granite Park Chalet,** 4 miles by trail, or the full-service 1915 **Sperry Chalet,** 6.8 miles by trail. Reservations are required.

Practical information

Site: Lake McDonald Lodge, Waterton-Glacier International Peace Park World Heritage Site, 32 miles east of Kalispell.

Recommended time: Late September.

Minimum time commitment: One day.

What to bring: Sunglasses with polarizing lenses to cut glare on the water when viewing Lake McDonald, warm jacket, sturdy walking shoes, binoculars, and camera with telephoto lens and polarizing filter.

Admission fee: Park entrance fees are $5.00 per person or $10.00 per vehicle for a 7-day pass, or $20 for an annual park pass, $50 per vehicle for a 12-month passport to all national parks, $10 for a Golden Age lifetime pass for seniors 62 and older, free for blind or disabled persons.

Hours: Lake McDonald Lodge is open from the fourth week in May to October 1. Glacier National Park is open year-round, but access and facilities are limited during winter months.

Directions: From Kalispell take U.S. 2 east 32 miles to West Glacier, then go 11 miles on Going-to-the-Sun Road to the lodge, near the north end of Lake McDonald.

For more information

Superintendent, Glacier National Park
West Glacier, MT 59936
(406) 888–7800
www.nps.gov/glac/home.htm

Glacier Park Inc.
The Viad Corporate Tower, Phoenix, AZ 85077-0928
(602) 207–6000, (800) 215–2395
www.glacierparkinc.com

Glacier Park Boat Company
P.O. Box 5262, Kalispell, MT 59903
(406) 257–2426
www.montanaweb.com/gpboats

Belton Chalets, Inc.
Highway 2 East, West Glacier, MT 59936
(406) 888–5000, (888) 235–8665
www.beltonchalet.com, www.ptinet.net/sperrychalet

39

A River Runs Through It
Lewis and Clark National Historic Trail Interpretive Center

Retrace the route of the "Corps of Discovery" as they struggled to portage not one but five great falls blocking navigation on one of the longest rivers in the world, and see the crystal clear waters of Lewis's discovery of the shortest river in the world.

The history

When Meriwether Lewis first saw the Great Falls of the Missouri on June 13, 1805, he described the view as the grandest sight he had ever seen. He then went on to see four other falls, each with its own character and beauty. On June 18 Clark also discovered a "giant springs" at the side of the river while he was surveying a portage route around the falls.

The Lewis and Clark Expedition had to make an 18-mile portage around these five falls. This portage was one of the greatest ordeals endured by the Expedition on its way to the Pacific. It required almost a month to plan and carry out and all the effort the men could muster. It was also here in north-central Montana that the Expedition discovered the cutthroat trout and the western meadowlark, both now Montana state symbols. The Expedition had several life-threatening encounters with the grizzly or "white bear" in this area, and they celebrated the young nation's independence here on July 4 by drinking the last of their grog.

The flow of Giant Springs into the Missouri has been dubbed the "Roe River" and is listed in the *Guinness Book of World Records* as the shortest river in the world. The spring is protected within Giant Springs Heritage State Park, one of a number of parks along the falls linked by the River's Edge Trail.

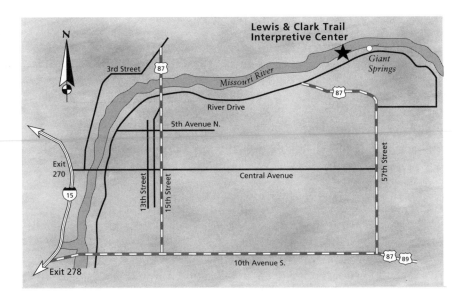

The fun

On a bluff overlooking the Missouri River, the Lewis and Clark National Historic Trail Interpretive Center is in the perfect place to interpret the Expedition's portage around the Great Falls. One of the best times to visit is in late September when the summer crowds are gone and the weather is still warm. Start your tour in the center's theater, which features a thirty-minute introductory film shown every hour. Then see the exhibits tracing the progress of the Expedition in Montana. Costumed interpreters also conduct demonstrations at the center. Don't miss the books and reproductions in the center's Portage Cache Store.

Pick up a *Great Falls of the Missouri* brochure at the center or the chamber of commerce. It contains a map and descriptions of the many sites associated with the Lewis and Clark Expedition near here. Make your next stop a half-mile north at Giant Springs, where 156 million gallons of crystal clear water pour out of the ground each day. The park here also includes a trout hatchery and a playground for children as well as a concession stand and picnic area.

Bike or drive another mile to the Rainbow Falls and Dam overlook. From here you can retrace your route past the interpretive center to River Drive and Black Eagle Falls Overlook. If you've brought a picnic lunch, Giant Springs and the River's Edge Trail are great places for picnics. The more adventurous can drive to Ryan and Morony Dams farther downstream. At Morony Dam you can launch your own pirogue or hike to Sulphur

Spring where Sacagawea was healed by drinking its water.

Next best

If you don't mind crowds and are hankerin' to try some period cuisine like fried beavertail, visit during the annual five-day Lewis and Clark Festival, held during the fourth week in June, the same month the portage was made. The festival includes interpretive walks and float trips, reenactments, Indian encampments, and living-history demonstrations in and around Giant Springs Heritage State Park.

Unique food and lodging

On weekdays try the "no-frills grill" at the **Club Cigar Saloon and Eatery,** 208 Central Avenue. One of Great Falls' oldest taverns, its gilded electric fans and massive mahogany back bar are worth a look. Or try the daily lunch special at the 1939-era **City Bar and Casino,** 709 Central Avenue, with its huge Brunswick back bar and nickel-plated hotel parlor stove. For overnight accommodations in an 1891 Queen Anne–style mansion, try the **Collins Mansion** bed-and-breakfast, 1003 Second Avenue North West.

Practical information

Site: Lewis and Clark National Historic Trail Interpretive Center and Giant Springs Heritage State Park, Great Falls.

Recommended time: Late September.

Minimum time commitment: Four hours, plus driving time.

What to bring: Sunglasses with polarizing lenses to cut glare on the water when viewing the Giant Springs, windbreaker, walking shoes, binoculars, and camera with telephoto lens and polarizing filter. A bicycle, in-line skates, or jogging shoes are also fun accessories if you want to follow the river along the paved River's Edge Trail.

Admission fee: The Interpretive Center is operated by the U.S. Forest Service. $5.00 adults, $4.00 seniors and students, $2.00 ages 6 to 17; free with Golden Age, Golden Access, or Golden Eagle pass. Giant Springs Heritage State Park admission is $1.00 per person age 6 and above.

Hours: The Interpretive Center is open daily from 9:00 A.M. to 6:00 P.M. Memorial Day weekend through September. Winter hours are 9:00 A.M. to 5:00 P.M. Tuesday through Saturday and noon to 5:00 P.M. Sunday. Giant Springs Heritage State Park is open from daylight to dusk year-round.

Rainbow Falls, one of five falls the Expedition had to portage around.

Directions: Take Interstate 15 to Great Falls Central Avenue West exit 270. Go east on Central Avenue to Third Street North West. Turn left and go to U.S. 87. Turn right and follow the brown directional signs to the Interpretive Center on Giant Springs Road.

For more information

Lewis and Clark National Historic Trail Interpretive Center
4201 Giant Springs Heritage Road, Great Falls, MT 59404
(406) 727–8733
www.fs.fed.us/r1/lewisclark/lcic.htm

Park Manager, Giant Springs Heritage State Park
4600 Giant Springs Heritage Road, Great Falls, MT 59405
(406) 454–5858
www.fwp.state.mt.us/parks

Great Falls Chamber of Commerce
P.O. Box 2127, Great Falls, MT 59403
(406) 761–4434
www.greatfallscvb.visitmt.com

Collins Mansion
1003 2nd Avenue North West, Great Falls, MT 59404
(406) 452–6798, (877) 452–6798
www.collinsmansion.com

40

I Will Fight No More Forever
Bear Paw Battlefield,
Nez Perce National Historical Park

> Here, only 40 miles from Canada, one of the most remarkable and tragic military campaigns in the annals of war ended with one of the most famous surrender speeches in history. Experience that cold blustery day in October 1877.

The history

On June 15, 1877, five bands of Nez Perce left central Idaho with 800 people, including 125–150 warriors, and more than 2,000 horses, on a 1,300-mile trek across the Rocky Mountains pursued by U.S. Army troops. Four months later, and only 40 miles from their goal of escaping to Canada, Chief Joseph and 431 Nez Perce surrendered here on October 5, 1877.

The Nez Perce homeland was overrun with encroaching prospectors and settlers when the military ordered them to move to a reservation in May 1877. They were preparing to move when three young warriors killed some settlers who had killed Indians. The Nez Perce left Idaho to seek refuge, first with their Crow allies on the plains, then with Sitting Bull's Sioux in Canada. On September 29, after surviving some twenty battles and skirmishes and losing many warriors and chiefs, the Nez Perce camped on the prairie here north of the Bear Paw Mountains. They named it "the place of the manure fire."

The next morning, Colonel Nelson A. Miles attacked the camp with thirty Cheyenne scouts and more than 400 troops of the 2nd and 7th Cavalries and the 5th Infantry. After heavy hand-to-hand fighting, casualties for the Army included twenty-three men killed and forty-five wounded, while the Nez Perce had thirty killed and forty-six wounded, including three

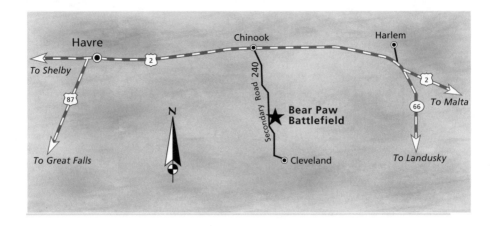

chiefs, and saw their horse herd captured. After a five-day siege with sharp-shooters and cannon fire, Chief Joseph surrendered his rifle and the remaining Nez Perce with his famous words, ". . . Hear me, my chiefs! I am tired. My heart is sick and sad. From where the sun now stands I will fight no more forever." The rifle is now on display at the Museum of the Upper Missouri in Fort Benton.

The fun

To fully appreciate the plight of the Nez Perce, you must visit this hallowed ground when they did, during the first week of October. Snake Creek is crusted with ice, the winds of October are spitting snow in your face, and you can hear a hungry coyote howl in the distance.

The Bear Paw Battle Commemoration is held by the Nez Perce during the first week of October. Call in advance to verify the time of the memorial activities on the battlefield, including the pipe ceremony, empty saddle ceremony, and traditional song and prayer. The battlefield also has interpretive signs, a 1-mile self-guided trail with eleven stops (pets are not allowed), picnic tables, and rest rooms. Tours of the battlefield should be scheduled in advance so as not to conflict with the ceremonies.

After the ceremonies and battlefield tour, arrange for a tour of the Blaine County Museum on the corner of Indiana and Fifth Streets in Chinook. Don't miss the audiovisual presentation *40 Miles to Freedom* detailing the events leading up to the battle. The museum has one paleontology room just for kids to touch the fossils; another showcases a 75-million-year-old *Albertosaurus* dinosaur skull. The museum gift shop has an excellent selection of books on the battle. Exhibits tell the story of the Nez Perce Indians, pioneer days, and hardships of the homestead era. You can even check out the

Chinook House ledger, which was saved when the local hotel burned in 1900. An entry for June 15, 1897, notes famous western artist Charlie Russell's bar bill of $20.75 and room bill of $3.50 for a three-day stay.

If that isn't enough western history for one day, drive a short 25 miles east on U.S. 2 to the Fort Belknap Agency Information Center. Call ahead and get a guided two-hour tour of the Gros Ventre (*grow vaunt*) and Assinniboine Indian Tribes' buffalo reserve and learn how native cultures depended on the bison.

Next best

If you can't visit the battlefield during the October battle commemoration, you can visit anytime from mid-June to early September when the weather is likely to be warm and the museum and visitor center have expanded hours. With limited staff, the National Park Service urges visitors to schedule ranger-led tours in advance.

Practical information

Site: Bear Paw Battlefield, Nez Perce National Historical Park, 16 miles south of Chinook.

Recommended time: First week in October.

Minimum time commitment: One day.

What to bring: Warm clothes, water, sunglasses, binoculars, and camera.

Admission fee: None.

Hours: The Bear Paw Battlefield is open daily year-round. The Blaine County Museum hours are Monday through Friday 1:00 to 5:00 P.M. from September through May, Monday through Saturday 9:00 A.M. to 5:00 P.M. and Sunday noon to 5:00 P.M. from June through August. The Chinook Visitor Information Center and National Park Service Office are open Monday through Thursday 9:00 A.M. to 2:00 P.M. from June through August.

Directions: From U.S. 2 in Chinook, go south on Indiana Street through town, then follow signs on Secondary Road 240 for 16 miles to the park entrance.

For more information

Nez Perce National Historical Park, Bear Paw Battlefield
P.O. Box 26, Chinook, MT 59523
(406) 357–3130
www.nps.gov/nepe

Blaine County Museum
501 Indiana Street, Chinook, MT 59523
(406) 357–2590

Chinook Chamber of Commerce
P.O. Box 744, Chinook, MT 59523
www.chinookmontana.com

Tribal Buffalo Tours
RR1, Box 66, Fort Belknap Agency, Harlem, MT 59526
(406) 353–2205

41

Growing Up Like Huckleberry Finn
Fort Benton National Historic Landmark

Walk through the cottonwood trees along the steamboat levee once known as "the bloodiest block in the west" to the adobe ruins of the old Fort Benton trading post, then explore the Museum of the Upper Missouri to learn why Fort Benton was called the birthplace of Montana.

The history

Established in 1846 by Alexander Culbertson of the American Fur Company, Fort Benton was known as the "birthplace of Montana" and the "Chicago of the Plains." First a fur trade fort, it soon became a hub for travel and trade to the Northwestern United States and Canada. From here, Lieutenant John Mullan built the military road across the continental divide to Fort Walla Walla in Washington. During the 1860s, millions of tons of freight were shipped through here to the goldfields. Fifty steamboats a season would dock along the levee, offloading traders, trappers, settlers, and soldiers as well as freight. From 1860, when the first stern-wheeler docked at the levee, until the last one came in 1890, 600 steamboats had reached the head of navigation here on the Missouri River.

In 1869 the U.S. Army bought the aging adobe-walled fort for a supply base for Forts Shaw and Ellis. During the Indian Wars of the 1870s, one of Benton's steamers, the *Far West,* carried Custer's wounded after the Battle of the Little Bighorn. In 1881 the first bridge was built across the river at this point, and in 1882 the Grand Union Hotel was built next to the levee. But in 1883 the first transcontinental railroad in Montana was completed at Gold Creek, dooming the steamboat trade and the future growth of Fort Benton.

Many famous and infamous folks lived and some died in Fort Benton. Charles and William Conrad, two brothers who immigrated here in 1868, became wealthy from the steamboat trade. The brothers started their careers with I. G. Baker in Fort Benton and William became its first mayor, while Charles relocated to the Flathead Valley when the freighting business declined. Eleanore Dumont, the pistol-packing mama known as "Madame Moustache," ran a saloon and brothel on the waterfront until she shot herself in 1879 over a gambling loss. In 1897, a petrified male corpse was dug up near the base of Signal Point next to the river north of town and put on display for years before he disappeared again. In 1908 the Daughters of the American Revolution rescued the Fort's blockhouse and adobe wall with donated funds, including $1,500 from the Montana legislature. The oldest building in Montana is still standing today because of their efforts.

The fun

Fort Benton is recognized as a National Historic Landmark because of the importance it played as the head of navigation on the Missouri River and the opening of the Northwest and western Canada. Call ahead to see the Museum of the Upper Missouri in Old Fort Park. Displays include some of the last wild buffalo, collected in 1886 by William Hornaday for the Smithsonian; Alexander Culberston's sword; and the rifle Chief Joseph surrendered with at the Bear Paw Battlefield. Nearby are Fort Benton's remaining adobe blockhouse and the reconstructed blacksmith shop, warehouse, and trade store.

Then get a walking tour guide and follow the levee along Front Street. Near the Lewis and Clark Memorial statue is the keelboat *Mandan* that was used in the movie *The Big Sky*. I. G. Baker's house on Front Street has been restored, and the old firehouse next to the steel bridge serves as a visitor center with a good bookstore and gift shop. A little farther on is the statue of the faithful dog Shep (see sidebar), who is buried on a hill just north of town. Finish your tour at the Grand Union Hotel, which has been restored to its former glory as a riverboat hotel. Some additional sights include the 1870s St. Paul Episcopal Church on Choteau Street and the Museum of the Northern Great Plains on 20th Street.

Next best

If you want company on your trip through Fort Benton, plan your visit for the last weekend in June during the annual Summer Celebration. Activities include living-history encampments, tours and floats, a pig roast, an art and quilting show, and a Saturday parade, street dance, and fireworks display. Most canoe concessions and the *Benton Belle* riverboat cruise operates during the summer as well.

The Old Steel Bridge on the Fort Benton Levee marks the official head of navigation on the Missouri.

Unique food and lodging

Restored after more than one hundred years, the 1882 **Grand Union Hotel** on the Fort Benton levee offers meals in the **Union Grille Restaurant** and has two floors of restored guest rooms with historic furnishings.

Practical information

Site: Fort Benton National Historic Landmark, 44 miles north of Great Falls.

Recommended time: Mid-October.

Minimum time commitment: Two hours, plus driving time.

What to bring: Light jacket and camera.

Admission fee: None for most activities.

Hours: The town is accessible year-round.

Directions: From Great Falls, go 44 miles north on U.S. 87, then turn right on Montana Highway 80 and go 2 miles to Fort Benton.

Shep's Vigil

One day in August 1936, a casket containing the body of a sheepherder was loaded onto a Great Northern Railroad baggage car at Fort Benton to be shipped back east for burial. Watching from a distance was a sheepdog of collie strain. From that day on, the faithful dog was there to meet every train that pulled in to Fort Benton. Three years later, train conductor Ed Shields finally pieced together enough clues to write Shep's story, as the dog continued to maintain his vigil at the train station. Once the story was known in 1939, Shep became a worldwide celebrity, sharing front-page headlines and offsetting news of the war in Europe and Asia.

Many sheepherders and others offered to adopt Shep and give him a home, but friends knew that Shep would never give up his vigil, waiting for his master to return. For five and a half years, Shep met every train no matter what the weather. Shep met his last train, Number 235, on January 12, 1942. The old dog did not hear the train until it was too late, and slipped on the snowy rails to his death. Mourned by all who knew his story, the townsfolk buried him on the bluff overlooking the train depot. Hundreds attended his funeral. School was dismissed so the children could attend, and the local Boy Scout troop sounded "Taps" and were Shep's pallbearers. As a tribute to Shep's faithfulness to his master, "Eulogy on the Dog" was read by a local reverend.

Great Northern employees marked Shep's grave with a concrete marker and his profile. Soon a spotlight was added so train passengers could see the grave at night. Later a heroic-size bronze statute of Shep was erected on the banks of the Missouri near the old river bridge. Shep is gone and the trains no longer stop at the depot, but his lighted gravesite on the bluff just north of town remains as a tribute to one man's best friend.

For more information

Fort Benton Chamber of Commerce
P.O. Box 12, Fort Benton, MT 59442
(406) 622–3864
www.fortbenton.com

Grand Union Hotel
P.O. Box 1119, Fort Benton, MT 59442
(406) 622–1882, (888) 838–1882
www.grandunionhotel.com

42

The Great Indian Council of 1855
Judith Landing Historic District

See the valley of the Judith in October and try to imagine it
filled with the lodges of 3,000 Plains Indians at the Great
Council of 1855, then see the remains of the homesteads and
the graves of the immigrants who tried to make a living in the
heart of the Indian hunting grounds.

The history

Of all the crossroads on the Northern Plains, the mouth of the Judith River
was probably the most significant. A major Blackfoot war trail led through
here south to Crow country. On May 29, 1805, William Clark named this
river in honor of Julia "Judith" Hancock of Fincastle, Virginia. In 1837 a boat
hauling trade goods upriver to Fort McKenzie stopped here after a case of
smallpox broke out, but then proceeded as demanded by the Indians. More
than 6,000 Indians died from the resulting epidemic. In 1843 Fort Chardon
was built on the north bank, but it was abandoned a year later.

In 1846 Father Pierre Jean DeSmet met with the Blackfeet and Salish on
the north bank to end their open warfare, and in October 1855 Washington
territorial governor Isaac I. Stevens, head of the Northern Pacific survey,
organized the largest peace conference on the Northern Plains. More than
3,000 Blackfeet, Gros Ventres, Nez Perce, and Salish assembled for the ten-day
meeting that featured many gifts to the Indians and terminated with the sign-
ing of the first treaty limiting their hunting grounds. In 1866 the army built
Camp Cooke on the south side of the river to protect travelers from Indian
attacks. It closed in 1870; Fort Claggett Trading Post was built from the
remains two years later. E. D. Cope also found some of the earliest fossils
found in Montana near here in 1876.

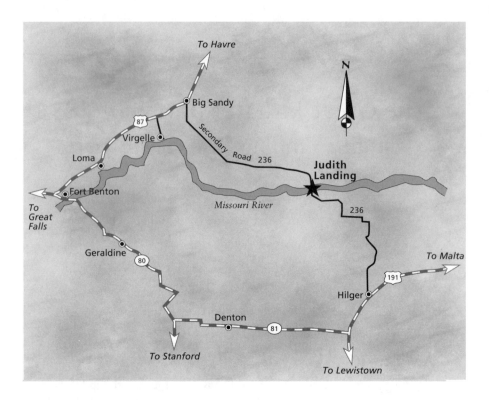

By 1885 the site was renamed Judith Landing and had a stone warehouse, saloon, hotel, stable, blacksmith shop, and store. During low water on the Missouri, Judith Landing became an important freight transfer point for steamboats, but like Fort Benton, the railroad soon made the town obsolete.

The fun

This is a great drive for a nice October day when the weather and the roads are dry. If you come from Big Sandy, watch for historical highway marker 89 on Fort Chardon before you get to the bridge. As you cross the bridge, you can look upstream on the south bank to where Judith Landing used to be. This is private property, so please don't trespass. As you drive to the base of Claggett Hill, watch for historical highway marker 90 on Judith Landing. To the east of the road near the base of Claggett Hill is the fenced headstone and grave of Matt Duncan, a young man from New York who wandered off and was killed by Indians here in 1881. Finally, drive 3 miles to historical highway marker 91 near the top of Claggett Hill. From here you can get a view of the wild and scenic Upper Missouri River country.

During the summer food and drinks are available at the Judith boat ramp store.

Next best

Another good but more crowded time to see Judith Landing is the first weekend in June when you can stop in Virgelle for Touch the Trail of Lewis and Clark, and at James Kipp Recreation Area for Lewis and Clark living-history encampment activities.

Practical information

Site: Judith Landing, Upper Missouri River Breaks National Monument, 63 miles north of Lewistown.

Recommended time: Mid-October.

Minimum time commitment: One hour, plus driving time.

What to bring: Sunglasses with polarizing lenses to cut glare on the water, warm jacket, sturdy walking shoes, binoculars, and camera with telephoto lens and polarizing filter. Bring along a copy of *The Journals of Lewis and Clark* and the two Bureau of Land Management river maps of the route.

Admission fee: None.

Hours: The area is accessible year-round, weather permitting.

Directions: To reach Judith Landing from Lewistown, drive 14 miles north on U.S. 191 to Hilger. Turn left on paved Secondary Road 236 and go 49 miles north to Judith Landing and the Missouri River. From Big Sandy, go southeast for 44 miles on Secondary Road 236, which is paved for the first 16 miles then becomes a gravel road.

For more information

Big Sandy Area Chamber of Commerce
P.O. Box 411, Big Sandy, MT 59520
(406) 378–2492, (406) 378–2176

Bureau of Land Management, Lewistown Field Office
P.O. Box 1160, Lewistown, MT 59457-1160
(406) 538–7461
www.mt.blm.gov/ido

Fort Benton Chamber of Commerce
P.O. Box 12, Fort Benton, MT 59442
(406) 622–3864
www.fortbenton.com

43

Christmas at the Mansion
The Charles Conrad Mansion

On the last weekend in October, a Victorian-era Christmas celebration benefits the Mansion Museum. Christmas craftwork, art, gifts, food, and decorating ideas are displayed for sale. Enjoy the smell of evergreen, the sounds of music, and the aroma of fresh-baked pies.

The history

Charles Edward Conrad—Montana pioneer, Missouri River trader, freighter, and founder of the City of Kalispell—was born near Front Royal, Virginia, in 1850. He and his older brother, William, fought with Mosby's Rangers during the Civil War. In 1868 they both came west to Fort Benton, Montana Territory, and went to work for the I. G. Baker Company, one of the largest mercantile enterprises in the northwest. They soon bought the company and prospered on steamboats and freight wagons for more than twenty-three years.

When the brothers saw that the completion of the Great Northern Railroad would put an end to their business, William moved to Great Falls, and Charles came to the Flathead Valley, where he founded the city of Kalispell in 1891.

As a trader in Fort Benton, Charles Conrad shipped hundreds of thousands of buffalo hides to St. Louis and witnessed the decimation of these majestic animals on the Great Plains, so one of his first projects in the Flathead Valley was to create a buffalo preserve. He paid trappers to collect some young animals and established the Conrad buffalo herd on what is now Kalispell's Buffalo Hill Golf Course. In 1908 his herd became the nucleus for the National Bison Range, 80 miles south of Kalispell.

Charles Conrad's wood-shingled three-story Norman-style mansion was designed and built in 1895 by Spokane Club and Davenport Hotel architect Kirtland Cutter. The mansion, long one of Kalispell's landmarks, contains twenty-six rooms, with an elevator linking all three floors and the basement. Be sure to check out the gaslights. Anticipating the future, Cutter had them wired for electricity as well. The rooms are furnished with Conrad's original belongings, even down to clothing, and offer one of the most complete examples of Victorian life in the Wild West. Conrad's youngest daughter, Alicia Conrad Campbell, donated the mansion to the city in 1975 as a historic site.

The fun

Although Queen Victoria died in 1901, her spirit lives on in the celebration of a Victorian-era Christmas at the Conrad Mansion on the last weekend in October. Since 1982, the mansion has hosted a juried craft, art, and bake sale to benefit the Mansion Museum. Fifty local craftspeople and organizations submit their best Christmas craftwork, art, gifts, food, and decorating ideas for display and sale. The mansion is full of the smell of evergreen, the sounds of music, and the aroma of fresh-baked pies. The highlight is the elaborate Victorian-era Christmas decorations and Christmas tree. Local musicians provide entertainment throughout the weekend, and a local caterer serves breakfast and lunch each day on the veranda. For a more intimate experience, call ahead for Friday evening tickets and come in your evening attire (Victorian if possible) for the champagne and hors d'oeuvres social. All of the craftspeople and staff dress in Victorian attire, and you get first choice at all the crafts and baked goods.

Plan to arrive early on Saturday to avoid the crowds, and to take advantage of the sunlight on the eastern front of the mansion grounds. Start the tour inside the eastern entrance to the house. Each room showcases Conrad's original Chippendale furniture, furnishings, and accessories. Extensive collections also include original Conrad family clothing dating from the 1880s to 1940s, and three generations of children's toys and dolls. The gift shop sells Victorian cards, books, gifts, jewelry, china, and decorations. Outside, you can stroll through beautifully landscaped lawns and gardens featuring thousands of flowers during the summer and handsome evergreens year-round.

Next best

You can also visit from mid-July to early September, when the mansion's flower beds are in full bloom and the weather is likely to be warm and sunny for the best outdoor photos.

The Conrad Mansion has a grand view of the Flathead River Valley.

Unique food and lodging

Well-known for its swinging doors, rustic atmosphere, and sawdust on the floor, **Moose's Saloon,** 173 North Main Street at the intersection of U.S. 2 and U.S. 93, has been a Kalispell landmark since the 1950s. The menu features homemade soup, pizza, and breadsticks. Within strolling distance of the mansion are some historic places where you can get a meal or a bed. The 1894 Central School Museum and **Blackboard Cafe,** 124 Second Avenue East, serves lunch. Farther west, you can get a room where the likes of artists and authors such as Charlie Russell, Frank Bird Linderman, and Irvin S. Cobb once stayed. The refurbished century-old **Kalispell Grand Hotel** occupies the corner of 100 Main Street. You may even want to drop in for breakfast, lunch, or dinner at the 1897 **Sykes' Grocery, Market, and Restaurant,** 202 Second Avenue West, where they say they have the cheapest coffee in town (10 cents a cup) and "nobody goes away a stranger."

Practical information

Site: The Charles Conrad Mansion, corner of Fourth Street East and Woodland Avenue, Kalispell.
Recommended time: Last weekend in October.

Minimum time commitment: Two hours, plus driving time.

What to bring: Camera (no flash allowed inside).

Admission fee: Tours are $7.00 adults, $6.00 seniors, $1.00 children under 12. Christmas at the Mansion is $5.00 adults, $1.00 children under 12. A limited number of $25 tickets goes on sale the second Saturday in September for the Friday evening Christmas at the Mansion social.

Hours: Open daily May 15 to June 14 from 10:00 A.M. to 5:30 P.M., June 15 to September 15 from 9:00 A.M. to 8:00 P.M., September 16 to October 15 from 10:00 A.M. to 5:30 P.M. Hours for Christmas at the Mansion are Friday from 7:00 to 9:00 P.M. (social), Saturday from 10:00 A.M. to 6:00 P.M., and Sunday from 11:00 A.M. to 4:00 P.M.

Directions: From Main Street in Kalispell, go 6 blocks east on Fourth Street East to Woodland Avenue and the mansion. The main entrance faces east on Woodland Avenue.

For more information

The Conrad Mansion
P.O. Box 1041, Kalispell, MT 59903
(406) 755–2166
www.conradmansion.com

Central School Museum
124 Second Avenue East, Kalispell, MT 59901
(406) 756–8381

Kalispell Grand Hotel
100 Main Street, Kalispell, MT 59901-4452
(406) 755–8100, (800) 858-7422
www.kalispellgrand.com

44

Last Chance Gulch Becomes the First City

Helena Historic District

> Montana's third major gold strike lasted long enough to turn a raw mining camp into Montana's third territorial capital and its state capital. See the legacy left behind by $3.6 billion in gold and fifty millionaires.

The history

Last Chance Gulch became the third major gold discovery in Montana Territory after Bannack and Alder Gulch. On July 14, 1864, Reginald Stanley and three other prospectors known as "the four Georgians" hit pay dirt on their "last chance" at panning for gold here before heading back to Alder Gulch. Soon Last Chance Gulch swarmed with miners, and in October the "more suitable" name of Helena was chosen. Named after a town in Minnesota (due to much politicking by a recent immigrant from there), by 1865 the town had a population of 3,000, with many coming from Virginia City. The end of the Civil War produced an even greater stampede from the states. By 1869 many of the placer claims had played out, but not before more than $17 million in gold had been washed from the gulches in the district.

Fortunately, the first lode claims were also discovered in 1864 in the hills south of Last Chance Gulch. By 1874, these mines had contributed enough to Helena's economic growth to have the territorial government moved here from Virginia City. Despite a disastrous fire in 1874, Helena continued to grow. When Montana became a state in 1889, the city was reported to have fifty millionaires, the most per capita in the nation. In 1894 the city won a bribe-filled contest with Anaconda to become the permanent state capital.

Some pioneer cabins on upper Last Chance Gulch are still occupied.

Most of Helena's grandest historic buildings, including the St. Helena Cathedral and the copper-domed capitol building, date from this prosperous period after statehood. Some historic buildings later succumbed to the earthquake and fire of 1935 and urban renewal efforts of the 1970s. During World War II, the Helena area became the training site for two unique war efforts, the American-Canadian First Special Service Force known as The Devil's Brigade, and dogsled teams at the "War Dog Reception Center."

The fun

One of the best times to visit Helena is in early November after the tourist season has ended and before the biennial legislative session begins. First, head for the Montana Historical Society Museum on Capitol Hill. The Montana history exhibits, archives, and Charles M. Russell art are unsurpassed. Pick up the tour guide *Montana's Capitol Building,* then cross the street for a forty-five-minute guided tour of the Greek Renaissance capitol building. Tours are given at noon, 1:00 and 2:00 P.M. and include the famous mural by Charles M. Russell in the House Chambers.

Afterward, head west to the old part of the city, stopping at the chamber of commerce to ask for *The Heart of Helena* self-guided walking tour guide, which describes many of the old buildings. Be sure to tour the Original Governor's

Mansion, restored to its 1888 Queen Anne–style splendor. Nearby is St. Helena's Cathedral, patterned after the great Cathedral in Cologne, Germany.

Downtown, a plaque on the Montana Club building marks the original gold discovery site, and there is a gold display in the Wells Fargo Bank building. Helena's Main Street is still named Last Chance Gulch, and part of it is now a walking mall with historic markers, statues, and one of Helena's old trolley cars. Walk the mall and then continue south on Park Avenue to the Pioneer Cabin and Reeder's Alley, one of the oldest sections of town. Today its restored cabins house craftsmen, retail shops, and a restaurant.

Continue south on Park Avenue until it becomes Main Street again and the canyon narrows. Here picturesque hand-hewn log, stone, and brick cabins, and one German Fachwerkbau-style house line the gulch in the old Chinatown section of the city. If you have time, take the scenic 9-mile Grizzly–Orofino Gulch loop drive past old limekilns, mine shafts, and mine tailings back to town. Finish your tour with a drive through the Mansion district on the upper west side of town, and a stop at the city's oldest cemetery along the old Fort Benton stage road across from Carroll College.

This time of year you can also see hundreds of migrating bald eagles on the Missouri River east of the city. For details and to learn the best places and times for viewing, call (406) 475–3128.

Next best

If you like a festive atmosphere and the sounds as well as the sights of the Old West, a great time to visit is the last week in July during the Last Chance Stampede Rodeo, Fair, and Parade. The Last Chance Tour Train runs daily during the summer.

Unique food and lodging

Homemade chili and milk shakes as well as chocolates are available at **The Parrot Confectionery,** 42 North Main Street, one of the oldest in town. Try the all-you-can-eat seafood buffet at **The Stonehouse Restaurant** in Reeder's Alley. Accommodations include several restored Victorian-style homes: **The Barrister** bed-and-breakfast (1874), 416 North Ewing Street; **The Sanders** bed-and-breakfast (1875), 328 North Ewing Street; **The Carolina** bed-and-breakfast (1906), 309 North Ewing Street; and the **Appleton Inn** bed-and-breakfast (1890s), 1999 Euclid Avenue.

Practical information

Site: Helena Historic District.

Recommended time: Early November.

Minimum time commitment: One day.

What to bring: Warm clothes, sturdy waterproof winter boots, hat, gloves, sunblock, sunglasses, camera, and binoculars.

Admission fee: None.

Hours: The Montana Historical Society Museum and the capitol building are open Monday through Friday 8:00 A.M. to 5:00 P.M. and Saturday 9:00 A.M. to 5:00 P.M. The Original Governor's Mansion is open Tuesday through Saturday noon to 5:00 P.M.

Directions: Helena is located at the crossroads of Interstate 15 and U.S. 12.

For more information

Helena Chamber of Commerce
225 Cruse Avenue, Helena, MT 59601
(406) 447–1530, (800) 743–5362
www.helenachamber.com, www.downtownhelena.com

Montana Historical Society
225 North Roberts Street, Helena, MT 59620-1201
(406) 444–2694
www.montanahistoricalsociety.com

The Appleton Inn
1999 Euclid Avenue, Helena, MT 59601
(406) 449–7492, (800) 956–1999
www.bbonline.com/mt/appleton

The Barrister
416 North Ewing Street, Helena, MT 59601
(406) 443–7330, (800) 823–1148
www.wtp.net/go/montana/sites/barrister.html

The Carolina
309 North Ewing Street, Helena, MT 59601
(406) 495–8095
www.carolinab-b.com

The Sanders
328 North Ewing Street, Helena, MT 59601
(406) 442–3309
www.sandersbb.com

The First Woman in Congress

When Jeannette Rankin was elected to the U.S. House of Representatives in 1916, most women in America were not even allowed to vote. She was the first woman to represent any state in the nation's capital. Rankin was an effective legislator for the cause of women's suffrage and rights, and was a leader in the feminist movement. She was also a lifelong pacifist, and was the only member of Congress to vote against America's entry into both World Wars.

Rankin was born in 1880, one of seven children who grew up on a ranch near Missoula. She graduated from the University of Montana in 1902 and worked as a social worker in New York and Seattle. While in Seattle, she worked with prominent suffragette Minnie Reynolds, who had a major impact on the remainder of Rankin's life. Rankin's speech to the Montana legislature in 1911 convinced Montana to give women the right to vote long before it happened in many other states. The speech also propelled her into a life of political activity that included serving two terms in Congress.

Elected as a Republican during her first term in 1917, she was called on to cast her vote on a resolution declaring war against Germany. She voted against the resolution with fifty-five other members of Congress, declaring, "I want to stand by my country, but I cannot vote for war." Despite the publicity she received for voting her convictions, she was decisively defeated in the next election and soon moved to Georgia to continue to lobby for peace and for women's and children's rights.

In 1940 she returned to Montana and again ran for Congress. She won the election under the slogan "Prepare to the limit for defense, keep our men out of Europe." Then on December 8, 1941, the day after the Japanese bombed Pearl Harbor, she was again called on to cast her vote on a resolution declaring war. Again she voted against it, saying, "As a woman, I can't go to war and I refuse to send anyone else." She voted her convictions again, but this time she was the lone dissenter, and the public viewed her vote as an act of treason. She did not run for reelection in 1942 and soon returned to Georgia. Rankin remained active in peace and women's rights movements until she died in 1973. Montana has yet to elect another woman to Congress.

45

The Cavemen of
Bitter Creek Coulee
Pictograph Cave State Park

*Ten thousand years ago, Montana was a different place—
but not too different. The ancients hunted giant bison instead
of bison, and trapped giant beaver, instead of beaver. See why
they made the caves of Bitter Creek their home.*

The history

The rock caves here in the sandstone rimrock of Bitter Creek housed some
of Montana's earliest families. Early residents of Billings called them
Inscription, or Indian Caves. Today the larger cave dwelling is called
Pictograph Cave; the other is Ghost Cave. Ten thousand years ago, after the
last glaciers had retreated and the climate warmed, early hunters occupied this
area, hastening the demise of woolly mammoths, giant bison, giant ground
sloths, and giant beavers. The caves and springs provided these and later
hunters with shelter, water, and a place where they could roast buffalo meat
and make bone and stone tools, pottery, baskets, and clothing.

The earliest artists also decorated the cave walls with more than one
hundred paintings, known as pictographs, of animals, people, and weapons.
A 3,500-year-old turtle design was painted with black and white paints,
which were probably made with ashes and clays. Later inhabitants added
shield-bearing warriors with red paints probably made from red clays and
animal fat. More recent Indians added pictures of horses, guns, and coups
sticks.

In 1937, local visitors found arrowheads, bones, and other artifacts in
the caves. A Works Progress Administration project eventually unearthed
more than 30,000 artifacts. A grid system enabled researchers to compare

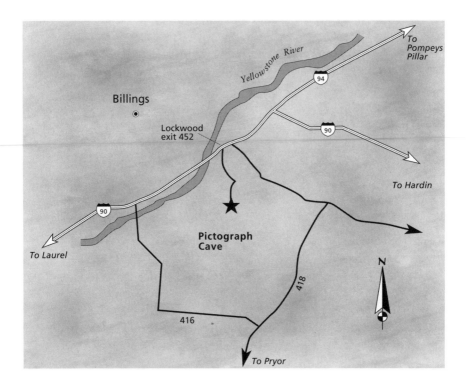

and date artifacts from other sites in the Northern Plains years before the carbon 14 dating process came into use. Pictograph Cave has been designated a National Historic Landmark, as no other sites on the Northern Plains have been found that were occupied so continuously for so long.

The fun

A trip to Pictograph Cave is a great way to get out of the city for a while and get some fresh air and exercise. By late fall the crowds are gone, the bugs are gone, and the rattlesnakes are gone. There are actually three caves at the park, although the Indians only inhabited the larger two. At this time of year you must call the Department of Fish, Wildlife, and Parks office before you go for a guided tour and trail maps.

When you arrive at the parking lot, take the short but steep paved trail on the right that goes past the rest room. Once you reach Pictograph Cave, the largest of the three, you can view the few pictographs that are still visible. The black dotted line on the cave wall indicates the floor level when the excavation began. Interpretive signs tell the story of Montana's first professional archaeological studies and excavations.

The sandstone rim rocks of Bitter Creek provided ideal shelter for ancient hunters.

Continue on the loop trail past the huge mound from the excavations to Middle Cave, which was not used as a dwelling, and Ghost Cave. From here you can see the ravine to the south of Pictograph Cave where the ancient spring still produces water. Stay on the paved trail and return to the parking lot. If you go in the morning or late in the evening, you will often see mule deer and birds of prey that also think the ancients picked a good place to live.

Next best

If you can't visit Pictograph Cave during the fall, try to visit during May or June when the road is open and the weather is likely to be warm. At this time of year the birds are singing, the deer have their fawns with them, the yuccas are in bloom, and the coulee is teeming with new life.

Unique food and lodging

Although the city of Billings didn't get going until the railroad arrived in 1882, it does have a downtown historic district and restaurants in historic buildings. **The Beanery,** 2314 Montana Avenue, in the 1909 Northern Pacific depot building, has lunches and dinners. **The Rex,** 2401 Montana Avenue, specializes in steak and prime rib. Also in Billings, **The Josephine**

Pictographs and Petroglyphs

There are basically two types of ancient rock art found in this region. The first is the pictograph, or rock painting. As the name implies, pictographs are images painted or drawn onto stone with materials derived from plants, soils, or animal products. Pictographs have been found in a number of colors, but red, black, and white are most commonly seen. In Montana you can see examples of pictographs at Pictograph Cave, the Gates of the Mountains, and Painted Rocks on Flathead Lake.

The second type of rock art is the petroglyph. These are images etched, carved, pecked, or scratched into soft rock with a sharpened tool. Captain William Clark's signature at Pompeys Pillar is a petroglyph. In Montana you can see other examples of petroglyphs at Pompeys Pillar, Medicine Rocks, Sleeping Buffalo Rock, and the Rosebud Battlefield.

Most rock art remains a mystery, although there are many theories about why the images were created. Some think that ancient people used rock art to record successful hunts or raids. Others think that they were more likely ceremonial and spiritual representations used to ask for divine help. For example, hunters who wanted to kill an elk may have painted the image on the rock to help them succeed. Shield-bearing soldiers may have been painted by warriors seeking the strength of the rock for their shields prior to battle.

Many pictographs and petroglyphs were made thousands of years ago. At Pictograph Cave one design is more than 3,500 years old. Yet modern man has done more damage to ancient rock art sites in a few decades than the forces of erosion over three millennia. Remember to respect these nonrenewable resources by leaving them untouched.

bed-and-breakfast, 514 North 29th Street, offers accommodations in a lovely historic home.

Practical information

Site: Pictograph Cave State Park and National Historic Landmark, 7 miles south of Billings.

Recommended time: Mid-November.

Minimum time commitment: Two hours, plus driving time.

What to bring: Warm clothes, hat, gloves, sturdy boots, water bottle, binoculars, and camera. A mountain bike is also a fun accessory if you prefer to ride rather than walk to the park.

Admission fee: $4.00 per vehicle or $24.00 for a state park passport. No fee for walk-ins.

Hours: Open daily 8:00 A.M. to 8:00 P.M. from May through September. Group tours available from October through April by calling (406) 247–2955.

Directions: From Interstate 90 in Billings take Lockwood exit 452, then follow signs 7 miles south on Coburn Road to the park entrance.

For more information

Montana Department of Fish, Wildlife, and Parks
Lake Elmo Drive, Billings, MT 59101
(406) 247–2940
www.fwp.state.mt.us/parks; www.pictographcave.org

Billings Area Chamber of Commerce
P.O. Box 31177, Billings, MT 59107
(406) 252–4016
www.wtp.net/bacc

The Josephine
514 North 29th Street, Billings, MT 59101
(406) 248–5898, (800) 552–5898
www.thejosephine.com

46

Teddy Roosevelt's Hunting Ground
Medicine Rocks State Park

No one who has seen the great sandstone pillars jutting from the prairie of southeastern Montana ever forgets them. Listen to the wind whistle through the pines as Teddy Roosevelt did when he camped here in the 1880s.

The history

Created from the drifting sands of 65 million years ago, the Medicine Rocks have always been a haven for travelers and hunters on the prairie. The Sioux Indians called them *Inyan-oka-la-ka* or "rock with a hole in it." The rocks have indeed been so sculpted by wind and rain that they are covered with innumerable crevices, hollows, and holes. Archaeologists have found ancient tools, weapons, medicine wheels, and tepee rings among the sandstone buttes and pillars. The ancients came to this magical place to ask for guidance from the spirits and to pray for courage, strength, and luck in the hunt and in war. The rocks and trees also provided shelter and fuel for travelers crossing the prairie.

One of the first white men to describe the Medicine Rocks was young outdoorsman and future president Teddy Roosevelt, who camped here for three days during a hunting expedition. In his words, "Altogether it was as fantastically beautiful a place as I have ever seen. . . ." But when he arrived, he found the last large herds of buffalo were gone and bear, elk, and bighorn sheep had virtually disappeared. Overgrazing by cattle was destroying even the grasslands in some areas. Conservation soon became one of his major concerns. Roosevelt's experiences here and in North Dakota allowed him to develop his philosophy of practical conservation. This philosophy, based on wise use of the nation's natural resources in the public interest, became the foundation for the national conservation policy of his presidency less than twenty years later.

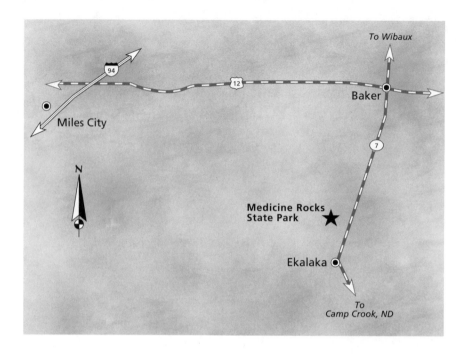

The fun

If you want to experience the vastness and solitude of the prairie the way Teddy Roosevelt did, come here in November, when the hoarfrost is thick in the morning and a crackling campfire feels and sounds good. Take a picnic lunch, some hot coffee, and firewood. When you enter the park, stop to read the rules and the map sign. If the water well is working, try some. The best drinking water for miles around, it comes right out of the sand here. Take a drive through the park on the gravel roads, but be careful to use a high-clearance vehicle if you drive on any primitive roads.

Toward the west end of the park are Castle Rock and Eagle Rock. Find a table and fire ring under the pines for your picnic, then park the car and take a long walk through the rock formations. Like Roosevelt, take in the magnificent views and keep your eyes open for deer, antelope, and prairie dogs, then head back to camp where you can build a fire and have a picnic.

After visiting Medicine Rocks, take a 10-mile drive south to Ekalaka. The town was established in 1884 by Claude Carter, who was hauling logs to build a saloon when his wagon broke down. "Hell," he said, "any place in Montana is a good place to build a saloon." Originally called Puptown after the numerous prairie dogs in the area, it was renamed Ijkalaka, an Ogalala Sioux name meaning "one who wanders." Ijkalaka was the wife of David

Ponderosa pines flourish in the shelter of the Medicine Rocks.

Russell, the first white man to settle in the area, and she was related to Chiefs Red Cloud and Sitting Bull. In Ekalaka, finish your trip with a visit to the Carter County Museum to top off your knowledge of local history and to see the photo of Teddy Roosevelt's signature on the Medicine Rocks. Polish master stonemason Nicholas Kalafatich built the museum in the 1920s as a garage from local quarried sandstone. It also has Indian artifacts, fossils, and a complete duck-billed dinosaur skeleton on display.

Next best

Another good time to visit is during the second weekend in September for the annual Medicine Rocks Black Powder Rifle Shoot when you can see period dress and hunting rifles of the 1800s. If you can't visit Medicine Rocks during the fall, you can visit anytime from mid-June to early September when the weather is likely to be warm and the Carter County Museum has expanded hours.

Practical information

Site: Medicine Rocks State Park, 25 miles south of Baker.

Recommended time: Mid-November.

Minimum time commitment: Four hours, plus driving time.

What to bring: Warm clothes, hat, gloves, sturdy boots, water bottle, firewood, binoculars, and camera.

Admission fee: None.

Hours: The park is accessible year-round, depending on snow conditions. The Carter County Museum is open Tuesday through Friday from 9:00 A.M. to 5:00 P.M., Saturday and Sunday from 1:00 to 5:00 P.M.

Directions: From Baker, go 25 miles south on Montana Highway 7 and look for the park entrance sign. Turn right onto the gravel park road.

For more information

Park Manager, Medicine Rocks State Park
P.O. Box 1630, Miles City, MT 59301
(406) 232–0900
www.fwp.state.mt.us/parks

Carter County Museum
P.O. Box 538, Ekalaka, MT 59324
(406) 775–6886

47

They Said It Couldn't Be Done
Fort Peck Dam

In 1933 some said it couldn't be done, but in less than seven years others were calling President Roosevelt's depression-era project the social, political, and engineering achievement of all time. Come and see why.

The history

Fort Peck Dam remains the world's largest hydraulically filled earth dam, backing up the Missouri River for 134 miles to create a lake shoreline longer than the coastline of Florida. The dam is 250 feet high, 4 miles long, and contains more than 125 million cubic yards of earth fill. It was the first dam built in the Upper Missouri basin, providing jobs for more than 7,000 men and women in the midst of the Great Depression in 1934 and 1935. During the dam's construction, the local population swelled from a few hundred to nearly 40,000.

The government built the nearby town of Fort Peck for workers, but the overflow population built eighteen "ragtowns" in the area. Workers gave the towns names that were symbolic of the hopes they had, such as Square Deal; others were called Roosevelt Heights and Wheeler after prominent men of the time. The work was hard, dangerous, paid as low as 50 cents per hour, and was carried out in temperatures that ranged from 60 degrees below zero to nearly 120 above. Eight men lost their lives in the landslide of 1938, and six are still buried in the dam itself. Despite all this, the project was considered a salvation for a populace desperate for work. For these reasons, Fort Peck has a special place in the hearts of the thousands who worked, lived, or were born in the area during this great project.

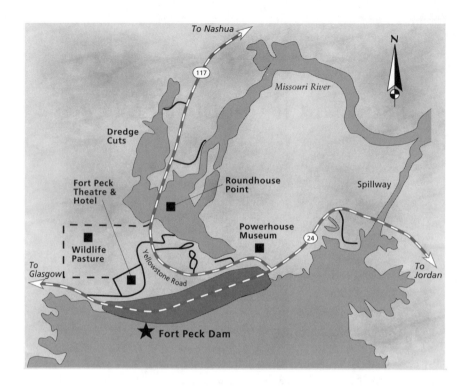

The fun

Stop at the visitor information kiosk on the west side of the dam to look at the map and pick up brochures on the dam and the wildlife auto tours. Any trip to Fort Peck has to start with a 4-mile drive across the dam itself to fully appreciate the magnitude of the project. Continue approximately 4 miles farther to see the massive spillway, designed to handle more water than a one-hundred-year flood.

Return to the east end of the dam, where you'll find a parking area, interpretive signs, and a good photo point, then drive down to the Powerhouse Museum. If you call ahead during the winter, you can take a tour of the museum and the power plant, which produces an average of 2.8 million kilowatt hours of electricity every day. There are models, exhibits, and pictures of the dam construction. The museum also has more than 400 local dinosaur and other fossils, including triceratops and giant Ice Age elk and bison skulls.

Continue your tour west on Yellowstone Road below the dam, past

The 1600-seat Fort Peck Theatre was built for a city of 20,000.

Downstream Campground and Kiwanis Park picnic area to Roundhouse Point on the right before the Dredge Cuts. This is one of the five best locations in Montana to watch the spring and fall waterfowl and bald eagle migrations. If the weather is right, you can observe eagles and thousands of ducks and geese that stop here during their annual migrations.

Turn around and go north again to the Leo Coleman wildlife pasture on the right just before the turnoff to the Fort Peck townsite. Turn right on New Deal Road and make a loop on the gravel road around this 250-acre enclosure. Be sure to take a camera and binoculars, as this is a great opportunity to see the area's native wildlife up close—elk, bison, antelope, and deer. Make the complete loop to make sure you haven't missed any. At the top of the hill on the right, opposite the wildlife pasture, you can also see the Texas longhorn pasture.

The road returns to the Fort Peck townsite near the historic and beautifully designed Fort Peck Theatre on the corner of Missouri Street and Sioux Avenue. Finish your drive through town and stop in at the historic Fort Peck Hotel, decorated just like it was in the 1930s. For the more adventurous, west of the dam you can visit Fort Peck Marina or take a drive to the Pines Recreation Area.

Next best

If you're a fisherman, you might want to visit on the second weekend in July, during the Governor's Cup Walleye Tournament. Events include fishing seminars, a youth fishing derby, and a fish fry. The Fort Peck Theatre is also open during the summer, with Friday through Sunday performances at 8:00 P.M. from June through early September. Tickets are $10.00 adults, $9.00 seniors, and $6.00 students (call 406–526–9943).

Unique food and lodging

For a scene reminiscent of the 1930s, stay in one of the seventy period rooms at the historic **Fort Peck Hotel** on the corner of Missouri Street and Osage Avenue. The hotel's **JJ's Restaurant** specializes in buffalo steaks, walleye fillets, and John's barbecued ribs. The hotel is open from May through November.

Practical information

Site: Fort Peck Dam, 17 miles southeast of Glasgow.

Recommended time: Late November.

Minimum time commitment: One day.

What to bring: Warm clothes, winter boots, hat, gloves, sunglasses, camera, telephoto lens, and binoculars.

Admission fee: None.

Hours: The dam is accessible year-round. The Powerhouse Museum is open 9:00 A.M. to 5:30 P.M. daily year-round. Free tours are given from 9:00 A.M. to 4:45 P.M. (call 406–526–3421 to arrange a tour during the winter season).

Directions: From Glasgow, take Montana Highway 24 south 17 miles to the project entrance. From Nashua, take Montana Highway 117 south 11 miles to the project entrance.

For more information

U.S. Army Corps of Engineers
P.O. Box 208, Fort Peck, MT 59223
(406) 526–3411

Valley County Pioneer Museum
U.S. 2, Glasgow, MT 59230
(406) 228–8692

Glasgow Chamber of Commerce
P.O. Box 832, Glasgow, MT 59230
(406) 228–2222

Fort Peck Hotel
P.O. Box 168, Fort Peck, MT 59223
(800) 560–4931

48

Victorian Christmas at the Ranch
Grant-Kohrs Ranch National Historic Site

*During the annual Christmas Open House you can
see authentic Victorian Christmas decorations, take a
Belgian draft horse hayride, sing Christmas carols, or try
your hand at making a pinecone bird feeder or an
old-fashioned Christmas ornament.*

The history

The Grant-Kohrs Ranch is a historic working ranch that commemorates America's frontier cattle era. In 1859 the Deer Lodge Valley was a 50-mile-long meadow when John Grant, the son of a Hudson's Bay Company trader, started the cattle ranching industry here by buying trail-worn stock from Oregon-bound settlers and marketing his Montana beef to the new gold camps in the region. In less than a decade, he built a herd of several hundred cattle and a fine house that still stands.

In 1866 Grant sold out for $19,200 and returned to Canada. The new owner was Conrad Kohrs, a German immigrant, miner, and butcher. He too had been selling beef to the mining camps, but he needed a base for his operations. Over the next forty years, Kohrs and his half brother, John Bielenberg, built the ranch into one of the largest and best-known in the region, with cattle grazing 10 million acres of open range in four states and Canada. As early as the 1870s they began raising registered Shorthorns and Herefords as breeding stock. The Kohrs Ranch was one of the few to prosper after the devastating winter of 1886–87 and the end of the open range. For a quarter century afterward, the ranch continued to ship 8,000 to 10,000 cattle to eastern markets each year.

The big red freight wagon greets visitors to the Grant-Kohrs Ranch.

In 1918 Kohrs and Bielenberg sold most of the ranch, which then languished until Kohrs's grandson, Conrad Kohrs Warren, took it over in the 1930s. He soon became widely known for his registered Hereford cattle and Belgian draft horses. Warren carefully preserved the old buildings, furniture, photos, and ranch documents. In 1972 he sold the historic ranch to the National Park Service.

The ranch house and other buildings have been restored and rejuvenated. The 1,500-acre site is maintained today as a working ranch and includes eighty-eight structures and 26,000 artifacts. Handicapped parking is available in the visitor center parking area, as is vehicular access to the ranch for the mobility impaired (inquire on arrival at the visitor center). Rest rooms are available near the visitor center and at the ranch.

The fun

The ranch is open year-round. Visitors can tour the ranch house with its original Victorian furnishings, many shipped west by steamboat, wagon, and later railroad. You can also see the bunkhouses, outbuildings, horse-drawn farm machinery, and registered cattle and horses.

A great time to visit is during the annual Victorian Christmas Open House on the first Sunday in December from 1:00 to 4:00 P.M. This is the only time of the year that you will see the house decorated for Christmas, including a Victorian Christmas tree with period ornaments, toys, games, and an incredible display of some of the ranch artifacts that are not shown at any other time.

For the young at heart, the Belgian draft horse hayride and Christmas caroling followed by hot apple cider and cookies should put anyone in the Christmas spirit. Children can make pinecone bird feeders and old-fashioned Christmas ornaments, or visit the blacksmith shop to watch the smithy make forged metal candy canes and tell an old blacksmith tale or two.

If you come early, you can participate in the Deer Lodge Christmas Stroll on Friday from 5:00 to 7:00 P.M. The downtown is decorated, and shops and businesses have open houses. Also downtown, the classic Rialto Theatre sponsors a free children's movie on Friday night and Saturday afternoon. You can even spend an entire day just visiting the Old Montana State Prison Museum Complex. See the visitor center, old territorial prison, antique auto museum, law enforcement museum, and "Little Joe," one of the last electric locomotives built to sell to Joseph Stalin's Russia.

Next best

You can see the Victorian Christmas decorations at the ranch all during the month of December, or visit during Western Heritage Days on the second weekend in July. Visits between mid-June and mid-September when the weather is likely to be warm and sunny are best for outdoor photos.

Unique food and lodging

Near the center of Deer Lodge is the 1891 Queen Anne Victorian-style **Coleman-Fee Mansion.** Located at 500 Missouri Avenue, the bed-and-breakfast offers five guest rooms with vintage decor.

Practical information

Site: Grant-Kohrs Ranch National Historic Site, at the north end of Deer Lodge off Interstate 90.

Recommended time: First Sunday in December.

Minimum time commitment: Three hours, plus driving time.

What to bring: Warm clothes, hat, gloves, and camera with flash.

Admission fee: None.

Hours: The ranch is open daily except Thanksgiving, Christmas, and New Year's Day. Hours are 8:00 A.M. to 5:30 P.M. from May to September, 9:00 A.M. to 4:30 P.M. the rest of the year.

Directions: Deer Lodge is 40 miles north of Butte and 80 miles southeast of Missoula. To get to the ranch, take the north Deer Lodge exit 184 from Interstate 90. Follow the signs 0.75 mile to the park entrance across the street from the Powell County fairgrounds.

For more information

Superintendent, Grant-Kohrs Ranch NHS
P.O. Box 790, Deer Lodge, MT 59722
(406) 846–2070, (406) 846–3388
www.nps.gov/grko

Old Montana Prison Museum Complex
1106 Main Street, Deer Lodge, MT 59722
(406) 846–3111

Chamber of Commerce of Deer Lodge
1171 Main Street, Deer Lodge, MT 59722
(406) 846–2094
www.powellpost.com

Coleman-Fee Mansion
500 Missouri Avenue, Deer Lodge, MT 59722
(888) 888–2507

49

Guideposts of the Great Plains
Sleeping Buffalo Rock

> Here in the vast openness and haunting landscapes of the prairie you can almost feel the silence. Touch the sacred rock that brought good fortune to generations of hunters on the Cree Trail and learn how the Milk River Valley has changed.

The history

Sleeping Buffalo Rock is one of many granite boulders that were scraped from the Canadian shield 10,000 years ago and deposited as glacial erratics on the Northern Plains. This sacred rock was originally part of a group of boulders that resembled a herd of sleeping buffalo on the crest of a ridge near Cree Crossing on the Milk River a few miles north of here. One Indian legend tells how a party of hunters spied a herd of buffalo on that ridge and was sneaking up on them when they all turned to stone. Over the years, Stone Age sculptors carved the boulder to further the resemblance. The boulder next to the sleeping buffalo was also found near the Cree Trail. It is a sacred "Medicine Rock," carved with symbols whose meanings are lost in antiquity but known to bring good fortune with the proper sacrifice. To early Indian tribes each unique medicine rock became a guidepost on the Great Plains.

One of the best fords across the Milk River lies just north of here. It became known as Cree Crossing even though it was used by many tribes, and later ranchers and homesteaders. Beginning in 1934 the crossing was improved and used extensively by trucks hauling tons of rock and gravel to build Fort Peck Dam on the Missouri. The ford carried traffic so well that it was sixty years before a bridge was built to replace it. Nearby in 1922 a wildcatter, exploring for oil, got 750 gallons per minute of 108 degree mineral water instead. With the help of Roosevelt's Works Progress Administration, in the 1930s the artesian well was developed into what is now Sleeping Buffalo Hot Springs.

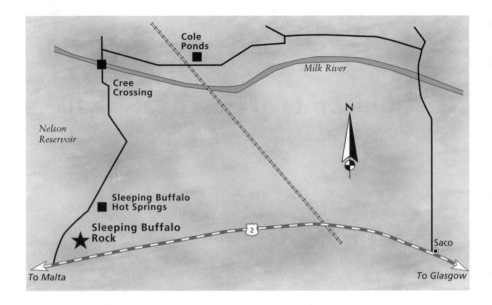

The fun

Stop first at Sleeping Buffalo and the Medicine Rock wayside exhibit and historical highway marker 130. Although the rocks have been targets for vandals, their etchings or "petroglyphs" are fascinating. Perhaps someday these sacred symbols can be returned to their places of origin and given the care and interpretation they deserve. From here you can take a 32-mile loop drive through the Milk River Valley. Continue 9 miles east on U.S. 2 to the town of Saco. Stop at the east end of town on U.S. 2 to see the restored one-room school once attended by TV newscaster Chet Huntley. Then return to the center of town to visit the restored Saco jail and museum. From Saco turn north at the easternmost junction of U.S. 2 and Secondary Road 243. Go 6.8 miles and cross the Milk River. Follow the paved road to the left and continue on the gravel road, turn left after 2.2 miles, and go another 4 miles to Cole Ponds. These ponds were a major quarry for Fort Peck Dam and today are popular for picnics and trout fishing.

Cross the railroad tracks and continue another 3 miles past the massive dredge piles left over from the 1930s dam building, turning left to the Cree Crossing Bridge and historical highway marker 129. Continue your loop drive on Secondary Road 243 south to Nelson Reservoir, a popular year-round walleye and pike fishery. Finish the day at Sleeping Buffalo Hot Springs with a dip in the hot mineral water and visions of eating the three-ton world record hamburger that was cooked here in 1999.

Stone Age sculptors finished what nature began on Sleeping Buffalo Rock.

Next best

If you like carnivals, be here during Saco Fun Days, held the Friday and Saturday before Labor Day. Events include a parade, free barbecue, pie and ice cream, games, petting zoo, craft and flower show, demolition derby, street dance, and carnival rides.

Unique food and lodging

You can stop for the popular Sunday smorgasbord at the **Buffalo Barn Supper Club** and stay in one of the 1930s-era cabins at the **Sleeping Buffalo Hot Springs Resort** 1.5 miles north of Sleeping Buffalo Rock on Secondary Road 243.

Practical information

Site: Sleeping Buffalo Rock, 18 miles east of Malta.

Recommended time: Early December.

Minimum time commitment: Three hours, plus driving time.

What to bring: Warm clothes, sturdy waterproof winter boots, hat, gloves, sunblock, sunglasses, swimsuit, camera, and binoculars. Cross-country skis or ice skates are also fun accessories, weather permitting.

Admission fee: There is a fee for using the pool at Sleeping Buffalo Hot Springs.

Hours: Accessible year-round. Sleeping Buffalo Hot Springs is open daily year-round. Pool hours are 9:00 A.M. to 8:00 P.M.

Directions: Sleeping Buffalo Rock is located 18 miles east of Malta at a signed wayside exhibit on the north side of U.S. 2 at its westernmost junction with Secondary Road 243 to Nelson Reservoir.

For more information

Phillips County Museum
431 Highway 2 East, Malta, MT 59538
(406) 654–1037

Sleeping Buffalo Resort
HC 75 Box 460, Saco, MT 59261
(406) 527–3370

50

The Bloody Bozeman
The Bozeman Trail

Only about 3,500 immigrants traveled the Bozeman Trail during its three short years of glory. Many met a violent death on the trail, including its founder, John Bozeman. Travel in one day what it took a month to do in a covered wagon and see the graves of some who didn't make it.

The history

In 1860 John Bozeman left his wife and three daughters and headed west to the Colorado goldfields. Failing to find his fortune, Bozeman and his partner, John Jacobs, pioneered a shortcut from the Oregon Trail at Fort Laramie, Wyoming, through the Northern Plains Indians' last and best hunting grounds, to the goldfields of Montana. Sioux Chief Black Elk correctly predicted, "It would scare the buffalo and make them go away, and it would let the other white men come in like a river." The trail also led to military occupation of the region and the Sioux War.

A wagon train led by Bozeman and Jacobs in 1863 had only traveled 140 miles when a large party of Cheyenne and Sioux warriors turned them back. In 1864, four wagon trains consisting of 1,500 people led by John Bozeman, Allen Hurlbut, and the famous guide Jim Bridger traveled the trail to the Montana settlements. A large Cheyenne and Sioux war party attacked one train east of present-day Kaycee, Wyoming.

In 1865 the Powder River Expedition commanded by General Patrick E. Connor attacked a nonhostile Arapaho village at what is now Ranchester, Wyoming, driving the tribe into alliance with the Sioux and Cheyenne. In 1866 about 2,000 people in numerous trains traveled the Bozeman Trail to Montana, and the Army built Forts Reno, Phil Kearny, and C. F. Smith. The Indians massacred the Thomas Party near Greycliff, Montana, in August, and wiped out the entire eighty-one-man command of Captain William Fetterman near Sheridan, Wyoming, on December 21. In 1867, Indian attacks near Fort C. F. Smith and Fort Phil Kearny caused the Army to abandon them and the Bozeman Trail the following year, after which the Indians burned the forts to the ground. In 1876 General George Crook used the trail again during the Sioux War, and during the 1880s it became a route for settlers and cattle drives coming into the region.

The fun

Approximately 285 miles of the original 530-mile Bozeman Trail route are in Montana, and you can drive on or near much of the original route. Travel the Bozeman Trail on the third weekend in December, when the "bloody Bozeman" took its most gruesome toll. You can start at Lodge Grass and go west like the pioneers did, or begin in Virginia City and go east. If you start in Lodge Grass, drive west on Secondary Road 463 to Secondary Road 313 to St. Xavier. Stop at the Fort C. F. Smith historical highway marker 152 at the turnoff to Fort C. F. Smith, then go west to Pryor on BIA Road 91, stopping at the Bozeman Trail ruts signpost at mile marker 19. You can also see another Bozeman Trail rut signpost a few miles east and south of the town of Pryor, then take the Pryor Creek Road and Secondary Road 416 north to Billings and Interstate 90 (exit 447) and go west.

Stop next at the Columbus rest area at milepost 419 to read the Columbus and Park City historical highway markers 112 and 113. Continue west on Interstate 90 to the Bridger Creek Road exit 384, 7 miles west of the town of Reedpoint. Go 2 miles west on the frontage road to the Thomas Party historical highway marker 109 marking the graves of three immigrants killed here on the Bozeman Trail. If you return to I–90 at exit 384, you can stop at the Greycliff rest area and read the Crazy Mountains historical highway marker 111. Continue 5 miles west to Greycliff exit 377 off I–90 and follow the signs to Greycliff Prairie Dog Town State Park to learn a little about these western residents.

Continue west on I–90 to Big Timber exit 367 and go a half mile east, stopping at the Bozeman Trail historical highway marker 108. Continue west again on I–90 to Bozeman Pass and historical highway marker 105. To see John Bozeman's grave in Bozeman, take Main Street exit 309 and go 1 mile west on Main Street. Turn left on Buttonwood Avenue and drive through Lindley Park to Sunset Hills Cemetery. Make an immediate right turn at the entrance and go to the marble columns marking the grave of pioneer cattleman Nelson Story. To the right overlooking his namesake city is a 4-foot-tall white obelisk marking Bozeman's grave.

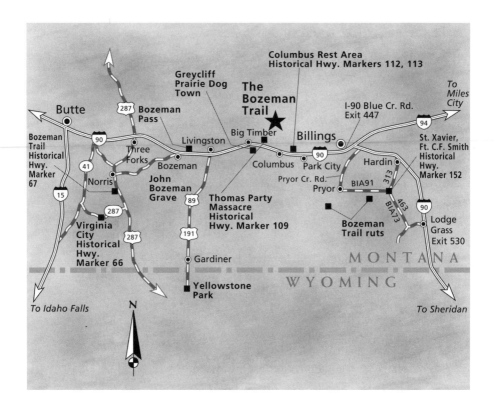

From Bozeman, you can also follow the Bozeman Trail west on Montana Highway 84 to Norris. Turn south on U.S. 287 and stop at the Bozeman Trail historical highway marker 67, 5 miles south of Norris. Finish up by taking Montana Highway 287 at Ennis to the end of the trail at Virginia City, stopping at the Virginia City historical highway marker 66 at milepost 14.

Next best

If you want to try the total immersion experience and you have a month to burn, meet up with Ben Kern's Bozeman Trail Wagon Train at Fort Laramie, Wyoming, on the second weekend in June. Travel with the wagon train by horse, foot, or wagon to Virginia City, arriving on the last weekend in July.

Unique food and lodging

For an old-fashioned meal and room, try **The Grand Hotel and 1890 Saloon,** 139 McLeod Street, Big Timber. For an even more western experience, **The Carriage House Ranch,** 7.5 miles north of Big Timber, offers year-round horseback trail rides at a historic bed-and-breakfast inn, with dining at the **Broken Spur Cafe** during events.

Practical information

Site: The Bozeman Trail, which extends 285 miles from Lodge Grass to Virginia City.

Recommended time: Third weekend in December.

Minimum time commitment: One day.

What to bring: Warm clothes, hat, gloves, camera, and binoculars.

Admission fee: None. Chief Plenty Coups and Greycliff Prairie Dog Town State Park fees are $1.00 per person, $4.00 per vehicle, or $24.00 for a state park passport.

Hours: The Bozeman Trail sites are accessible year-round, depending on snow conditions.

Directions: From the east, begin at Lodge Grass exit 530 on Interstate 90. From the west, begin at Virginia City and go east on Montana Highway 287.

For more information

The Frontier Heritage Alliance
P.O. Box 27, Buffalo, WY 82834
www.frontierheritage.org, www.bozemantrail.org

Sweet Grass Chamber of Commerce
P.O. Box 1012, Big Timber, MT 59011
(406) 932–5131
www.bigtimber.com

The Grand Hotel and 1890 Saloon
139 McLeod, Big Timber, MT 59011
(406) 932–4459
www.thegrand-hotel.com

Carriage House Ranch
P.O. Box 1249, Big Timber, MT 59011
(406) 932–5339, (877) 932–5339
www.carriagehouseranch.com

51

Lewis and Clark Reach
the Headwaters
Missouri Headwaters State Park

Reach down and touch the rock that Meriwether Lewis stood on when he termed this "an essential point in the geography of this western part of the Continent." Then look up and around at the living reminders of the natural wonders they encountered and the remnants of man's struggle to tame the Wild West.

The history

Here, 2,500 miles above the Gulf of Mexico, the Jefferson, Madison, and Gallatin Rivers converge to form the Missouri River. For centuries, Native Americans, explorers, trappers, fortune seekers, farmers, and settlers all passed through this geographical hub. On July 25, 1805, when the Lewis and Clark Expedition stopped here, they had to determine which river would take them to the mountains. The three forks of the Missouri were roughly the same width and appearance, so they chose to follow the western fork, naming it the Jefferson River for "the author of our enterprise." The eastern fork was named for Albert Gallatin, Jefferson's treasury secretary. The middle river was named for Secretary of State James Madison, who had been instrumental in gaining support for and negotiating the Louisiana Purchase.

A large stone outcropping called Fort Rock stands over the confluence of the three forks. Clark noted, "Between these two forks, and near their conjunction with that from the southwest, is a position admirably well calculated for a fort." Three years later, former Expedition members Private John Colter and John Potts were caught here by the Blackfeet. Potts was killed and Colter

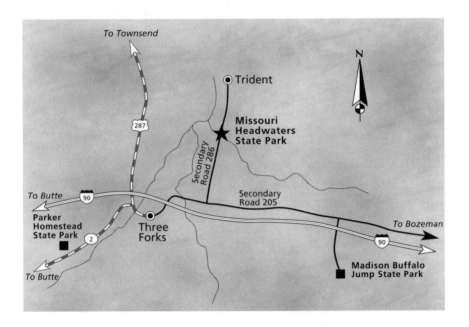

barely escaped with his life. In 1810 the Blackfeet also killed trapper George Drouillard, who had been with the Expedition here.

Beaver trapping continued until the 1840s, and by the 1860s gold seekers, cattlemen, and settlers arrived on the scene. The town of Gallatin City was founded here in 1865. Today, although railroads and highways now cross where grizzly bears and Indians once roamed, much of the landscape looks remarkably the same as it did when Lewis and Clark first saw it.

The fun

The Missouri headwaters can be visited any time, but one of the best times to visit is in late December, well after the tourist season (and the mosquito season) is over and you can hear the silence of the centuries, broken only by the sound of water coming together to form the mighty Missouri River.

Start your tour at the orientation sign at the park entrance, then continue driving north to the interpretive area at Fort Rock, where several signs and a survey marker provide interpretive information for the area, including its importance to the tribes, the Expedition, and later to trappers. From here take the short climb past the fenced graves of pioneer children who died in the diphtheria epidemic of the 1870s, then climb to the top of the hill for a first-rate view of Lewis Rock to the north and the surrounding mountains. If you like to walk, the park has several miles of trails for hikers, bicyclists, and equestrians between the many viewpoints.

Across the highway from Fort Rock is Ling Rock, where you can look upstream to the confluence of the Jefferson and Madison Rivers and the actual beginning of the Missouri River. As you return, finish your trip by stopping again at the park entrance for a look at the remains of the Gallatin City Hotel. Across the highway are a popular campground and picnic area. For a longer outing, include a side trip to Parker Homestead southwest of Three Forks, or the prehistoric 2,000-year-old Madison Buffalo Jump 14 miles east of Three Forks off of the Logan exit on Interstate 90.

Next best

You can also visit during the summer to experience the river by boat. From June through August the park offers Saturday evening campfire talks at 7:00 P.M. on a variety of topics. Call ahead and time your visit to coincide with the Lewis and Clark Honor Guard encampment in Three Forks, usually held on the last weekend in July, or the John Colter Run on the second Saturday in September.

Unique food and lodging

For a bite of the Old West, stop in the town of Three Forks and try the buffalo Italian sausage burger at the **Historic Headwaters Restaurant,** 105 South Main Street.

Practical information

Site: Missouri Headwaters State Park and National Historic Landmark, 3 miles north of Three Forks.

Recommended time: Late December.

Minimum time commitment: Two hours, plus driving time.

What to bring: Warm clothes, hat, gloves, camera, and binoculars.

Admission fee: $4.00 per vehicle or $24.00 for an annual state park passport.

Hours: Open daily from daylight to dusk.

Directions: The park is 28 miles west of Bozeman off of Interstate 90. Take Three Forks exit 278, then follow the signs 2 miles east on Secondary Road 205. Turn left on Secondary Road 286 and go 1.5 miles to the park entrance.

For more information

Park Manager, Missouri Headwaters State Park
1400 South 19th Street, Bozeman, MT 59718
(406) 994–4042
www.fwp.state.mt.us/parks

John Colter's Last Marathon

The Lewis and Clark Expedition passed the three forks of the Missouri again in 1806 on their way to the Yellowstone River and back to St. Louis. Expedition member John Colter had no idea that two years later he would be running a footrace here. As the Expedition neared its destination, Colter received permission to leave and become a guide for trappers headed back to the Upper Missouri River country.

In the spring of 1807, Colter left the Mandan villages on the Missouri with Manuel Lisa to build a fur-trading post at the confluence of the Yellowstone and Bighorn Rivers. Lisa then sent him out to inform the Crows and other tribes that the store was open for business.

In the fall of 1808, Colter and his trapping companion, John Potts, were floating down the Jefferson River just above the three forks of the Missouri when a large Blackfoot war party saw them and ordered them ashore. When Potts shot one of them, he was riddled with arrows. Colter did not resist; he was stripped naked and brought before the chief. They decided to make a game out of killing him. The chief asked if he could run, and Colter signed that he couldn't, guessing what was in store for him. So the Indians gave him a head start across the flats between the Jefferson and Madison Rivers and the race was on. His only hope was to run barefoot and naked across 6 miles of cactus-infested flats to the Madison and jump in before they could catch him.

Despite being barefoot, he outdistanced all but one warrior. When the warrior was closing in for the kill, Colter stopped, turned, grabbed his lance, and killed him. He made it to the river and hid under a beaver lodge until dark. But his trip was only beginning. Eleven days later, the naked, barefoot, freezing, starving Colter had managed to walk 250 miles to Fort Lisa. Two years later Colter left the Rocky Mountains, never to return.

Three Forks Chamber of Commerce
P.O. Box 1103, Three Forks, MT 59752
(406) 285–4753
www.threeforksmontana.com

52

Prairie Tycoon with a Vision
The Moss Mansion

They say that the Northern Pacific brought prosperity
to Billings, and prosperity brought Preston B. Moss. Learn what
he did for Billings and what his elegant house has in common
with New York's Waldorf-Astoria Hotel.

The history

Billings financier Preston Boyd Moss built his handsome red sandstone mansion in 1903 for $105,000 at a time when the average home cost $3,000 or less. The red-tile-roof home was designed by one of New York's finest architects, Henry Janeway Hardenbergh, who also designed such hotels as the Waldorf-Astoria, Plaza, Willard, and Copley Plaza.

Moss was born in Missouri and worked for his banker father for a while after leaving school. In 1892 he came to Billings at the age of twenty-nine and soon became president of what was to become the city's largest bank. He became wealthy by investing in the future of the city. His enterprises included the *Billings Gazette* newspaper, the Northern Hotel, water and electric utilities, a meat packing plant, sugar refinery, telephone company, irrigation project, farming, and sheep ranching.

Moss's friends called him PB, and his 14,400-square-foot home and sandstone horse barn became a symbol of wealth and power as well as Billings's cultural center during the first half of the twentieth century. The interior is even more lavish than the exterior with colorful Oriental and Persian carpets, silk wall fabrics, elaborate light fixtures, and Moorish decor. The mansion includes Louis XVI French parlors, a formal oak-paneled Empire dining room, an Art Nouveau sitting room, and an Art Moderne kitchen. When PB died in 1947 at the age of 83, his daughter continued to live in the mansion until her death in 1984. Local preservation efforts managed to purchase and restore the building.

The red sandstone Moss Mansion was a symbol of wealth and power.

The fun

The best way to step into P. B. Moss's shoes is with a Christmas tour of the mansion, offered during December. The mansion is decorated outside and inside with Christmas lights, ornaments, and of course, a Christmas tree. The one-hour guided tour of the three-story mansion captures early turn-of-the-century life as the Preston Boyd Moss family lived it. It begins with a short video on Moss and his family, then a tour guide will show you PB's symbols of wealth and power, including original draperies, fixtures, furniture, Persian carpets, and family heirlooms. There is also a bookstore and gift shop.

If you would like to see more nearby historic sites, get a copy of the *Billings Vacation Guide,* or ask about Christmas lights trolley tours. If you want to extend your knowledge of the Billings area even more, try the Western Heritage Center Museum, 2822 Montana Avenue, or the Yellowstone County Museum across from Logan International Airport.

The Legendary Calamity Jane

The city of Billings had more than one famous resident during its early years. One who was more on the infamous side was Martha Jane Canary, better known as Calamity Jane. Her life became a legend as reality was mixed freely with romance to the point that sorting fact from fiction is almost impossible. It is believed that she was born in Missouri around 1852 and came west with her parents in 1864 to the Montana goldfields in Virginia City.

Her parents either died or left, and she may have taken care of her brothers and sisters for a while. Whenever there was a fever, epidemic, or other calamity, they say that she was always helping take care of the sick, earning her the nickname Calamity Jane. No one knows when she left the mining camps, but she turned up in a number of places, working at various jobs, sometimes posing as a man to get jobs that females were not allowed to do. She claimed she could ride and shoot better than any man, and said she had been an Army scout, stagecoach driver, and bullwhacker. In 1876 she was a wagon driver with General Crook's army column until they discovered she was a woman.

Some say Calamity Jane was married to Wild Bill Hickok, other reports say she had as many as twelve husbands, and still others say her involvement with men was more likely for money. She drove the stage in Junction City for a while, and in 1893 Buffalo Bill Cody hired her for his Wild West Show. It must have been a short tour, because in 1895 she moved upriver to Canyon Creek near Billings. To make a living, she continued to drive stagecoach, haul wood, and cook. Some say she stole horses for extra spending money, keeping them on a butte near her place in Canyon Creek.

Calamity was frequently in one scrape or another. She once clerked at the Yegen Brothers Mercantile, the largest store in Billings, but was fired after pulling a knife on a customer. In 1901 she was jailed for being drunk and attacking two store clerks with a hatchet. Her last wish was to be buried next to her old friend, Wild Bill, in South Dakota, so in 1903 she boarded a train to Deadwood—without buying a ticket, of course. The passengers chipped in to pay the fare and her final wish was granted. Will history call her a foul-mouthed, tobacco-chewing, cigar-smoking, belligerent drunkard, or a heroine with a heart of gold who could ride and shoot better than any man and yet was a saintly nurse in times of illness? Only time will tell.

Next best

If you like parties, the third Friday in July is the "In the Mood at the Moss" summer party. You can dine from a picnic basket full of gourmet treats, listen to great music, and dance under the stars. The second weekend in December is the Christmas Open House family event. Children enter free when accompanied by a parent. There are special holiday displays, music, and activities.

Unique food and lodging

Although the city of Billings didn't get going until the railroad arrived in 1892, it does have a downtown historic district and restaurants in historic buildings. **The Beanery,** 2314 Montana Avenue, in the 1909 Northern Pacific Depot Building, has lunches and dinners. **The Rex,** 2401 Montana Avenue, specializes in steak and prime rib. Also in Billings, **The Josephine** bed-and-breakfast, 514 North 29th Street, offers accommodations in a lovely historic home.

Practical information

Site: Moss Mansion, 914 Division Street, Billings.

Recommended time: Late December.

Minimum time commitment: Two hours, plus driving time.

What to bring: Camera.

Admission fee: $6.00 adults, $5.00 seniors and children over 13, $3.00 children 6 to 12.

Hours: Open daily except Thanksgiving, Christmas, and New Year's Day. Winter hours are 1:00 to 3:00 P.M. Hours from June through Labor Day are Monday through Saturday 10:00 A.M. to 4:00 P.M., Sunday 1:00 to 3:00 P.M., with Wednesday evening tours at 7:00 P.M.

Directions: From Interstate 90 in Billings, take North 27th Street exit 450. Go north on 27th Street to Third Avenue North, a one-way street. Turn left on Third Avenue North and go west to the mansion at the corner of Division Street.

For more information

Moss Mansion
914 Division, Billings, MT 59101
(406) 256–5100
www.mossmansion.com

Billings Area Chamber of Commerce
P.O. Box 31177, Billings, MT 59107
(406) 252–4016
www.billingschamber.com

The Josephine
514 North 29th Street, Billings, MT 59101
(406) 248–5898
www.thejosephine.com

Best Bets by Chapter

Best Trips for Families

2   Four Billion Years of History
4   The Ghosts of Garnet
5   Monuments in Conservation
8   High Plains Buffalo Culture
12   Lewis and Clark's Indian Highway
14   The Cradle of Montana Civilization
18   Steamboat's a Comin'
22   Bear's Tooth Meets Sleeping Giant
29   The Sheriff Was a Road Agent
30   The Golden Gulch
32   Surprise Attack on the Nez Perce
33   They Call Them the Apsaalooke
36   The Steel Rail Crosses the West
38   Reflections of Glaciers
39   A River Runs Through It
46   Teddy Roosevelt's Hunting Ground
51   Lewis and Clark Reach the Headwaters

Best Trips for Scenery and Photography

1   Looking for the Mother Lode
4   The Ghosts of Garnet
5   Monuments in Conservation
7   The Gold Is Gone but the Elk Aren't
13   Captain Clark Leaves His Mark
17   The Valley of the Mission
18   Steamboat's a Comin'
19   If Cattle Were Kings, Sheep Were Queens
22   Bear's Tooth Meets Sleeping Giant
24   Fur Traders and Free Trappers
28   Nation of the Plains Indian
32   Surprise Attack on the Nez Perce
33   They Call Them the Apsaalooke
38   Reflections of Glaciers
39   A River Runs Through It
45   The Cavemen of Bitter Creek Coulee
46   Teddy Roosevelt's Hunting Ground

Best Trips for Living-History Demonstrations

13 Captain Clark Leaves His Mark
20 General Miles's Frontier Outpost
24 Fur Traders and Free Trappers
25 Custer's Last Stand
26 Homesteading the Medicine Line
27 The Wild Bunch Goes Shopping
28 Nation of the Plains Indian
29 The Sheriff Was a Road Agent
30 The Golden Gulch
31 Liver Eatin' Johnston Slept Here
33 They Call Them the Apsaalooke
36 The Steel Rail Crosses the West
39 A River Runs Through It
48 Victorian Christmas at the Ranch
51 Lewis and Clark Reach the Headwaters

Best Trips for Avoiding the Crowds

1 Looking for the Mother Lode
4 The Ghosts of Garnet
5 Monuments in Conservation
7 The Gold Is Gone but the Elk Aren't
8 High Plains Buffalo Culture
10 Towns Where the West Is Still Wild
12 Lewis and Clark's Indian Highway
13 Captain Clark Leaves His Mark
14 The Cradle of Montana Civilization
18 Steamboat's a Comin'
23 Where the Sister Saved Her Brother
35 The Last Chief of the Crows
40 I Will Fight No More Forever
42 The Great Indian Council of 1855
45 The Cavemen of Bitter Creek Coulee
46 Teddy Roosevelt's Hunting Ground
47 They Said It Couldn't Be Done
48 Victorian Christmas at the Ranch
51 Lewis and Clark Reach the Headwaters

Best Trips for the Mobility Impaired

2   Four Billion Years of History
3   Homeland of "The People"
8   High Plains Buffalo Culture
9   From Cowboy to Artist
22 Bear's Tooth Meets Sleeping Giant
25 Custer's Last Stand
27 The Wild Bunch Goes Shopping
32 Surprise Attack on the Nez Perce
35 The Last Chief of the Crows
36 The Steel Rail Crosses the West
39 A River Runs Through It
41 Growing Up Like Huckleberry Finn
47 They Said It Couldn't Be Done
48 Victorian Christmas at the Ranch
49 Guideposts of the Great Plains
50 The Bloody Bozeman
51 Lewis and Clark Reach the Headwaters
52 Prairie Tycoon with a Vision

Best Trips for a Tight Budget

1   Looking for the Mother Lode
7   The Gold Is Gone but the Elk Aren't
10 Towns Where the West Is Still Wild
16 Pioneers in Forestry
17 The Valley of the Mission
21 Guarding the Whoop-Up Trail
23 Where the Sister Saved Her Brother
24 Fur Traders and Free Trappers
27 The Wild Bunch Goes Shopping
34 The Frenchman Becomes a Cowboy
40 I Will Fight No More Forever
41 Growing Up Like Huckleberry Finn
42 The Great Indian Council of 1855
44 Last Chance Gulch Becomes the First City
45 The Cavemen of Bitter Creek Coulee
46 Teddy Roosevelt's Hunting Ground
47 They Said It Couldn't Be Done
48 Victorian Christmas at the Ranch

49 Guideposts of the Great Plains
50 The Bloody Bozeman

Best Trips for Native American Culture

2 Four Billion Years of History
3 Homeland of "The People"
8 High Plains Buffalo Culture
25 Custer's Last Stand
28 Nation of the Plains Indian
32 Surprise Attack on the Nez Perce
33 They Call Them the Apsaalooke
35 The Last Chief of the Crows
40 I Will Fight No More Forever
45 The Cavemen of Bitter Creek Coulee
46 Teddy Roosevelt's Hunting Ground
49 Guideposts of the Great Plains

Best Trips for Explorer Trails

12 Lewis and Clark's Indian Highway
13 Captain Clark Leaves His Mark
18 Steamboat's a Comin'
21 Guarding the Whoop-Up Trail
22 Bear's Tooth Meets Sleeping Giant
24 Fur Traders and Free Trappers
26 Homesteading the Medicine Line
39 A River Runs Through It
41 Growing Up Like Huckleberry Finn
42 The Great Indian Council of 1855
50 The Bloody Bozeman
51 Lewis and Clark Reach the Headwaters

Best Trips for Forts and Fights

14 The Cradle of Montana Civilization
20 General Miles's Frontier Outpost
21 Guarding the Whoop-Up Trail
23 Where the Sister Saved Her Brother
24 Fur Traders and Free Trappers
25 Custer's Last Stand
32 Surprise Attack on the Nez Perce

40 I Will Fight No More Forever
41 Growing Up Like Huckleberry Finn
50 The Bloody Bozeman

Best Trips for Ghost Towns

1   Looking for the Mother Lode
4   The Ghosts of Garnet
7   The Gold Is Gone but the Elk Aren't
10 Towns Where the West Is Still Wild
26 Homesteading the Medicine Line
29 The Sheriff Was a Road Agent
30 The Golden Gulch

Best Trips for Frontier Architecture

1   Looking for the Mother Lode
4   The Ghosts of Garnet
5   Monuments in Conservation
6   A Company Town Grows Up
7   The Gold Is Gone but the Elk Aren't
9   From Cowboy to Artist
11 Still the Richest Hill on Earth
14 The Cradle of Montana Civilization
15 Raising the Fastest Horses in the World
17 The Valley of the Mission
19 If Cattle Were Kings, Sheep Were Queens
21 Guarding the Whoop-Up Trail
24 Fur Traders and Free Trappers
26 Homesteading the Medicine Line
29 The Sheriff Was a Road Agent
30 The Golden Gulch
31 Liver Eatin' Johnston Slept Here
34 The Frenchman Becomes a Cowboy
37 Where Low Rent Means High Spirits
38 Reflections of Glaciers
41 Growing Up Like Huckleberry Finn
43 Christmas at the Mansion
44 Last Chance Gulch Becomes the First City
48 Victorian Christmas at the Ranch
52 Prairie Tycoon with a Vision

Further Reading

1. Looking for the Mother Lode

Meloy, Harriet C. "Marysville: Hub of Commerce." *More from the Quarries of Last Chance Gulch*. Helena, Mont.: Helena Independent Record, 1995.

Wolle, Muriel Sibell. *Montana Pay Dirt: A Guide to the Mining Camps of the Treasure State*. Athens, Ohio: Sage Books, 1963.

2. Four Billion Years of History

Alderson, Nannie T., and Helena H. Smith. *A Bride Goes West*. Lincoln: University of Nebraska Press, 1969.

Horner, John R., and James Gorman. *Digging Dinosaurs*. New York: Harper Collins, 1990.

Linderman, Frank B. *Pretty-Shield: Medicine Woman of the Gros Ventre*. Lincoln: University of Nebraska Press, 1972.

3. Homeland of "The People"

Bigart, Robert, and Clarence Woodcock, eds. *In the Name of the Salish and Kootenai Nation: The 1855 Hell Gate Treaty and the Origin of the Flathead Indian Reservation*. Pablo, Mont.: Salish Kootenai College Press, 1996.

Holliday, Jan, and Gail Chehak. *Native Peoples of the Northwest: A Traveler's Guide to Land, Art, and Culture*. Seattle: Sasquatch Books, 2000.

4. The Ghosts of Garnet

Hammond, Helen. *Garnet: Montana's Last Gold Camp*. Missoula, Mont.: Acme Press, 1983.

Munn, Debra D. *Big Sky Ghosts: Eerie True Tales of Montana*. Vol. 2. Boulder, Colo.: Pruett Publishing Company, 1994.

5. Monuments in Conservation

Blevins, Winfred. *Roadside History of Yellowstone Park*. Missoula, Mont.: Mountain Press Publishing Company, 1989.

Spritzer, Don. *Roadside History of Montana.* Missoula, Mont.: Mountain Press Publishing Company, 1999.

6. A Company Town Grows Up

Morris, Patrick F. *Anaconda Montana: Copper Smelting Boom Town on the Western Frontier.* Bethesda, Md.: Swan Publishing Company, 1997.

Wolle, Muriel Sibell. *Montana Pay Dirt: A Guide to the Mining Camps of the Treasure State.* Athens, Ohio: Sage Books, 1963.

7. The Gold Is Gone but the Elk Aren't

Florin, Lambert. *Montana-Idaho-Wyoming Ghost Towns.* Seattle: Superior Publishing Company, 1971.

Wolle, Muriel Sibell. *Montana Pay Dirt: A Guide to the Mining Camps of the Treasure State.* Athens, Ohio: Sage Books, 1963.

8. High Plains Buffalo Culture

Danz, Harold P. *Of Bison and Man.* Boulder: University Press of Colorado, 1997.

Hungry Wolf, Adolf, and Beverly Hungry Wolf. *Indian Tribes of the Northern Rockies.* Summertown, Tenn.: Book Publishing Company, 1989.

Whitaker, John C. *Flint Knapping.* Austin: University of Texas Press, 1994.

9. From Cowboy to Artist

Russell, Charles M. *Trails Plowed Under: Stories of the Old West.* Lincoln: University of Nebraska Press, 1996.

Shirley, Gayle C. *Charlie's Trail.* Helena, Mont.: Falcon Publishing Company, 1996.

Taliaferro, John. *Charles M. Russell: The Life and Legend of America's Cowboy Artist.* Boston: Little, Brown & Company, 1996.

10. Towns Where the West Is Still Wild

Costello, Gladys, and Dorothy Whitcomb Klimper. *Top O' The Mountain.* Malta, Mont.: Gladys Costello, 1976.

Costello, Gladys. *The Golden Era of the Little Rockies.* Zortman, Mont.: John and Candy Kalal, 1991.

Wilson, Gary. *Outlaw Tales of Montana.* Havre, Mont.: High-line Books, 1996.

11. Still the Richest Hill on Earth

DeHaas, John N. Jr. *Historic Uptown Butte.* Bozeman, Mont.: John DeHaas, 1977.

Freeman, Harry C. *A Brief History of Butte, Montana.* Chicago: The Henry Shepard Company, 1900.

Workers of the Writers Program. *Copper Camp: Stories of the World's Greatest Mining Town, Butte, Montana.* New York: Hastings House, 1943.

12. Lewis and Clark's Indian Highway

DeVoto, Bernard, ed. *The Journals of Lewis and Clark.* Boston: Houghton Mifflin Company, 1981.

Discovery Writers. *Lewis & Clark in the Bitterroot.* Stevensville, Mont.: Stoneydale Press, 1998.

Wilfong, Cheryl. *Following the Nez Perce Trail: A Guide to the Nee-Me-Poo National Historic Trail with Eyewitness Accounts.* Corvallis: Oregon State University Press, 1990.

13. Captain Clark Leaves His Mark

Ambrose, Stephen E. *Undaunted Courage.* New York: Touchstone Press, 1996.

Clauson, Roger. *Pompey's Pillar: Crossroads of the Frontier.* Billings, Mont.: Prose Works, 1992.

Howard, Harold P. *Sacajawea.* Norman: University of Oklahoma Press, 1971.

14. The Cradle of Montana Civilization

Allen, Harold. *Father Ravalli's Missions.* Chicago: Good Lion Publishing, 1972.

Carriker, Robert C. *Father Peter John DeSmet: Jesuit in the West.* Norman: University of Oklahoma Press, 1995.

Evans, Lucylle H. *St. Mary's in the Rocky Mountains.* Stevensville, Mont.: Montana Creative Consultants, 1976.

15. Raising the Fastest Horses in the World

Jones, Carolyn, and Georgiana Porter. *Shamrocks among the Bitterroots.* Hamilton, Mont.: Jones and Dayton, 1990.

Malone, Michael P. *The Battle for Butte.* Helena, Mont.: Montana Historical Society Press, 1981.

Powell, Ada. *The Dalys of the Bitterroot.* Hamilton, Mont.: Ada Powell, 1989.

16. Pioneers in Forestry

Cohen, Stan. *The Tree Army, A Pictorial History of the CCC, 1933–42.* Missoula, Mont.: Pictorial Histories Publishing Company, 1998.

Koch, Elers. *Forty Years a Forester.* Missoula, Mont.: Mountain Press, 1998.

Mullan, Capt. John. *Report on the Construction of a Military Road from Fort Walla-Walla to Fort Benton.* Fairfield, Wash.: Ye Galleon Press, 1998.

17. The Valley of the Mission

Obersinner, Rev. S. J., and Judy Gritzmacher. *St. Ignatius Mission: National Historic Site.* St. Ignatius, Mont.: Jesuit Fathers, 1977.

Spritzer, Don. *Roadside History of Montana.* Missoula, Mont.: Mountain Press Publishing Company, 1999.

18. Steamboat's a Comin'

Arthur, Jim. *Retracing Kipp Trails.* Lewistown, Mont.: Central Montana Publishing, 1997.

Vestal, Stanley. *The Missouri.* Lincoln: University of Nebraska Press, 1996.

19. If Cattle Were Kings, Sheep Were Queens

Rostad, Lee. *Fourteen Cents & Seven Green Apples: The Life and Times of Charles Bair.* Great Falls, Mont.: C. M. Russell Museum, 1992.

20. General Miles's Frontier Outpost

Brown, Mark H., and W. R. Felton. *The Frontier Years: L. A. Huffman, Photographer of the Plains.* New York: Holt, 1955.

Brown, Mary, and W. R. Felton. *Before Barbed Wire*. New York: Holt, 1956.

Miles, Nelson A. *Nelson A. Miles, a Documentary Biography of His Military Career, 1861–1903*. Edited by Brian C. Pohanka in collaboration with John M. Carroll. Glendale, Calif.: Arthur H. Clark Company, 1985.

21. Guarding the Whoop-Up Trail

Hart, Herbert M. *Pioneer Forts of the West*. New York: Bonanza Books, 1981.

Miller, Don, and Stan Cohen. *Military and Trading Posts of Montana*. Missoula, Mont.: Pictorial Histories Publishing Company, 1978.

Seckie, William H. *The Buffalo Soldiers: A Narrative of the Negro Cavalry in the West*. Norman: University of Oklahoma Press, 1962.

22. Bear's Tooth Meets Sleeping Giant

Cutright, Paul R. *Lewis & Clark: Pioneering Naturalists*. Urbana: University of Illinois Press, 1969.

Hilger, Bryan, with Wendy Wollett and Patricia Kane. *Building the Herd*. Helena, Mont.: Tailight Studio, 1989.

MacLean, Norman. *Young Men and Fire*. Chicago: University of Chicago Press, 1972.

23. Where the Sister Saved Her Brother

Mangum, Neil C. *Battle of the Rosebud: Prelude to the Little Bighorn*. El Segundo, Calif.: Upton and Sons, 1987.

Vaughn, J. W. *With Crook at the Rosebud*. Lincoln: University of Nebraska Press, 1988.

24. Fur Traders and Free Trappers

Barbour, Barton H. *Fort Union and the Upper Missouri Fur Trade*. Norman: University of Oklahoma Press, 2001.

Larpenteur, Charles. *Forty Years a Fur Trader*. Lincoln: University of Nebraska Press, 1989.

Thompson, Erwin N. *Fort Union Trading Post: Fur Trade Empire on the Upper Missouri*. Williston, N.D.: Fort Union Association, 1994.

25. Custer's Last Stand

Gray, John S. *Centennial Campaign: The Sioux War of 1876.* Fort Collins, Colo.: Old Army Press, 1976.

Hardoff, Richard G. *Cheyenne Memories of the Custer Fight.* Lincoln: University of Nebraska Press, 1995

26. Homesteading the Medicine Line

Kelly, Charles. *The Outlaw Trail: A History of Butch Cassidy and His Wild Bunch.* Lincoln: University of Nebraska Press, 1996.

LaDow, Beth. *The Medicine Line: Life and Death on a North American Borderland.* New York: Routledge Publishing Company, 2000.

27. The Wild Bunch Goes Shopping

Meadows, Anne. *Digging Up Butch and Sundance.* Lincoln: University of Nebraska Press, 1996.

Patterson, Richard. *Historical Atlas of the Outlaw West.* Boulder, Colo.: Johnson Publishing Company, 1985.

28. Nation of the Plains Indian

Grinnell, George Bird. *Blackfoot Lodge Tales.* Lincoln: University of Nebraska Press, 1962.

Jackson, John C. *The Piikani Blackfeet: A Culture Under Siege.* Missoula, Mont.: Mountain Press Publishing Company, 2000.

Schultz, James Willard. *Blackfeet and Buffalo.* Norman: University of Oklahoma Press, 1962.

29. The Sheriff Was a Road Agent

Dimsdale, Thomas J. *The Vigilantes of Montana.* Butte, Mont.: McKee Printing Company, 1950.

Mather, R. E., and F. E. Boswell. *Hanging the Sheriff: A Biography of Henry Plummer.* Missoula, Mont.: Historic Montana Publishing Company, 1998.

Silverberg, Robert. *Ghost Towns of the American West.* New York: Ballantine Books, 1968.

30. The Golden Gulch

Grant, Marilyn. *Montana Mainstreets.* Vol. I, *A Guide to Historic Virginia City.* Helena, Mont.: Montana Historical Society Press, 1998.

Langford, Nathaniel P. *Vigilante Days and Ways.* 1890. Reprint, Missoula, Mont.: University of Montana Press, 1957.

Pace, Dick. *Golden Gulch: The Story of Montana's Fabulous Alder Gulch.* Virginia City, Mont.: Dick Pace, 2nd ed. 1970.

31. Liver Eatin' Johnston Slept Here

Crutchfield, James Andrew. "Liver-Eating Johnston's Gruesome Revenge, 1843." *It Happened in Montana.* Helena, Mont.: Falcon Publishing Company, 1992.

Lampi, Leona. "Red Lodge and the Festival of Nations." *Montana: The Magazine of Western History* 11 (Summer 1961): 26–41.

32. Surprise Attack on the Nez Perce

Brown, Mark H. *The Flight of the Nez Perce.* Lincoln: University of Nebraska Press, 1967.

Haines, Aubrey L. *An Elusive Victory: The Battle of the Big Hole.* West Glacier, Mont.: Glacier Natural History Association, 1991.

McWhorter, Lucullus V. *Yellow Wolf: His Own Story.* Caldwell, Idaho: The Caxton Printers, Ltd., 1983.

33. They Call Them the Apsaalooke

Hoxie, Frederick E. *Parading Through History: The Making of the Crow Nation in America, 1805–1935.* Cambridge, England: Cambridge University Press, 1995.

Medicine Crow, Joseph. *From the Heart of the Crow Country.* New York: Orion Books, 1992.

34. The Frenchman Becomes a Cowboy

"Pierre Wibaux." *Hoofprints from the Yellowstone Corral of the Westerners,* vol. 23, no. 2 (fall/winter 1993).

Welsh, Donald H. *Pierre Wibaux, Cattle King.* Reprint. Bismarck, N.D.: State Historical Society of North Dakota, 1953.

35. The Last Chief of the Crows

Fitzgerald, Michael Oren, ed. *Yellowtail: Crow Medicine Man and Sun Dance Chief.* Norman: University of Oklahoma Press, 1991.

Linderman, Frank B. *Plenty Coups: Chief of the Crows.* Lincoln: University of Nebraska Press, 1962.

36. The Steel Rail Crosses the West

Malone, Michael. *James J. Hill. Empire Builder of the Northwest.* Norman: University of Oklahoma Press, 1996.

McCarter, Steve. *Guide to the Milwaukee Road.* Helena, Mont.: Montana Historical Society Press, 1992.

Riegel, Robert. *The Story of the Western Railroads.* Lincoln: University of Nebraska Press, 1998.

37. Where Low Rent Means High Spirits

Spritzer, Don. *Roadside History of Montana.* Missoula, Mont.: Mountain Press Publishing Company, 1999.

Wilson, Gary A. *Honky Tonk Town: Havre Bootlegging Days.* Havre, Mont.: High-Line Books, 1985.

38. Reflections of Glaciers

Djuff, Ray, and Chris Morrison. *Glacier's Historic Hotels and Chalets: View with a Room.* Helena, Mont.: Farcountry Press, 2001.

Gallagher, Eileen, et al. *Insiders' Guide to Glacier National Park.* Guilford, Conn.: The Globe Pequot Press, 2001.

39. A River Runs Through It

Howard, Ella Mae. *Lewis and Clark, Exploration of Central Montana.* Great Falls, Mont.: Lewis and Clark Interpretive Association, 1993

Murphy, Dan, and David Muench. *Lewis & Clark, Voyage of Discovery: The Story Behind the Scenery.* Las Vegas: KC Publications, 1977.

40. I Will Fight No More Forever

Beal, Merrill D. *I Will Fight No More Forever: Chief Joseph and the Nez Perce War.* Seattle: University of Washington Press, 1963.

Greene, Jerome. *Nez Perce Summer of 1877.* Helena, Mont.: Montana Historical Society Press, 2000.

Josephy, Alvin M., Jr. *Chief Joseph's People and Their War.* Yellowstone National Park: The Yellowstone Association, 1964.

41. Growing Up Like Huckleberry Finn

Casler, Michael M. *Steamboats of the Fort Union Fur Trade.* Williston, ND: Fort Union Association, 1999.

Gratz, Rick, and Suzie Gratz. *Montana's Upper Missouri River Breaks National Monument: The Wild and Scenic Missouri.* Helena, Mont.: Northern Rockies Publishing, 2001.

Lepley, John G. *Birthplace of Montana: A History of Fort Benton.* Missoula, Mont.: Pictorial Histories Publishing Company, 1999.

42. The Great Indian Council of 1855

Ewers, John C. *Indian Life on the Upper Missouri.* Norman: University of Oklahoma Press, 1968.

Sunder, John E. *The Fur Trade on the Upper Missouri: 1840–1865.* Norman: University of Oklahoma Press, 1965.

43. Christmas at the Mansion

Christiansen, Albert. *The Conrad Buffalo Ranch.* Kalispell, Mont.: Albert Christiansen, 1991.

Murphy, James E. *Half Interest in a Silver Dollar: The Saga of Charles E. Conrad.* Missoula, Mont.: Mountain Press Publishing, 1988.

44. Last Chance Gulch Becomes the First City

Baucus, Jean. *Helena: Her Historic Homes.* Helena, Mont.: Jean Baucus and Gayle Shanahan, 1976.

Liffring, Bob. *The Tour Train Companion: A Trivia Guide to Helena, Montana's Capital City.* Helena, Mont.: Manx Publishing Company, 1992.

Paladin, Vivian, and Jean Baucus. *Helena: An Illustrated History.* Norfolk, Va.: Donning Company, 1983.

45. The Cavemen of Bitter Creek Coulee

Clawson, Roger, and Katherine A. Shandera. *Billings, The City and The People.* Helena, Mont.: American and World Geographic Publishing, 1993.

Jensen, Joyce M. *Pieces and Places of Billings History (Historic Sites Around Town).* Billings, Mont.: Western Heritage Press, 1994.

46. Teddy Roosevelt's Hunting Ground

Hagedorn, Hermann. *Roosevelt in the Bad Lands.* New York: Houghton Mifflin, 1921.

Morris, Edmund. *The Rise of Theodore Roosevelt.* New York: Coward, McCann & Geoghegan, Inc., 1979.

Roosevelt, Theodore. *Hunting Trips of a Ranchman: Sketches of Sport on the Northern Cattle Plains.* New York: G. P. Putnam's Sons, 1885.

47. They Said It Couldn't Be Done

Federal Writers' Project. *The WPA Guide to 1930s Montana.* Tucson: University of Arizona Press, 1994.

Quinn, Kevin R., ed. District News. *Fort Peck: A half-century and holding.* Vol. 11, No. 2. Omaha, Neb.: U.S. Army Corps of Engineers, Summer, 1987.

48. Victorian Christmas at the Ranch

Kent, Phillip. *Montana State Prison History.* Deer Lodge, Mont.: Powell County Museum and Arts Foundation, 1979.

Madsen, Betty, and Brigham Madsen. *North to Montana.* Provo: Utah State University Press, 1998.

Meikle, Lyndel, ed. *Very Close to Trouble: The Johnny Grant Memoir.* Pullman: Washington State University Press, 1996.

49. Guideposts of the Great Plains

Bryan, William L., and Michael Crummitt. *Montana's Indians: Yesterday and Today.* 2d ed. Helena, Mont.: American and World Geographic Publishing, 1996.

Willard, John. *Adventure Trails in Montana.* Helena, Mont.: Montana Historical Society Press, 1971.

50. The Bloody Bozeman

Burlingame, Merrill G. *John M. Bozeman: Montana Trailmaker.* Bozeman, Mont.: Museum of the Rockies, 1983.

Johnson, Dorothy M. *The Bloody Bozeman: The Perilous Trail to Montana's Gold.* Missoula, Mont.: Mountain Press Publishing Company, 1983.

Murray, Robert A. *The Bozeman Trail: Highway of History.* Fort Collins, Colo.: Old Army Press, 1988.

Walter, Dave. "The Thomas Tragedy on the Yellowstone." *Montana Campfire Tales.* Helena, Mont.: Falcon Publishing Company, 1997.

51. Lewis and Clark Reach the Headwaters

Burroughs, Raymond D., ed. *The Natural History of the Lewis & Clark Expedition.* East Lansing: Michigan State University Press, 1995.

Harris, Burton. *John Colter, His Years in the Rockies.* Lincoln: University of Nebraska Press, 1993.

52. Prairie Tycoon with a Vision

Great American Homes. Reader's Digest's Explore America Series, vol. 14. Pleasantville, NY: Reader's Digest Association, 1997.

Wiencek, Henry, and Donna M. Lucey. *National Geographic Guide to America's Great Houses.* Washington, D.C.: National Geographic Society, 1999.

Index

A

Alder Gulch 137, 138, 142
Anaconda, 32–35
Appaloosa horses, 63
Apsaalooke (*see* Crow Indians)
artists, 44–47
Assinniboine Indians, 99, 113, 117, 191

B

Bair, Charles, 91–94
Bannack, 137–41
Bear Paw Battlefield, 189–92
Big Hole National Battlefield, 152–56
Blackfoot Indians, 72, 113, 117, 133–36
Blaine County Museum, 190–92
Bozeman, 16, 234
Bozeman Trail, 233–36
Bucking Horse Sale, 96–97
buffalo, 40–42, 229
Butte, 32, 54–57

C

Calamity Jane, 243
Carter County Museum, 218
Charles Conrad Mansion, 201–4
Cheyenne Indians, 109–10, 118, 120
Chief Joseph, 189, 190
Chief Plenty Coups, 167–68
Chinese population, 145
Clark, Captain William, 58–63, 64–67, 85, 95, 184, 213, 237
Clark, William Andrews, 32, 54
Colter, John, 237, 239, 240
Conrad, Charles, 193–94, 201–2
Conrad Mansion, 201–4
Copper Kings, 32, 54
County splitters, 125
Cree Indians, 99, 102, 113, 229

Crook, General George, 109–10, 118
Crow Indians (Apsaalooke), 113, 117, 157–61, 167–71
cultural sites, 13, 44, 55, 69–70, 73–75, 92–93, 124–25, 134–35, 138–39, 148–49, 153–54, 158–60, 163–66, 168–71, 177–78, 189–92, 194, 198–99, 202–3, 206–7, 226–27, 241–42
Curry, Kid, 48, 51, 127, 129, 131
Custer, George A., 95, 109, 110, 118–22
Cutter, Kirtland, 180, 202

D

Daly, Marcus, 32, 54, 73–74, 76
Deer Lodge, 224–28
DeSmet, Father, 68, 72, 197
Dillon, 140

E

Ekalaka, 216–18
Elkhorn, 36–39

F

Flathead Indians (see Salish Indians)
forestry, 77–80
Fort Assinniboine, 99–103
Fort Benton, 89, 193–96
Fort Keogh, 95
Fort Owen, 68–72
Fort Peck Dam, 219–23
Fort Union Trading Post National Historic Site, 113–17
frontier architecture, 8, 9, 23, 25, 33–35, 37, 49, 51, 69–70, 138–39, 143–44, 163, 165, 202, 206, 226, 241–42

G

Gardiner Roosevelt Entrance Arch, 27–31
Garnet, 22–26
Gates of the Mountains, 104–8, 213
ghost towns, 8–12, 22–26, 36–39, 48–53, 137–41, 143
Glacier National Park, 180–83
Glendive, 165
Going-to-the-Sun Road, 180
gold mining methods, 52
Grant, John, 224
Grant-Kohrs Ranch National Historic Site, 224–28
Great Falls, 184
Great Train Robbery, 127–32
Gros Ventre Indians, 191

H

Havre, 176–79
Heinze, Fritz Augustus, 54
Helena, 11, 36, 205–8
homesteaders, 16, 123–25, 172, 176, 180, 229
horses, 63, 76

I

Indian cultural sites, 40–42, 113–16, 118–21, 158–60, 167–71, 210–14, 215–18, 229–32
Indian Wars, 16, 95, 102, 109, 119–20, 152–53, 189–90

J

Judith Landing, 117, 197–200

K

Kalispell, 201

Kohrs, Conrad, 224, 226
Kootenai Indians, 18–21

L

Lake McDonald Lodge, 180–83
Landusky, 48–53, 127
Last Chance Gulch, 205–6
Lewis and Clark, 58–63, 64–67, 85, 97, 104, 129, 184–87, 237–38
Lewis, Captain Meriwether, 58, 85, 104, 184, 237
Lewistown, 172, 173, 175
Little Big Horn Battle, 118–22
living-history demonstrations, 66–67, 114–15, 120, 121, 124–25, 129, 139–40, 143, 144, 190–91, 226
Lolo Trail, 48–53

M

Malta, 129
mansions, 73–76, 201–4, 206–7, 241–45
Marysville, 8–12
Medicine Rock, 229
Medicine Rocks State Park, 213, 215–18
Miles, General (Colonel) Nelson A., 95, 189
Miles City, 95–98
Milk River, 129, 130, 229, 230
mining, 8–9, 22, 32–33, 36, 48, 49, 51, 52, 54–55, 137–38, 142, 145, 147, 150, 205, 243
missions, 68–72, 81–84
Missouri Headwaters State Park, 237–40
Missouri River, 85–90, 113, 117, 219, 237
monuments, 27, 29–30, 40, 85–90, 118–22, 169
Moss Mansion, 241–45

museums, 13–17, 33, 44–47, 78, 82, 96, 114–15, 120, 123–24, 129, 130, 134, 136, 153, 163–66, 168, 190, 191, 218, 220, 230

N

Nevada City, 142–46
Nez Perce Indians, 58–59, 152–56, 189–92

O

outlaws, 48, 51, 127–32, 137, 142, 174

P

Pend d'Oreille Indians, 18–21
People's Center, 18–21
Pershing, General John J., 99, 102
Phillips County Museum, 129, 130, 131
Pictograph Cave State Park, 210–14
Pictographs and Petroglyphs, 213
pioneers, 14, 16, 123–26, 176–77
Plummer, Henry, 137
Pompeys Pillar, 64–67, 213
Powerhouse Museum, 220, 222

R

railroads, 32, 95, 127, 172–75
ranching, 77, 83, 95–96, 123, 162, 224, 226
Range Riders Museum, 96, 97
Rankin, Jeannette, 209
Ravalli, Father, 68, 69, 70, 72
Red Lodge, 147–51
Rendezvous, 148
riverboats, 85–90, 193, 194, 195
Roosevelt, Teddy, 215
Rosebud Battlefield, 109–12, 213
Russell, Charlie, 44, 172

S

Saco Museum, 230
Salish (Flathead) Indians, 18–21, 68–69, 72
Savenac Tree Nursery, 77–80
Scobey, 123–26
Sidney, 115
Sioux Indians, 95, 99, 102, 109–10, 113, 118, 120, 123, 215
Sleeping Buffalo Rock, 229–32
St. Ignatius Mission, 81–84
St. Mary's Mission, 68–72
State Parks, 37, 40–43, 109–12, 137–41, 167–71, 210–14, 215–18, 237–40

T

Tammany, 32, 76
traders and trappers, 113–17, 193

U

Ulm Pishkun State Park, 40–43

V

vigilantes, 141
Virginia City, 142–46, 243
vision quest, 170

W

Wibaux, Pierre, 162–63

Y

Yellowstone National Park, 27

Z

Zortman, 48–53

Acknowledgments

I would like to thank all those who provided information and helped with the editing, including the protectors, managers, and chroniclers of these early times and vanishing resources. My special thanks to Gayle Shirley, Randy English, all the staff at The Globe Pequot Press, and to my family—Mary, Dacia, and Chris—for their research and editing help as well. Finally I will always be grateful to Dr. Merrill Burlingame, Dr. John N. DeHaas, Jr., Dr. Carling Malouf, Sister Genevieve McBride, O.S.U., J. Ken Ralston, and the many students, teachers, and makers of Montana history for passing on to me their passion for the place they call Montana.

About the Author

A Montana resident for more than thirty years, author Dave Conklin is a retired park ranger who lives in the Flathead Valley. Although he has B.S. and M.S. degrees in Forestry and Wildlife Management, and an M.B.A., one of the first professional assignments he took was writing the *Montana Historic Preservation Plan*. As a historic preservation planner, he was instrumental in nominating many of the historic sites in this book to the National Register of Historic Places. As a park ranger, he worked to preserve Montana's historic parks. While in Helena, Dave lived in a log cabin he built at the headwaters of Last Chance Gulch near the old mining town of Unionville. His hobbies include writing, photography, dogsledding, and Indian Wars cavalry reenactments.

Help Us Keep This Guide Up to Date

Every effort has been made by the author and editors to make this guide as accurate and useful as possible. However, many things can change after a guide is published—establishments close, phone numbers change, facilities come under new management, etc.

We would love to hear from you concerning your experiences with this guide and how you feel it could be improved and kept up to date. While we may not be able to respond to all comments and suggestions, we'll take them to heart and we'll also make certain to share them with the author. Please send your comments and suggestions to the following address:

The Globe Pequot Press
Reader Response/Editorial Department
P.O. Box 480
Guilford, CT 06437

Or you may e-mail us at:

editorial@globe-pequot.com

Thanks for your input, and happy travels!